What should Catholics think of the American founding? Most observers have argued either that Catholics can reconcile the founding with their Faith, or that the founding, and the republican government in general, are contrary to the Catholic Faith. Tim Gordon makes a strong case for a third option: our republican founding "appropriated" a Catholic understanding of reality and can rest secure only on an explicitly Catholic foundation. Anyone interested in this debate should acquaint themselves with the details of Gordon's fascinating argument.

— Jay Richards
Executive Editor, The Stream

In this intellectually stimulating and thought-provoking book, Tim Gordon highlights that the very source of America's political and cultural salvation is the Catholicism that has been eschewed and even persecuted from the first days of the republic. Catholic moral thought, with its declaring of natural law, needs a fresh look in the world of American politics and culture.

— Michael Voris
Church Militant

Tim Gordon is, without doubt, an intellectual heavyweight with a deep understanding of, and love for, the Catholic Church. He is also a good husband, father, and educator who is just as at home lifting weights at the gym as he is standing in front of a group of teenagers, teaching them the intricacies of the *Summa*. In an era bereft of leaders, Tim is a throwback to the days of yore, where godly men would not only have an intimate relationship with Christ and His Church but would be willing to stand up and defend it, regardless of the consequences.

— Matthew Marsden
Catholic Actor and Producer

The framers held "these truths to be self-evident." Timothy Gordon does a deep dive into the intellectual sources of their assertion in *Catholic Republic: Why America Will Perish without Rome* and finds, inter alia, a treasure trove of crypto-Catholicism. Not for the faint of heart, this book exposes popular presuppositions imbibed by many conservatives, while handing readers on both sides of the culture war a slew of provocative insights.

— Patrick Coffin
Host, The Patrick Coffin Show

Timothy Gordon impressively substantiates the crypto-Catholic political philosophy present in the American Revolution and founding of the United States of America. Saint Thomas Aquinas asserted that "man cannot attain his end by nature, but only by grace because of the exalted character of the end." Gordon demonstrates that the Natural Law tradition of America, in which she was conceived, must also be perfected by this grace. Without turning to the supernatural graces of Catholicism, America will not heal, elevate, or perfect her created nature. Gordon is provocatively accurate: America will perish without the philosophical and theological tradition of Catholicism.

— Taylor Marshall
Best-Selling Author

Catholic Republic

TIMOTHY GORDON

CATHOLIC REPUBLIC

Why America Will Perish without Rome

An imprint of Sophia Institute Press

Manchester, New Hampshire

Sophia Institute Press
Box 5284, Manchester, NH 03108
1-800-888-9344

www.SophiaInstitute.com

Sophia Institute Press® is a registered trademark of Sophia Institute.

Library of Congress Cataloging-in-Publication Data
To come.

First printing

Nothing is more to be feared than too long a peace. You are deceived if you think that a Christian can live without persecution. He suffers the greatest persecution of all who lives under none. A storm puts a man on his guard and obliges him to exert his utmost efforts to avoid shipwreck.

—Saint Jerome

Hope has two beautiful daughters; their names are Anger and Courage: Anger at the way things are and Courage to see that they do not remain as they are.

—Saint Augustine

Contents

Catholic Republic

PIPPIN: *"Why are they still guarding [the Tree of the King]?"*

GANDALF: *"They guard it because they have hope, a faint and fading hope that one day it will flower, a King will come, and the city will be as it once was, before it fell into decay. The old wisdom borne out of the West was forsaken. Kings made tombs more splendid than the houses of the living, and counted the old names of their descent dearer than the names of their sons. Childless lords sat in aged halls musing on heraldry, or in high cold towers asking questions of the stars. And so the people of Gondor fell into ruin. The line of Kings failed. The White Tree withered. The rule of Gondor was given over to lesser men."*

—J. R. R. Tolkien, *The Return of the King*

We have thought it fitting . . . that this letter should be addressed specially to you. It will also be our care to see that copies are sent to the bishops of the United States, testifying again to that love by which we embrace your whole country, a country which in past times has done so much for the cause of religion, and which will by Divine assistance continue to do still greater things. To you, and to all the faithful of America, we grant most lovingly, as a pledge of Divine assistance, our apostolic benediction.

—Pope Leo XIII, *Testem Benevolentiae Nostrae*

An Introduction Important Enough to Be a Chapter

America is wired Catholic, labeled Protestant, and currently functioning as secular. In this book, I will show that this is true and explain how this confusion has caused most of our country's major problems.

Moreover, I will show that, ideologically, every American — Protestant, Jew, Muslim, or atheist — is actually Catholic. That's because America is a republic, and, to the extent that they are successful, all true republics rely on a citizenry that holds Catholic principles. When — as America has done — a republic strays from its fundamental principles, fatal problems ensue. Today's widespread immorality and ever-increasing tyranny are, in fact, symptoms of a much deeper problem: our nation has ceased to be a republic.

One solution — and only one — can restore our republic and recover America's greatness: Catholicism.

Only the true source of republican principles — Catholicism — bears the answer to the problem *underlying* the six American symptoms to which I dedicate the chapters of this book.

Although Catholic apologetics usually seeks to convert others to the Faith, these pages aim for something less ambitious: revealing America's *hidden* Catholicism, which I call crypto-Catholicism.

That's it.

Doing this alone could be enough to save America.

* * *

Many religious and political conservatives long for a "return to principles." That's nothing new. The purpose of this book is first to demonstrate the *real source* of American principles—Catholicism—and *only then* to return to them.

Hoping to reverse cultural degeneration and the expansion of the state, patriots note that our republic can go in only one of two ways. Either it will *disappear* (as did the vast Roman Republic, which slowly disintegrated), or it will *perdure* (as has the Roman Catholic Church, which has remained fundamentally the same despite a series of superficial changes). We'll follow either the Roman republic or the Roman Church, for all roads really do lead to Rome.

Just as the fading Roman Empire wound up needing Catholicism in the fifth and sixth centuries, so, too, does America, the republic founded expressly against Catholicism. In these pages, I engage in a new form of "apologetics," showing that the ideas Americans have long embraced about republican politics and Western culture have always been Catholic, but secretly so.

Not to sound like Gus Portokalos in *My Big Fat Greek Wedding*, who reduces every nicety of modern life to his Greek heritage, but seriously: *all true republican principles are Catholic in origination*.[1]

---

[1] Undeniably, the primordial form of the republic hails to pre-Christian Greece and Rome. As we will see, the Natural Law underlying such republican elements as local rule and popular

It's undeniable, and I will show how.

I'll repeat it time and again: *America is wired Catholic, labeled Protestant, and currently functioning as secular*. No wonder it has devolved into a secular state rife with bacchanalia, eugenics, and collectivism — symptoms of a republic in name only.

Don't misunderstand me. I hold that *all* genuine, successful republics — not only the American one — are rooted in certain Catholic ideas and are doomed to fail without them. It's not just an American thing.

Also, I don't hold that *in addition to Protestantism*, Catholicism fosters republicanism. Rather, I show how *Catholic principles alone* can sustain genuine republicanism. Protestantism can't do it, nor, as we shall see, can Enlightenment ideas.

These claims may shock the average American, for we are not accustomed to thinking of this republic as Catholic, but as Protestant. My thesis turns out to be the equivalent of showing you that your favorite basketball team, when seen up close, has been populated by an opposing team's players, secretly in your colors.

Moreover, given the fervent anti-Catholicism of the Puritan American founders, this book will be more like a *Lakers* fan coming to find his team populated by *Celtics* clad in gold and purple![2] But

---

morality in Greece and Rome — remarkably well-developed in many ways — proved to need what culminated in Christian revelation: a more specific reason (*logos*) and goal (*telos*) for the republic.

[2] "About 1,800 years into her often stormy history, this Church found herself as a very small group in a new country in Eastern North America that promised to respect all religions because the State would not be confessional; it would not try to play the role of a religion. This Church knew that it was far from socially acceptable in this new country. One of the reasons the country was established was to protest the king of England's permitting

fear not: America has been blessed to have such secret "Celt-ics" on its side. Their team plays work. America needs only to return to the fundamentals they bring—this time *knowing the source* of those fundamentals—in order to regain the form of a true republic.

The Two Camps That Formed America

Russell Kirk wrote that "the Protestant and Catholic Reforma-tions of the 16th century were both reactions against the excesses of the Renaissance." I disagree. It's more like the later Renaissance (i.e., the early, early Enlightenment) and the Protestant Reforma-tion were both sixteenth-century reactions against some aspects of Catholicism. For the purposes of this book, you should think of "the Enlightenment" simply as a *secular* (i.e., anti-religious) rejection of Catholicism; for that matter, any time you see "the Protestant Reformation," define it for yourself as a *Christian* (i.e., religious) rejection of Catholicism.

---

the public celebration of the Catholic Mass on the soil of the British Empire in the newly conquered Catholic territories of Canada. He had betrayed his coronation oath to combat Ca-tholicism, defined as 'America's common enemy,' and protect Protestantism, bringing the pure religion of the Colonists into danger and giving them the moral right to revolt and reject his rule. Nonetheless, many Catholics in the American colonies thought their life might be better in the new country than under a regime whose ruling class had penalized and persecuted them since the mid-sixteenth century. They made this new country their own and served her loyally. The social history was often contentious, but the State basically kept its promise to protect all religions and not become a rival to them, a fake church. Until recent years." Francis Cardinal George, O.M.I. "A Tale of Two Churches." *Catholic New World*, September 7–20, 2014.

What follows is an explanation of the *basis* for the rejection of Catholicism by these two camps: Protestant and Enlightenment thought.

By pretty much everyone's account, ideas from the Enlightenment and the Reformation[3] combined to form the American Founding. It's an old narrative that finds no challenge here, although many of its implications and presumptions will be challenged throughout this book.

The great irony is that those two America-forming camps, the Reformation and the Enlightenment, rejected precisely that element in Catholicism that America *requires* in order to thrive as a republic: *Catholic Natural Law*.[4]

Natural Law is God's moral model for human behavior, evident in nature. As we shall see, in America and in all the other corners of the West influenced by the Reformation and the Enlightenment, reception of Catholic Natural Law has been altogether *schizophrenic*: "on paper" it has been rejected, while behind the scenes, it has been embraced (because it proves necessary!).

---

3 "Early in America's history, many Protestants who came to America believed that they were extending the Reformation; God's special hand of blessing was upon them as they hoped to realize the postmillennial dream: bringing God's kingdom to earth ... they assumed that they were the new people of God embarking on a new exodus — an errand in the wilderness — to do theocracy the right [Protestant, Calvinist] way." John Goldingay, *Old Testament Theology: Israel's Gospel*, vol. 1 (Downers Grove, IL: IVP Academic, 2015).

4 In most places in this book, this term appears as "Catholic Natural Law," while sometimes it appears as simply "Natural Law." The latter should be understood as the former, unless otherwise stipulated.

CATHOLIC REPUBLIC

The schizophrenic[5] American reception of Catholic Natural Law is this book's proper subject. Its six chapters describe six ways in which America has plagiarized Catholic Natural Law. We shall see that these six ways turn out to be the six elements of the true, classical definition of a *republic*: (1) a natural rights regime (2) headed by limited government and (3) peopled by a moral citizenry, who are (4) able to properly conceive of personhood and humanism, (5) of the family and the economy, and (6) of scientific and technological advancement.

In other words, if a republic devolves into a republic in name only, as I claim ours has done, those six elements become measures of its six *symptoms of decay*. That's because Catholic Natural Law is necessary not only for any republic to *come to exist* or to *thrive*, but even to *survive*.

Bear in mind as we define "Catholic Natural Law" that the Enlightenment rejected it on a *secular* basis and Protestantism did so on a *Christian* basis. Each camp rejected Catholic Natural Law as a centermost aspect of its own philosophy in the late sixteenth and the early seventeenth centuries.

So really, only one dimension in all of this contradicts anything you learned in the sixth grade. Everyone was taught rightly

---

[5] "Today, especially in the United States, evangelical Protestants find themselves *reconsidering* [emphasis added] the issue of Natural Law. Their interest seems to be occasioned by two things. First, the political success of evangelical Protestantism has made it necessary to frame an appropriate language for addressing civil politics and law. Second, evangelicals find themselves in dialogue with Catholics, with whom they share many common interests in matters of culture and politics—interests that would seem amenable to Natural Law discussion." Louis Bouyer, "Catholic Moral Theology," in *Principles of Catholic Moral Life*, ed. William E. May (Chicago: Franciscan Herald Press, 1980).

that the Declaration of Independence founded America on the basis of the universal principles known as the Natural Law. And everyone was taught rightly that those founders were almost exclusively Protestant. Further, everyone was also properly instructed that most of the newer ideas of self-government imported into America—such as the "social contract"—were products of the European Enlightenment.

All that really contradicts what you learned in sixth grade is my claim that the republic that Protestantism and the Enlightenment combined to form—America—*had always expressly rejected the Natural Law, so that when early America found that it needed Natural Law to make a proper republic, its two big camps had to plagiarize from their worst enemy, Catholicism.*

Both camps, Protestant and Enlightenment, muted their objection to Catholic Natural Law temporarily during the American Founding and even endorsed it. Of course, they never admitted what was afoot. Why would they?

So, the question is: *What in the world is going on?*

Here's what. America has a secretly Catholic wiring (i.e., a Catholic Natural Law wiring), even as the two camps that produced it were doctrinally devoted to rejecting the Natural Law (since it lay at the core of hated Catholic social, political, and moral teachings). Remember, America is that conspicuous nation, *wired Catholic, labeled Protestant, and currently functioning as secular.*

But don't worry, you're not "behind" in your lessons. No one has yet gotten past the paradox of Protestant and Enlightenment ambivalence toward Natural Law Catholicism in America. This is why our country is failing. Most have not even confronted it as a paradox: they've only recognized the undeniable *symptoms* of a republic in decline. And clearly, solving the paradox involves some historical twists and philosophical turns. It is rough ground, and the map has not thus far been open to the American public. Until now.

Catholic Natural Law and the "Prot-Enlight" Tradition That Rejected It

Let's slow down now, before going on. What exactly have we established? Two "opposite" camps of thought — Protestantism and the Enlightenment — rejected Catholicism's Natural Law principles but secretly and heavily drew on these principles in the making of early America. Let's call this phenomenon of codependent, American plagiarism "Prot-Enlight"[6] because it involves the two camps' secret ripping off of their hated rival,[7] Catholicism.

But, what *is* this Catholic Natural Law, rejected yet secretly plagiarized by Prot-Enlight? Basically, Catholic Natural Law amounts to three properties that its Catholic proponents ascribe to nature.[8] (Too often, Catholic Natural Law is thought of as

---

[6] Only upon the final edit of this book, I came across the thought of Father Vincent Miceli, who posed the Church's *bête noir*, Modernism, as something very, very similar to what I've coined *Prot-Enlight*: "Its religious ancestor is the Protestant Reformation; its philosophical parent is the Enlightenment; its political pedigree comes from the French Revolution." Vincent Miceli, *The Antichrist* (Harrison, NY: Roman Catholic Books, 1981), p. 133.

[7] It's just another name for what Pope Pius X has called "Modernism, the sum of all heresies."

[8] One brief caveat, before proceeding to an explication of the ways in which each of these properties was rejected by both Protestantism and the Enlightenment: The Catholic rendition of Natural Law is not the only one in history. While Enlightenment and Protestant thought rejected Natural Law, not everyone else besides the Catholics did. The Jews had their own iteration of the Natural Law, from the days following the Babylonian Exile, at which point Judaism became dispersed throughout the

having only the first of these three properties. But it comprises all *three together*.) Each of these properties of the Natural Law was in turn rejected by Prot-Enlight thought. Here they are:

1. *Nature as moral (free)*: within nature, mankind is free and morally accountable, because intelligent.
2. *Nature as intelligible (meaningful)*: man, because he is intelligent, can learn from and about his surroundings.
3. *Nature as teleological (oriented to a purpose)*: mankind is wired to see the moral purpose of his surroundings.

Why is Catholic Natural Law so central to republics? As a form of government, republicanism is the only type in which unchanging truth *matters*. In a republic, truth delicately counterbalances the ever-fluctuating tempers of the ballot. As Pope Benedict XVI said, "Truth is not determined by a majority vote." True republics presuppose truth. On the other hand, in pure democracies, the mathematical majority rules with zero regard for the immutable, timeless truths of Catholic Natural Law.

Democracy is the relativism of the many.

Mediterranean, where it became Hellenized. And the Greeks (who Hellenized those Jews) had several changing conceptions of it, spanning the time from Homer through Alexander the Great. There was a nebulous Homeric-tragic Greek version of it, forerunning Aristotle's and underpinning some of Aristotle's basic assumptions about nature. And this Aristotelian version was carried into the young Roman Empire, where Romans also formed their own distinctive iteration, in both pagan and later Christian forms. It was that matured Aristotelian iteration of Natural Law that Thomas Aquinas came to modify very slightly, and which went on to become the single aspect of Catholicism most objected to by Enlightenment and Reformation thought. (Thus, one could call Aristotle almost as indispensable for republics as Thomas Aquinas is!) This Catholic rendition of Natural Law is the thing! It is the seat of all earthly republics.

Similarly, in a monarchy, the country centers not on a fixed set of Natural Law principles, but rather around the whims of the king. A good one gives good laws; a despotic one gives despotic laws.

Monarchy is the relativism of the one.

At the risk of redundancy, the reader should bear in mind that these three inherently Catholic properties of Natural Law are each *indispensably* necessary for all republics. This point cannot be overemphasized. The two camps that formed the American republic — Enlightenment secularism and Protestant Christianity — should *generally* be seen as rejecting each one of these three properties.

The term "generally" does not mean "without exception."

Among more than thirty-eight thousand sects of Protestantism and hundreds of differing Enlightenment thinkers, this book does not make the unqualified claim that no Protestant or Enlightenment thinkers have embraced something they call the Natural Law. Many of these thinkers have, in fact, done so; every so often, a luminary from either camp will refer to something he misguidedly calls "Natural Law."

Indeed, making such a claim would require the impossible: the scouring of every thinker who could possibly fit into either category. As Carl E. Braaten once wrote in *First Things*: "Reformation thinkers have swung erratically between absolute denial of Natural Law and conditional acceptance of it." And the exact same can be said of the hugely disparate group of thinkers designated by the term "Enlightenment."

One more time, the reader should be spared any suspense: some fraction of each camp definitely *does* claim to affirm some idiosyncratic (self-contradictory) rendition of the Natural Law. But few thinkers of either camp accept the version of Natural Law emanating from Aristotle's thought. Even fewer accept the modifications and adjustments made to the former by Saint Thomas Aquinas. The three prongs of the Natural Law in this book summarize the Aristotelian-Thomist version—what I call Catholic Natural Law. Generally, the Catholic Natural Law position remains the closest thing to the mainstream version.

At the most conservative and least ambitious, my thesis could be phrased that America and all republics *heavily* depend upon the Catholic version.

But here phraseology does not matter much: each of the *six elements of American crypto-Catholicism* (*the six elements of the definition of the true republic*) in these chapters increasingly confirms the point that *all* republics need Catholic Natural Law, which is summarized by these three prongs. Let's examine each of the three properties, what they mean, and the distinctive ways in which both the Reformation and the Enlightenment ("Prot" and "Enlight") rejected them.[9]

---

[9] Pope Benedict XVI, as Joseph Cardinal Ratzinger, spent much of his career defending the notion that the West's "dehellenization," or removal of two of Aristotle's four causes from nature, by the Reformation, altered the modern view of *reality* as well as of *theology*. Pope Benedict states it most simply in the Regensburg address, in which he identifies the Reformation as the first of three moments of dehellenization in the West, for its Enlightenment-styled ontological removal of the formal cause (*logos*, *eidos*) and the final cause (*telos*) of nature (that is to say, the second prong of Catholic Natural Law, nature as intelligible, and also the third prong, nature as purpose oriented). Pope Benedict's claim of the Protestant denaturalizing of the Natural Law of the West was a claim he openly made about their take on the *world*—not only about theological points such as salvation or the sacraments or even God's attributes. This point is firmed up by Pope Benedict's identification of the second moment of dehellenization: the Kantian takeover of the European view of

CATHOLIC REPUBLIC

Human Nature as Moral, Free

The first property of the Natural Law is that it holds human nature as moral and free. In other words, the Natural Law proponent suggests that man's will is naturally free to make moral choices in the world. Man is the intelligent animal. Even after the lowering of his will by concupiscence — the human inclination toward evil, resulting from the Fall of Adam and Eve — it remains natural for him to recognize and desire moral good.

---

nature. While Kant never "took over" English-speaking Europe, John Locke did, to a virtually identical effect. Both Kant and Locke — Protestants themselves and powerful philosophical Protestantizers of Europe — were making claims about ontology, not theology. And both Kant and Locke represented a second step not only of Western dehellenization, but very arguably, a second natural step of Protestantism itself (but this latter point is merely the cherry on top). Since I've already addressed the Protestant dehellenization of Catholic Natural Law prongs two and three, I might as well tend to prong one.

Protestants argue among themselves about the degree to which man is determined by sin, making him both immoral and unfree. But at the simplest level, *all* Protestants believe in a far more sin-deterministic view of man's day-to-day life than Catholics do. Even a specific recourse by Reformers to "Natural Law" proves a radically different thing from the Catholic Natural Law needed in republics for self-rule. For instance: "There remain in man since the fall the glimmerings of natural light, whereby he retains some knowledge of God, of natural things, and of the difference between good and evil, and shows some regard for virtue and for good outward behavior. But so far is this light of nature from being sufficient to bring him to a saving knowledge of God and to true conversion *that he is incapable of using it aright even in things natural and civil*" (Synod of Dort, 1618). Another instance: "As man is enclosed by the darkness of error, the natural law gives him scarce an inkling of the kind of service which is pleasing to God" (John Calvin).

In combination with his intelligence, man possesses free will to pursue the moral good, which he is able to understand. Nature provides many opportunities for man to exercise his free will. Therefore, knowing and following God's moral law is *not* unnatural, as the post-Enlightenment, post-Reformation world portrays. On the contrary, it is altogether natural.

Pope Benedict XVI wrote of this first property of the Natural Law: "In reality, the fundamental intuition about the moral character of Being itself ... and the message of nature is common to all the great cultures, and therefore the great moral imperatives are likewise held in common."

With Aristotle, the Catholic Church reasons that we have the *capacity* for moral goodness and true happiness by nature, but we must *become* good by choice.[10] Aristotle certainly does not mean that moral virtue happens automatically. Moral virtue happens by man's will; nature is morally neutral. But we are nevertheless adapted by God's nature and our own rational nature to make a habit of virtue, if we so desire. Even after the Fall, we are not so concupiscent that we cannot make virtue habitual.[11] Only when

---

[10] Aristotle. *Nicomachean Ethics* (*EN*). Book V makes continual reference to this proposition. In a nearby place in the *EN* (1141a20–22; see 987b20–27), Aristotle remarks that if man were the highest being, politics would be the highest science. Commenting on this passage, James V. Schall notes that "it suggests that there is a relation between the truth of man and the freedom of man." James V. Schall, "The Uniqueness of the Political Philosophy of Thomas Aquinas," http://faculty.georgetown.edu/schallj/WS11BJVS.html.

[11] "Freedom is the power, rooted in reason and will, to act or not to act, to do this or that, and so to perform deliberate actions on one's own responsibility. By free will, one shapes one's own life. Human freedom is a force for growth and maturity in truth

we begin to be virtuous do we properly serve our end as human beings. This is what I mean by "moral and free."

But Protestantism does not accept human nature as moral *or* free. At first, the Protestants generally broke into two camps: Luther's and Calvin's. Each camp rejected man's post-Fall freedom within nature. Calvin's rejection of this prong of the Natural Law, however, was both more severe and more influential in America. Calvinists saw man as utterly predestined and therefore entirely without free will. To Calvin, man was "totally depraved"[12] and, even against the workings of his own intellect, totally committed to sin. Luther and his adherents, on the other hand, viewed human will somewhat more openly but still as "in bondage."[13] Luther provided a faith-based caveat against *complete* determinism: through grace, the Christian is capable of some highly limited freedom, upon conversion to faith. Nevertheless, even as Luther's slightly more liberal view provided a condition whereby man's will might be freed up in faith, it was not free within the state of nature. Thus, it can be said that even the more moderate Reformers such as Lutherans rejected natural freedom and natural morality.[14]

---

and goodness; it attains its perfection when directed toward God, our Beatitude." *Catechism of the Catholic Church* (CCC), no. 1731.

[12] John Calvin used this term to designate a sense of human will that could not be governed by the intellect, such as to turn from sin, even temporarily.

[13] Martin Luther, *On the Bondage of the Will* (1525), trans. J.J. Packer and O.R. Johnston (Grand Rapids, MI: Baker Academic, 2012).

[14] This book will continually refer to both Protestantism and Enlightenment thought as rejecting ontological realism, since being is portrayed as unintelligible by both camps.

And, on the other hand, Enlightenment thinkers all posited one form or another of *naturalism*, which states precisely that human nature is not moral or free. Indeed, naturalism dictates that all things within nature, including man, are predetermined to act blindly and irrationally, not according to any sort of intelligent structure. For the naturalist, anything made of matter — the whole world and everything in it — is randomly assembled, amoral, and unfree. Everything is a mechanism and a system. Thus, for Enlightenment thinkers, man was neither free nor moral within the forum of nature, because it simply does not afford such an opportunity. Nor does man's thinking apparatus (which, for Enlightenment thinkers, was not "intellect" or "mind," but just "brain" or "neurons"); it was merely one more material mechanism of nature.

Enlightenment thinkers supposed that everything that exists has been predetermined to act without freedom as a system. Therefore, to any adherents of this point of view, political and moral freedom is utterly impossible within nature or within society.

Now, republican self-rule is utterly impossible without natural freedom. The former is based upon the latter. Self-rule presupposes the liberty, the morality, and the intelligence of the citizenry. So, given the hostility of both of the Prot-Enlight halves to the doctrine of free will, how did young, Prot-Enlight America incorporate the idea of social and political freedom?

It borrowed secretly from Natural Law Catholicism!

Chapter 2 will discuss this fact in great detail.

Nature as Intelligible, Meaningful

The second property of the Natural Law is that nature is intelligible. This means that Creation (nature, being) was fashioned by

God to be understandable—and reality to be discernible—both in itself and to human beings.

"Being is intelligible," Aristotle famously held.[15] Also, the Catholic view is that the order and design evident in nature is precisely that which makes natural science possible. If nature were not ordered, there would be no reason for natural things to be the way we observe them to be.[16]

Therefore, for Catholics, science and philosophy are consistent with Truth (capital T)—that is, with theology—because, as Thomas Aquinas says, "[lower, scientific] truth cannot contradict [higher, theological] truth." Recalling this Thomistic principle, Hans Urs von Balthasar adds that "Thomas never fails to remember the way in which being points critically to the eternal, hidden God nor the way in which reason points noetically to the possible revelation of that God, and consequently he wants all metaphysics to be seen as oriented towards theology."[17] That is to say, man uses his natural intellect with science and philosophy to discern the order and intelligibility of the universe. And he can even derive *theological* meaning from it.

The Protestants—both the Lutheran and the Calvinist prototypes—held that *sola scriptura*, the Bible alone, turns out to be intelligible. Nothing on earth can be made any real sense of, except for the supernatural revelation of Scripture. The more

---

[15] Aristotle, *EN*. Book V of the *Ethics* is seen pervasively as standing for the position of Natural Law realism.

[16] See Michael W. Tkaca, "Aquinas vs. Intelligent Design," *Catholic Answers Magazine*, November 1, 2008, https://www.catholic.com/magazine/print-edition/aquinas-vs-intelligent-design.

[17] Hans Urs von Balthasar, *The Glory of the Lord: A Theological Aesthetics*, vol. 4: *The Realm of Metaphysics in Antiquity*, trans. Brian McNeil (San Francisco: Ignatius Press, 1989), p. 396.

extreme and popular American Protestantism, i.e., Calvinism, rejected as idolatrous any attempts to link the intelligibility of the universe with theology.[18] The Bible is, for such Protestants, the single manner of knowing about God or reality altogether. Obviously, neither the philosophical nor the scientific examination of the created universe is included in *sola scriptura* (e.g., the Bible mentions neither the philosophical principle of noncontradiction nor the scientific theory of gravity). Therefore, for the Protestant, nature is unintelligible. Chapter 6 will deal with this.

From the Protestant camp, the knee-jerk reaction to this book's thesis will be quite familiar. Again, many people will loudly point out that Luther and other Reformers affirmed the Natural Law; similarly, they reason that Luther's *sola scriptura* must not be opposed to Natural Law. Yet in reality, Luther affirmed something radically different, which he called the Natural Law: a very badly misdefined Natural Law.

The eminent Lutheran scholar Dr. Thomas D. Pearson noted precisely this confusion in a December 2007 article titled "Luther on Natural Law" in *The Journal of Lutheran Ethics*: "Although Luther does indeed directly mention natural law in a number of his writings, he does not employ any vestige of the traditional apparatus of classical natural law theory as it existed prior to the nominalist movement." Nominalism, which grew out of late Scholasticism and into early Protestantism, denied the existence of all objective and universal principles within the order

---

[18] In some quarters, Protestants claim that the Reformation did not pull away from ontological realism. They allege that *sola scriptura* restricts its skeptical claims only to what is knowable about theology, not about philosophy or science. But this claim will end up being contradicted both by extrapolations and by the early (Calvin, Luther) and late (Karl Barth) Reformers themselves.

of reality, citing their "fabricated" categorization in the human mind. Pearson continues that "Luther and Melanchthon — and by extension, Lutheran theological practice in general — depart from the classical natural law tradition in significant ways."

Applied to the will of God and to the order of creation, nominalism led directly to the Protestant view of a creation that could not be intelligible. It is an anti-Thomistic reversal of the traditional ordering of the primacy of God's intellect over His will, from which Catholic Natural Law derives. As Pearson continues: "If the divine law issues from God's will rather than from his reason, then there is no cause to affirm that human reason is the obvious instrument for intuiting the natural law that follows from the divine law." This is the keystone to understanding Luther's opposition to true Natural Law, as this book discusses it. It is also why, for Protestants, Scripture really is the only instrument at human disposal that affords a comprehensible view of the world.

On the secular side, Enlightenment thinkers rejected nature's order with a reinvigorated form of materialism, a philosophy denying anything that we cannot see, hear, touch, feel, or taste — which had been around since the ancient Greeks. All material functions reduce to the smallest bit of matter, randomly strewn together but not created. This was called "corpuscular reductionism" or sometimes just "atomism." For the materialist Enlightenment thinkers, nothing immaterial — God, metaphysics, ethics, or even our ideas — could be said to exist. Without meaning or order, nature must be considered *beyond understanding*, even if, quite ironically, the "new science" that stemmed from the Enlightenment created more nuanced tools for measuring nature than ever.

"Whatever would there be to measure, after all, if there are no immaterial or mathematical truths?" the Natural Law Catholic asks the Enlightenment thinker. But Enlightenment science did not ask itself this question, and so it remained in a state of perpetual self-contradiction.

So, both of the Prot-Enlight halves posited the meaninglessness of reality and thereby rejected nature's intelligibility. But republican self-rule is simply impossible without meaning. After all, meaning confers upon the citizen his conception of principles such as liberty and justice. *How do we know, for example, that living under just government is better than living under tyranny, if the invisible principle of justice does not make sense to us in the first place?*

The Catholic answer, of course, is that our natural intellect tells us so. The intelligibility of the natural universe renders it knowable! But, given the hostility of both Prot-Enlight halves to this proposition, we infer that they secretly borrowed from Natural Law Catholicism!

Nature as Teleological, Purpose-Driven

The third and final property of the Natural Law is that nature is *teleological.* This five-dollar word simply means that nature has a purpose. The goal of nature, as designed by God, is to get us back to Him through Jesus Christ, who created nature and entered it as a man. The Catholic worldview has always been that both philosophy and science should be grounded in this goal. Thomas Aquinas writes in the *Summa Theologiae:*

> All things partake somewhat of the eternal law, insofar as, namely, from its being imprinted upon them, they derive their respective inclinations *to their proper acts and ends.* Now among all others, the rational creature is subject to divine providence in a more excellent way, insofar as it

partakes of a share of providence, by being provident for itself and for others. Wherefore it has a share of the eternal reason, whereby it has a natural inclination *to its proper act and end,* and this participation of the eternal law in the rational creature is called the natural law.[19]

But in the sixteenth century, both halves of Prot-Enlight rejected this third aspect of the Natural Law. Both the Protestants and the Enlightenment thinkers rejected any purpose in nature. In other words, they rejected the "inclinations [of created things] to their proper acts and ends."

The Protestants — even as they have always agreed with Catholics that Christ is the final goal of existence — held that He *no longer has anything to do* with the universe (aside from His thirty-three historical years of dwelling in it). About this, Louis Bouyer writes that "in Protestantism, everything . . . seems to go on, as if the Incarnation had ended with the Ascension of the Savior."[20] Chapter 4 will explain how Christ continues to be connected to nature: via the sacraments, most especially through the consecrated host in His real presence. This is an explanation of how the Natural Law leads right up to the supernatural law.

But for Protestants, the universe points us in no way to anything about Him as creation's purpose. Only the Bible, not nature, does that. So, it can be said that what's missing in Reformation theology is the *teleological connection* linking Christ and the universe, the natural clue about the purpose of all things. In a word, most Protestants hold all the rest of the world outside the Bible to

---

[19] Thomas Aquinas, *Summa Theologiae* I-II, 91, 2.

[20] Louis Bouyer, *Introduction to Spirituality,* trans. Mary Perkins Ryan (Notre Dame, IN: Ave Maria Press, 2013), p. 25.

be wicked, misleading, predetermined, and pointless. That's what *sola* (only) indicates, after all.[21] They do not believe, alongside the Natural Law Catholic, that the human being "partakes of a share of providence." For Protestants, then, man is unable not only to perceive the intelligibility of the universe but also to use such intelligibility for detecting its *goal*, Christ.

On the other hand, Enlightenment thinkers, following one of their luminaries, Francis Bacon, specifically removed from the study of science the purpose of nature.[22] This is a bit simpler to see. Under Bacon's "new science," nature became a subject to be studied (for the first time in human history) with the expectations of both meaninglessness and purposelessness. Science immediately thereafter came to contradict its own truth-seeking purpose. Further, post-Enlightenment scientists became deeply dishonest as to their own motivations for doing science at all.[23]

---

[21] Admittedly, saying "only," "all," or "none" is always a huge commitment. But whenever in this book the reader takes issue with the appearance of these, please recall that the central idea of the Protestant Reformation (*sola scriptura*) did so first.

[22] Aristotle had posed four types of causes (material, efficient, formal, and final), which were accepted by medieval Catholic thinkers. The Enlightenment removed the most important two of these (formal and final) from the way in which modern science proceeds. Afterward, it could no longer be presumed that the natural universe had any goal (*telos*, or final cause) or intelligibility (formal cause) at all. In fact, the proposition of a *natural goal* was explicitly rejected by the Enlightenment, which brought about the irony that the "scientific explosion" of the Enlightenment produced far *less* good science than it might have, had it not removed final and formal causation. Chapter 6 will explore this paradox of Enlightenment science.

[23] Again, prongs two and three of the Natural Law described in this section correspond closely with the two most important

Obviously, the sciences seek after a natural goal, although they still do not admit it!

Until science reinstates its natural purpose, its modern practitioners cannot in earnest resume its quest for truth. Chapter 6 will investigate this dilemma in greater detail.

So, this book will show how these three properties of nature—its moral freedom, intelligibility, and teleology—are must-haves for citizens of republics. Specifically in America, these secretly wired properties of Natural Law bear out in six ways. Each chapter of this book covers one of the six.

Six Ways (in Six Chapters) Catholic Natural Law Has Been Miswired in America

Although the Reformation and the Enlightenment *began* as allies (as Christian and secular versions of rejecting the Natural Law and Catholicism), their intellectual "grandchildren" grew into bitter twenty-first-century rivals in America. In fact, you know these grandchildren as the "religious Right" and the "secular Left," respectively. Today they are more bitter rivals with one another than *either one* ever was with Catholicism!

So, you've been forewarned: this book exposes irony after irony in American history. Ex-bedfellows make the bitterest rivals. After all, the descendants of the Reformation and the Enlightenment—the religious Right and the secular Left—today seem to hate one another with that fury that is particular to former fellow

---

Aristotelian causes, formal and final, which also happen to be those two causes removed from investigation by Enlightenment science and the Protestant Reformation. Formal cause corresponds with the intelligibility (prong two), and final cause corresponds with the teleology (prong three) of nature.

travelers. In the last analysis, one must even conclude that the Reformation was *part and parcel of* the Enlightenment.[24]

This is really no surprise, considering that both camps rejected the Natural Law so vigorously. For the secular Enlightenment thinker, science replaced the old, goal-oriented view of nature. For the Protestant thinker, naturally a bit closer to the Catholic worldview, *sola scriptura* offered all the information required about nature.

As the closest thing yet to a "Natural Law republic," America has given republicanism a real run for its money — the best yet. But as noted in my opening pages, that run is quickly nearing its end, unless there is drastic change. The fly in the ointment is what you have read above: *America is a republic wired Catholic, labeled Protestant, and currently functioning as secular.* Its wiring was almost adequate — but secretly and dishonestly hidden. Thus, the hidden wiring became ineffective prematurely, since certain Catholic precepts could not be openly embraced or honored in early America. The problem is that America's mostly correct principles got lost in translation from *wiring* to *labeling*, and then even more so from *labeling* to *functioning*.

The list of our current problems is longer than the mere *symptoms* of tyranny and popular immorality. The longer list includes six specific marks of decay, stemming from the Prot-Enlight misunderstanding of the Natural Law described in the previous

---

[24] The identical goals of each were the demystification, the desacralization, and the democratization of individuals from the "hegemony" of the Catholic Church. Put another way, Protestantism is just Enlightenment thought — with Christ tacked on. The Reformation jettisoned all the aspects of the "bygone" Catholic era as the Enlightenment did, but unlike the Enlightenment, it retained a single item: Christ.

section. These comprise the six chapters of this book. And these six marks of decay can be countered only with an unwavering acceptance of the *Catholicity* of the Natural Law. In America, the best we have had to offer, to this point, has been *crypto*-Catholic (rather than outright Catholic). This must change.

In each of the six elements of crypto-Catholicism below, note how Natural Law Catholicism emerges with clear answers that fall between two bickering, confounded "opposites"—the secular Left ("Enlight") and the religious Right ("Prot"):

• Chapter 1 takes a look at the crypto-Catholicism of the natural rights appearing in Thomas Jefferson's Declaration of Independence. This covers the first step in any republic's life: *breaking the old regime*. Natural rights, it turns out, do not exist for their own sake: according to the Natural Law, we have natural rights only in order to fulfill our moral duties. Chapter 1 examines the British suppression of American natural rights in the 1770s and the ensuing revolution. The upshot is that the Prot-Enlight American colonists wanted natural rights without the source, Natural Law Catholicism. You can't have your cake and eat it too, especially if you're a Prot-Enlight thinker, whose two constituent philosophies *each reject* the Natural Law, as we now know. Following the Catholic model, Thomas Jefferson kept the original list of such rights in his Declaration very short. Today we find those rights inverted, perverted, and subverted by a far longer list of false new "rights" created by Prot-Enlight. Crypto-Catholic in their approach, the American founders lacked the *open* Catholicity to correctly access the Natural Law. *Americans accept natural rights as catholic, but not as Catholic.* You can't do that. Chapter 1 shows why.

• Chapter 2 zooms in on the framing of the crypto-Catholic American Constitution and on its primary author, James Madison. This is the second step in a republic's life: *making the new regime.* Chapter 2 further examines one of the three natural rights in greater detail: liberty. In what way does true liberty function? The Catholic answer, subsidiarity, holds that matters should be handled at the level most local, the closest to home. Chapter 2 takes a look at the false, secular copy of subsidiarity operative in the U.S. Constitution, explaining why local rule eventually broke down in America. Prot-Enlight plagiarized and mongrelized this primary Catholic social principle; with it, Madison wound up establishing something opposite to liberty: *license.* The republican culture degenerates if it forgets the *moral object* of its freedom. And so in our day, even most political conservatives who love freedom express it wrongly. They say that government should be done by a system of "local rule," rather than by subsidiarity. (Political liberals don't say it at all.) Because we've secularized a religious-political principle, the present version operates improperly, actually disabling local rule in our country.[25] Chapter 2 shows why.

Chapters 3 through 6 describe the third, longest, and final step — the cultural one — in a republic's life: *staking the Catholic Natural Law regime within the republican culture.*

---

[25] So, in sum, the first two chapters of this book cover the first two, out of three, phases in the life cycle of a republic. Chapter 1 focuses on the first phase, founding, as a subset of Jefferson and his influence, Locke; chapter 2 focuses on the second phase, framing, as a subset of Madison and his influence, Montesquieu.

• Chapter 3 examines the crypto-Catholic element of popular morality in America. After the founding and framing of a republic (described in chapters 1 and 2), only a republic's *people*, not its *governors* or *lawmakers*, can maintain it. Both halves of the Prot-Enlight worldview deny any possibility of a truly moral citizenry. Luther and Calvin ("Prot") reduced all human behavior to inevitable sin; secular thinkers Hume and Hobbes ("Enlight") did basically the same, while refusing to name it sin! And without a moral citizenry, a nation is not truly a republic, because, as Saint Augustine explained, wicked men are slaves to sin and cannot self-govern. Good men exercise their citizenship simply by leading virtuous lives and by tending the God-given moral authority over their families. Chapter 3 closes by asking whether, after good laws have been established, the *people* or the *government* of the republic are what continue to make the regime and the culture good. The Catholic answer must be that only properly formed culture, rather than government, makes a republic truly moral. Forced morality is, as Aristotle taught, "accidental morality." Only free choice begets "true morality." Chapter 3 shows why both halves of American Prot-Enlight deny the Natural Law proposition that culture is capable of sustaining morality.

• Chapter 4 assesses the historically catastrophic American misdefinition of "personhood" (operative in, say, slavery and abortion). It looks at the view that Americans hold about the role of ... well ... themselves. Which *view of the human person* (i.e., humanism) should be embraced in a true republic? Various conceptions of humanism — Protestant, Enlightenment, Catholic — compete for the citizen's attention in the years after the death and Resurrection of the One True Man. The answer is that the correct humanism, like everything else that this book examines, must come from Catholic Natural Law. Any semblance of correct humanism in America is therefore crypto-Catholic. To be *fully* human, our experience must extend to the supernatural—and this can be accomplished only through *sacrament*. The fostering of a sacramental humanism can be done only through the natural community of church, a notion that was often falsely embraced by American Prot-Enlight. The concept of church reminds us that our connection to the supernatural remains natural: a republic simply cannot be populated by fully *humane* citizens (each recognized as persons) without the daily role of sacramental grace. In turn, this is why the Prot-Enlight "separation" between church and state in America has proven so disastrous.[26] The Natural Law insinuates that the unique role of mankind (the only intelligent members of the universe, with souls to be nurtured) cannot be honored when church is ostracized by the state. Chapter 4 explains it all.

• Chapter 5 takes a look at the Natural Law connection of family and economy needed in true republics (united into the term "family economy" by Aristotle). The moral economy of the family is the natural community, which

---

[26] With a *remarkably* nonpartisan look at the jurisprudence of separation of church and state in America, famous legal scholar Philip Hamburger (who does not approach the topic as a Catholic) comes to a *remarkably* similar conclusion about the *mésalliance* between American Protestantism and post-Enlightenment secular thought in the nineteenth century.

must serve as the "original cell" and the center of any republic, as the *Catechism of the Catholic Church* affirms (CCC 2207). As such, the Natural Law charges each family with self-determination, making its own decisions—moral, spiritual, *and* economic. But in America, the merely supportive role of labor and wealth grew and supplanted the true goal of family: sanctity.[27] On this basis, Chapter 5 shows why economic liberty can be properly conceived only by Natural Law Catholicism, not by the religious Right or the secular Left, who mischaracterize it. It is quite simple: economic liberty does not *always* end in consumerism and careerism, as the materialistic Prot-Enlight conception of it does. True republicanism is rule by family (subsidiarity, as introduced in chapter 2), involving a system of moral capitalism, wherein government is disallowed to interfere in the private property and private contracts of family life. A true republic will always require the citizen's dependence upon family, not government (CCC 2207). Chapter 5 shows why.

• Chapter 6 examines the way in which modern science has been upended by the two sixteenth-century rejections of the Natural Law: the Reformation and the Enlightenment. *True* science must be done in accordance with the three prongs of Catholic Natural Law described in the beginning of this introduction. And as such, only Natural

---

[27] We will see this same Prot-Enlight shift from *freedom as means* to *freedom as the end*, in chapter 2. In chapter 5, we will see how and why each half of Prot-Enlight, for differing reasons, violated the Catholic Natural Law by making economic freedom into the goal itself, replacing family sanctity, which it is geared to serve.

Law Catholicism can offer republics such as America the sixth and final element of true republicanism: *right-minded science and technology*. The dictates of Catholic Natural Law contrast sharply with the pseudoscientific claims made by the religious Right and the secular Left: the former vilifies science as the latter deifies it. Science is particularly important in an age of technological innovation and discovery, rendering us increasingly dependent upon it. In this sense, technology alienates us from spirituality. And we must therefore treat it cautiously. The pagan dangers inherent in science and technology cannot continue to be ignored in Prot-Enlight America: chapter 6 puts forward the solution.

Conclusion

The whole point of this book is that the Reformation and the Enlightenment cannot be taken on their own terms: *if you reject Catholic Natural Law, then you can't make or maintain a republic.*

Period.

No lengthy conclusion is necessary; that's the easy part.

The premises, properly conceptualized, bespeak an obvious implication: true republicanism involves a certain view of man amidst a free, intelligible, and goal-driven nature.

So, America must choose either its Prot-Enlight philosophy or its Catholic Natural Law. But it can no longer afford to sustain both quasi-loyalties.

If America were to opt for an upgrading from *crypto*-Catholic Natural Law to *outright* Catholic Natural Law, then indeed things could be turned around. This would be optimal.

If, conversely, America were to stand more openly and consistently against Catholic Natural Law ... best of luck. For both

CATHOLIC REPUBLIC

America's religious Right and its secular Left, if they're being honest, the rejection of Catholic Natural Law means that government must be coercive and non-republican. Go get a king and hope for the best. (But at least this would be open and honest.)

As stated in the opening paragraph, this is not a book of philosophy or theology. It is a book about *what republicanism requires.* The limited philosophy and theology (and even history) that make appearances in this book are geared toward explaining the present republican decline. How could what began with the Virginian genius of Washington, Jefferson, and Madison wind up with ... the options foisted upon the voter by the last, say, eight general presidential elections?

This book, by adverting to *some* philosophy and *some* theology, will explain how.

Too often, authors of books of philosophy and theology put readers into an uncomfortable dilemma: "Believe either me (the author) or your own lying eyes." This book does not do that: it does not toil hours to "prove" propositions that contradict what easily can be observed. *Yes, America (or Europe) really is as bad it looks today!*

One needs not extensive philosophy and theology to see that; one needs just a small dose of each to get out of the hole and see things afresh.

Chapter 1

Breaking the Old Regime

The Crypto-Catholicism of the Natural Rights in the Declaration of Independence

Here, the pale clergyman piled up his library, rich with parchment-bound folios of the Fathers, and the lore of Rabbis, and monkish erudition, of which the Protestant divines, even while they vilified and decried that class of writers, were yet constrained often to avail themselves.

—Nathaniel Hawthorne, *The Scarlet Letter*

The idea of formulated "rights" comes from Western civilization. Specifically, it comes not from John Locke and Thomas Jefferson—as many might assume—but from the Canon law of the Catholic Church.

—Thomas Woods

Today in the United States and in the West in general, the role of the government has grown intolerably large. The space left for individual rights and for the authority of family, in turn, has shrunk drastically. Such a thing could not come to pass in a true republic, the form of government that once seemed to describe the United States.

Nowadays, the most accurate way we can refer to our nation is as a republic in name only. This term designates nations like ours, bearing a tenuous relationship with Catholic Natural Law, described in the introduction.

But, as we shall see, even republics in name only, such as the United States, claim to affirm individual rights. Given our rights-centered founding, even today's comparatively lax citizenry is somewhat vigilant, disallowing overt rights stripping by the government.

Even today's citizens, asleep at the wheel, would probably notice such an obvious breach. Something a bit subtler must be at work. You are about to see just what.

The *hidden* (crypto) Catholicity of natural rights imagined by the American founders sped the growth of government we see culminating today. Even though those founders created the republic to be far healthier than present-day America, it was nevertheless crypto-Catholic all along. And their plagiarism set in motion the eventual erosion of those rights.

This first chapter, *on the natural rights in the Declaration of Independence*, and the next one, on the Constitution, will describe how and why the rights' source (Catholicism) put forth by the founders was hidden *in the first place*.

But first, we must look at which rights have been removed and what exactly replaced them.

Once we investigate which natural rights were removed and replaced, we will conclude that ours is a republic in name only. It is what is suggested by the term "tyrannical government." American founders such as Thomas Jefferson felt exactly the same about England in the late eighteenth century as the opening paragraphs of the Declaration of Independence evidence. "Whenever any form of government becomes destructive to these ends," the Declaration asserts, "it is the right of the people to alter or abolish it."

But, in using language so closely mirroring Catholic Natural Law, Thomas Jefferson was only bootlegging from another, even greater Thomas: Aquinas.

One might accurately say that America ceased to be a true republic because government grew too large and because the people's natural rights were taken away and supplanted by false rights. More on this below.

Imagine the opening scene from the Indiana Jones movie *Raiders of the Lost Ark*, when "Indy" swiftly snatches the booby-trapped gold talisman and replaces its weight on the booby trap with a finely calibrated bag of sand. In that way, he sought to prevent the talisman from being missed. (Recall how the collapse of the entire structure immediately ensued!)

In a similar fashion, the American government has snatched our talismanic rights and replaced them with idols as worthless as Indy's bag of sand. But our political and moral situation in America today is bizarre precisely because, when the government removed the people's natural rights, the substitutes they offered were *anything but* finely calibrated to seem like those they stole. Unlike Indy's bag of sand, the false rights substituted by the government were not of sufficiently similar heft to have fooled anyone ... and yet they did.

After all, these pseudo rights proffered by the government turned out to be not only *false* but even "anti-rights": perfect opposites of what they replaced. One would assume that the American people should have caught on to such cheap fraud!

But we have been utterly duped.

CATHOLIC REPUBLIC

If the Prot-Enlight American founders of the 1760s and 1770s had been candid about the new republic's secret wiring—which turns out to be unequivocally Catholic—then these anti-rights would never have been placed before the American people!

Beginning with the Declaration of Independence, the secret *wiring* of the American republic was necessarily Catholic, but the young republic's *label* was as Protestant as its colonial authors were. And Protestantism had long before rejected the Catholic Natural Law doctrines that it would eventually come to need in America.

Because the impasse between America's Catholic wiring and its Protestant label was never sorted out, the republic currently functions *secularly*. In other words, American ambivalence about Catholic Natural Law put the germ into the host. And this gradually secularized society. To function secularly is to see our God-given rights removed. Our rights are not worldly, but rather otherworldly; to treat them as worldly is to take the first step in forfeiting them.

Even in a republic openly wired to Catholic Natural Law, eventual disintegration is the certain end. Along a wide-enough time span, any republic will fail. But America, on account of its false view of rights, seems to be dying prematurely. As James Madison once said, "Liberty may be endangered by abuses of liberty as well as abuses of power."[28] Saint Augustine in his *City of God* reminds us that decline is the eventual fate of all earthly

---

[28] James Madison, *Federalist* No. 63. In chapter 2, we will discuss the connection with another famous founder's quote: "A general dissolution of principles and manners will more surely overthrow the liberties of America than the whole force of the common enemy.... Once they lose their virtue they will be ready to surrender their liberties to the first external or internal invader."

republics.[29] But again, this should not happen so soon after the founding, as in America—and certainly not by such obvious counterfeits of natural rights!

We twenty-first-century Americans bear a share of the blame for forfeiting the house that the founders built, on account of our less-than-stellar vigilance. But this chapter and the next will show how there was a fundamental problem with the American understanding of the *source* of those rights—Catholic Natural Law—*evident even at the founding and framing*, which led us here.

The Prot-Enlight founders failed to understand the rights they fought for (and eventually "constitutionalized") as stemming from nature, which would have required a genuine, Catholic belief in Natural Law. Such natural rights, of course, are the products of a Catholic Natural Law with which the young Prot-Enlight republic could not square itself![30]

That is, the founders wanted natural rights without the source. They wanted to enshrine catholic (i.e., universal) liberty without acknowledging the doctrine of Catholic liberty. This cannot work. Natural rights come only from the Natural Law; universal liberty, too, comes only from the Catholic view of free will.

Ultimately, only a Prot-Enlight, crypto-Catholic understanding of natural rights could have produced this convoluted American rights regime we see in the twenty-first century.[31]

---

[29] Augustine reminds us that the City of God lasts forever; the City of Man is doomed to decline.

[30] Recall that both halves of Prot-Enlight, Protestant and Enlightenment thinkers, rejected all three aspects of the Natural Law.

[31] Insofar as such rights were *truly* Catholic, they were correct conclusions about nature and man; insofar as they were

CATHOLIC REPUBLIC

Remember from the introduction: America is that conspicuous republic *wired* Catholic, *labeled* Protestant, and currently *functioning as* secular. Such a cover-up has brought about the devolution from a true to a false republic, a republic in name only. Image perceived is image achieved: despite America's mostly correct Catholic wiring, its Protestant self-labeling gradually changed the way it functioned.

America sees Martin Luther instead of Thomas Aquinas staring back in the mirror. It shouldn't.

The Declaration's Natural Rights
versus Modern Anti-Rights

Let's get down to it. Which American rights has the government taken from its citizens? The answer is comprehensive: the government has inverted *each* of the rights described in the Declaration of Independence. Absolutely crucial to note here is their small number: "life, liberty, and the pursuit of happiness." The British violation of these three rights instigated the entire American Revolution. And by implication, we can argue that these three violations ought to prompt a just revolution *anywhere* (for reasons discussed at the end of this chapter).

The twenty-first-century American startles to hear that he has "only" three natural or true rights. His very surprise is a symptom of the problem. Not only has government taken and then fabricated three substitutes for our real rights, but to add extra garnish to the plate — to keep us from noticing the removed main course — more and ever more pseudo rights are tossed our way. We now believe we have *dozens* of natural rights.

---

crypto-Catholic, their basis within nature was convoluted and covered up, leading to their popular misapprehension in America.

We do not.

The Declaration lists only three natural rights. Here's the most certain checklist for failing republics in name only. Just ask if the government protects:

- the right to life
- the right to liberty (pursuing happiness[32])
- the right to private property

That's the test, which is quite simple.[33] And any honest, contemporary American response to all three questions will be no. Moreover, what exists in each natural right's place is a perfect anti- or pseudo right. Here's why.

The right to life. As guaranteed by the Declaration, the right to life in modern America is dead on arrival. Presently, it is *illegal* for any one of the fifty states to uphold the right to life by outlawing abortion. The present abortion jurisprudence of *Roe v. Wade* (1973),[34] *Doe v. Bolton* (1973),[35] and *Planned Parenthood v. Casey*

---

[32] Because, as we shall see, *liberty* and the *pursuit of happiness* wind up being the same thing, we also must ask if the right to *private property* is honored by the government. Locke included property as the third natural right; for reasons of expediency, Jefferson substituted *pursuit of happiness*, which was redundant of liberty, for Locke's property.

[33] Here is an excellent summary by founder and framer George Mason: "That all men are by nature equally free and independent, and have certain inherent rights, of which, when they enter into a state of society, they cannot by compact deprive or divest their posterity; namely the enjoyment of life and liberty, with the means of acquiring and possessing property, and pursuing and obtaining happiness and safety." George Mason, Virginia Bill of Rights (June 12, 1776), Article I.

[34] Roe v. Wade 410 U.S. 113 (1973).

[35] Doe v. Bolton 410 U.S. 179 (1973).

(1992)[36] collectively requires all fifty American states to sanction and defend the legal murder of young humans. It's that simple.

In other words, a pregnant mother presently holds a pseudo right to abort that nullifies the natural right to life. This is a sort of "right to kill." Think of it this way: not a single American person is conceived with a recognized *right to life*. Each of us "survived" pregnancy through either good fortune or good maternal choices, but *not* on account of the protection of life described in the Declaration, which is all but overthrown. Think about that grim fact as crowning evidence of America's pseudo republicanism.

By definition, a true republic must recognize and require the right to life. The American right to life weakens regarding *the end* of life, as well. Two cases of such a pseudo right—euthanasia and suicide—further illustrate our country's fixation with death. Both of these are fast gaining popularity in the culture.

Recall our Indiana Jones analogy: the American right to life was not surreptitiously or furtively removed through Indy's swift sleight of hand and carefully measured replacement. It was blithely inverted—stood on its head—and turned into an unmasked *right of death*.

In a parody of this scene, the comedy *UHF* portrays "Weird Al" Yankovic as Indy, carefully assessing the weight of the gold talisman, only to grow frustrated, impatiently shrug his shoulders, toss the bag of sand over his shoulder, and snatch the talisman without replacing its weight on the trap—*open* and *unhidden* theft far more like the government's snatching of the right to life in America.

This is the first symptom that the United States is a republic in name only. And it's a big one, practically sufficient proof on

---

[36] Planned Parenthood v. Casey 505 U.S. 833 (1992).

its own. Just as American colonists broke away on account of the British violations of the natural right to life, the same usurpation has come to pass under our own American watch.

Next is the right to liberty. In the infamous 1992 Supreme Court decision *Planned Parenthood v. Casey*, upholding *Roe v. Wade*, Justice Kennedy wrote: "At the heart of liberty is the right to define one's own concept of existence, of meaning, of the universe, and of the mystery of human life."

According to Kennedy's Enlightenment-style mischaracterization of natural rights, a citizen may use his "right" to liberty to violate another's right to life. Wrong!

Clearly, the government and the popular culture in America have inverted the right of liberty, such that its common understanding is now liberty's complete opposite: *license*. Whereas liberty, out of the Catholic tradition, is defined as the freedom to pursue the good, license is just freedom with no moral purpose (or constraints).

As if rebutting Justice Kennedy from ninety-three years before, Pope Leo XIII wrote:

> These dangers, viz., the confounding of license with liberty, the passion for discussing and pouring contempt upon any possible subject, the assumed right to hold whatever opinions one pleases upon any subject and to set them forth in print to the world, have so wrapped minds in darkness that there is now a greater need of the Church's teaching office than ever before, lest people become unmindful both of conscience and of duty.[37]

---

[37] Leo XIII, Encyclical *Testem Benevolentiae Nostrae: Concerning New Opinions, Virtue, Nature and Grace, with Regard to Americanism* (January 22, 1899).

License, or "freedom for its own sake," sounds much more like Justice Kennedy's expression of American relativism. Commentators have long noted that this is just the difference between *freedom directed* (at a moral purpose) and *freedom undirected*—which more starkly shows the contrariety between the two terms. "Liberty" and "license" tend to sound more like synonyms.

Once more, the universal recognition of the right to liberty is a necessary condition of the true republic.[38] As stated in the introduction, republics are the one form of government rooted in Catholic Natural Law morality. When the true sense of liberty is absent, one should feel confident calling his country a republic in name only.

Next up is the right to pursue happiness. Thomas Jefferson called this the third natural right in the Declaration. But as the reader may now see, the right to pursue happiness is actually the same thing as liberty. True happiness, as disclosed by Catholic Natural Law, means fulfilling human existence by freely choosing the

---

[38] The right to liberty becomes a sort of polestar of all the other political rights—the means by which they are captured or measured. In other words, liberty enables the capture of the others. Both life and property are also named in the Due Process Clauses of the Constitution, since the framers, like the founders, well knew the small number of natural rights. But liberty *enables* the furtherance of both life and property rights. And on that constitutional basis, the chapter following this one, on the crypto-Catholicism of the American Constitution, will make even clearer the perversion of the idea of freedom in American jurisprudence. Before it could be taken from us, liberty was first transformed into a pseudo doctrine of license. But for the moment, it should suffice to say that in both the legal and the popular context, American liberty has been supplanted and perverted by American license. The symptom is the rampant pleasure seeking we see all around us.

moral good.[39] This should strike the reader as nearly identical in meaning to the true definition of liberty: freedom to pursue the good. In both the ancient Greek and the Catholic sense,[40] happiness and the good end up being the same thing.

Man is truly happy when he acts as God intended him to act — morally. But in a failing or a failed republic, populated by immoral people, the pursuit of happiness is misunderstood as the immoral pursuit of *pleasure*. (Moral cultures, by definition, do not allow immoral government. Plato wrote that "the penalty that good men pay for their indifference to public affairs is to be ruled by wicked men"[41] — the very men who create such misdefinitions.)

Once again, pleasure seeking is an utter misconception of liberty.

This does not mean that no one in America honors the higher sense of happiness. It just means that the *popular understanding* fails to do so.

Sometime after the founding era, American culture stood on its head the natural right of pursuing of happiness (liberty), yielding the pseudo right to pursue *pleasure* (license).

---

[39] The concept of *eudaimonia*, as taught by Aristotle in the *Nicomachean Ethics* (*EN*), is the Natural Law's first model of human happiness, especially that of the high medieval period. This indicates not pleasure but rather a moral happiness, whereby humans note the effect of filling their proper function. Plato, *Republic* I, 347c.

[40] The sense of "happiness" intended by the founders of our republic came somewhat nearer than today's conception to the Greek word *eudaimonia*. Thomas Aquinas rightly understood *eudaimonia* to mean a particular kind of happiness: the morally ordered kind of human life, described above.

[41] Plato, *Republic* I, 347c.

Perhaps now the reader can see the high degree of similarity between the two rights of *liberty* and *pursuit of happiness*. Both terms, when rightly understood, designate properly ordered freedom; *license* and the *pursuit of pleasure* designate, conversely, wrongly ordered freedom. For the remainder of this book, we will assume: *liberty:license; pursuit of happiness:pursuit of pleasure*.

The takeaway principle is simply that true republics require citizens who pursue bona fide (moral) happiness, not just materialistic pleasure. A republic is a government of self-rule, after all. And it is a hopeless dream without a self-possessed, virtuous citizenry.

The right to private property. The third and final right indispensable to republics is that of private property. This was John Locke's third right, changed by Jefferson. A nation cannot be called a republic unless its government protects the private property of its citizens. In America, the current jurisprudence of private property, stemming from *Kelo v. City of New London*,[42] allows the government to transfer private property not only to the public domain but also to other private property owners as well.

In short, today's America honors an unjust pseudo right to *public property* running beneath the surface of private-property ownership. People are now thought to have a right in property *that is not their own*.[43]

Owning real estate is not the full extent of the natural right of property.

---

[42] Kelo v. City of New London 545 U.S. 469 (2005).

[43] Whereas the formal foundation of republicanism lies in the rights of life and liberty, the material foundation of any republic, as the Declaration of Independence recognizes, is the governmental defense of private-property ownership by citizens.

There is also financial-property ownership. Any system of taxation that does not enact a simple equality of proportionality (e.g., a "flat tax"), requires too much tax revenue from some and too little from others. And this has the same effect as transferring property from a deserving to an undeserving owner. As Aristotle writes, "Awards should be according to merit: for all men agree that what is just in distribution must be according to merit, in some sense."[44]

Both Saints Augustine and Thomas Aquinas follow Aristotle by acknowledging that a government that overtaxes its citizens immediately becomes a "thief." Thomas Aquinas[45] and Augustine[46] (rejecting egalitarian redistribution) agree that it is not only properly *legal* but also *moral* for man to keep what he earns. Thomas Aquinas asserts that "if possessions were equalized among families ... [it] would lead to the corruption of the polity."[47] For

---

[44] Aristotle, *Nicomachean Ethics* V, 3.
[45] Thomas Aquinas, *De Regimine Principum*.
[46] Augustine, *City of God* 19, 13: Justice is defined considering "the disposition of equal and unequal things, giving to each what it deserves." It is as unjust to make equal things unequal as it is to make unequal things equal, as Aristotle affirms in the *Nicomachean Ethics*.
[47] Thomas Aquinas, *De Regimine Principum* 4, 9: "Further, nature does not fail in necessities, as I said above, and therefore neither does the art of civil government, but this would happen if possessions were equalized among families, because citizens would die of penury, which would lead to the corruption of the polity. It also follows that the equalization of possessions is unsuitable from a consideration of the gradation of personages, as well as from human nature. There is a difference between citizens just as there is between members of a body, to which I compared a polity above: moreover, the virtue and function of different members is different. It is well known that someone

his own part, Augustine asks: "If justice is taken away, what are kingdoms but massive robberies?"[48]

In America, of course, we do not have the flat tax — the simplest mathematical way to honor the equality of proportion. Certain taxpayers are discriminatively taxed at higher rates than others. How much we are allowed to retain from our earnings is dictated arbitrarily by the government. Therefore, the right of financial property is widely inverted in today's society. And this, too, violates Catholic Natural Law.

The Supreme Court has added lots of pseudo rights to the short list of three true natural rights (life, liberty, property). Presently, the supreme law of the land holds that individual American states cannot outlaw the following pseudo rights: the "right" to purchase and use contraception;[49] the "right" to pornography;[50] the "right" to sodomy;[51] the "right" to gay marriage.[52]

And further, the Court recognizes a whole litany of entitlements that are not in any sense *natural*. These pseudo rights have been created out of whole cloth in order to distract the citizenry from the thievery of our true, few, natural rights. Just because the Court has rendered these takings *legal*, it does not follow that they should be considered *moral*.

---

who is noble must make greater expenditures than one who is not noble — it is for this reason, for example, that the virtue of liberality is called magnificence in a ruler on account of the great cost involved. This could not happen where possessions were equal." Here is the spot where Thomas cites Matthew 25:15.

[48] Augustine, *City of God*.
[49] Griswold v. Connecticut 381 U.S. 479 (1965).
[50] Stanley v. Georgia 394 U.S. 557 (1969).
[51] Lawrence v. Texas 539 U.S. 558 (2003).
[52] Obergefell v. Hodges 576 U.S. _ (2015).

In sum, only three rights formed the basis for the Declaration of Independence and the ensuing American Revolution. "Odd" or "curious" are not strong enough terms to express the perversity of the proposition that: (1) these three rights have been supplanted by their opposites and (2) that Americans enjoy scores of additional "fundamental rights" that turn out to be phonies. Both of these are, of course, egregious symptoms that America, the former republic — if it ever qualified as a true republic at all — is now dead.

This is the recipe for revolution. Let's have a look at how the American founders worked it out.

Revolution: The Spirit of '76 and Reclaiming Natural Rights

On that muggy, July morning in Philadelphia when the Declaration of Independence was signed, all that was *really* being expressed was the set of ideas contained by the pages appearing above: the British government had violated life, liberty, and property rights.

And this, in turn, convinced the American founders that they no longer lived under the laws of the republic of England,[53] which itself had been "restored" after a revolution during the previous century — the Glorious Revolution of 1688.

So, the American founders broke away from England.

The American colonists came to see that they were essentially being treated as "outlaws" or people with no rights. Obviously, the colonists had not violated any laws at all; the *English government* had in *its* offenses against colonial rights violated Catholic

---

[53] James Madison, in *Federalist* No. 39, proposes that England has "been frequently placed on the list of republics."

Natural Law. On this basis, a revolution was justified. The British citizenship of the American colonists, in other words, was already dead, *whether they liked it or not*.

Thomas Jefferson and the eventual signers of his document had, in the first place, to convince their fellow colonists of the somewhat obvious tyranny afoot. Afterward, Jefferson declared in the Declaration that the violation of these three natural rights led to a fourth, fundamental, but contingent right: *revolution*.

Revolution must be called a natural right because it pertains to citizens of all countries. But it must also be distinguished as a contingent right, because it "kicks in" only upon violation of life, liberty, and property. And, as Thomas Aquinas had long before urged, it must be undertaken in proportion to the state's violation of those rights. One does not have the right to revolt simply because he happens to suffer a minor or temporary lapse in his rights.

To connect with the spirit of the preceding pages, the reader should ask: If this book's argument is consistent, then shouldn't the fourth fundamental right — revolution — have been perverted as well?

Of course! Presently in America, the right to revolution also finds itself inverted because it is popularly understood as a one-time, nonrepeatable proposition from 1776. Such "one and done" reasoning should not be applied to natural rights, which are always with us.

To qualify as a right, revolution must be widely observed as a "fallback" option for all ages, but especially for the future. By its very nature, that's what a right is — future oriented! Thomas Jefferson wrote of Shays' Rebellion:

> God forbid we should ever be twenty years without such a rebellion.... If [the people] remain quiet ... it is a lethargy,

the forerunner of death to the public liberty. We have had thirteen states independent eleven years. There has been one rebellion. That comes to one rebellion in a century and a half for each state. What country ever existed a century and a half without a rebellion? And what country can preserve its liberties if their rulers are not warned from time to time that their people preserve the spirit of resistance? Let them take arms.... What signify a few lives lost in a century or two? The tree of liberty must be refreshed from time to time with the blood of patriots and tyrants. It is its natural manure.[54]

One cannot even begin to apply Jefferson's reasoning to America today: it's simply unfathomable according to most Americans. While Jefferson hoped that America "should never be twenty years without" rebellion—which verifies his belief in it as a natural right—the modern "patriot" ardently relegates rebellion to the pages of eighteenth-century history. For the modern-day American, who apparently would suffer any amount of tyranny rather than revolt, revolution is a one-time proposition.

Once more, what in the world is going on here?

We've been taught that the republican theory of the American founders was thoroughly and clearly in line with these four rights—life, liberty, property, and revolution. The English violations of these led to the *breaking* with the British regime and the *making* of the American one.

But, as we saw in the introduction, the Prot-Enlight reasoning of the founders and framers acknowledged as truly natural

---

[54] Thomas Jefferson, letter to William S. Smith, November 13, 1787, Paris.

none of the rights they pressed. The philosophy of the founders, therefore, *cannot* have been perfectly square with a proper natural rights regime. What would that proper natural rights regime have looked like?

Well … it would have looked *more* Catholic.

Thomas Aquinas: True Champion of Limited Government

We have all been led to think of "small government" as a new invention in the late sixteenth and early seventeenth centuries by the Enlightenment or by Reformation Protestants, or both. But in reality, neither of these Prot-Enlight halves could sustain the regime of natural rights upon which small government must be based. As the introduction to this book shows, both the Enlightenment and the Protestant Reformation were fundamentally based on the *rejection* of Catholic Natural Law!

Thus, any claims by them to support limited government must be faulty.

Take a brief moment and absorb that thought. Prot-Enlight *rejects* Catholic Natural Law. I am hardly the first to "ask how human beings, without using reason, can form moral judgments about the many particular [political or ethical] questions on which the Bible is silent or unspecific."[55] Without using the natural intellect described by Thomas Aquinas, one cannot navigate even the most basic political or ethical questions. It's that simple. But Protestants (and certainly Enlightenment thinkers) stop short of absorbing this implication, especially when it comes to the American founding, which they gladly count among their achievements.

[55] Richard J. Regan, introduction to Thomas Aquinas's *Treatise on Law* (Cambridge, MA: Hackett Publishing; 2000), p. xxi.

As will be shown below, only Catholic teachings can *truly* affirm the right of revolution—through Thomas Aquinas's interpretation of the Aristotelian Natural Law tradition. The Catholic tradition following Aquinas taught that all just revolutions are based upon violations of life, liberty, and property.

The main point of this chapter is that neither half of Prot-Enlight should have taken credit for the American Revolution. One would need to affirm the three prongs of Catholic Natural Law (described in the introduction) to do that!

Excepting only one Catholic founder, Charles Carroll, it was these American Protestants and Enlightenment thinkers—not Catholics—who wrote, ratified, and set into motion the Declaration of Independence. And the Declaration is, of course, famous for its beautiful articulation of natural rights. This means that the founders contradicted their Prot-Enlight philosophy: they plagiarized from their sworn enemy the Catholic Church and its Natural Law, which they refuted most ardently in other places.

It turns out that all these natural rights *require* Thomas Aquinas's understanding of nature itself. Ironic!

Thomas operates on the notion that government exercises God-given, *natural*—not just "socially contracted"—control over its citizens. But for Thomas, that governmental control was to be *heavily* restrained. Thomas strongly viewed the family as the primary unit of society. He believed that the child belongs to the father, not to the state.[56] Consequently, the father, not the government, is responsible to provide for his family.

---

[56] "Paternal authority can be neither abolished nor absorbed by the state; for it has the same source as human life itself. 'The child belongs to the father,' and is, as it were, the continuation

On that basis alone, Thomas must be seen as one of the very earliest advocates of limited government. But the evidence gets even more convincing.

In addition to this, Thomas beat modern libertarians to the punch by asserting that not all virtues should be required by the state, nor all vices prohibited. Also, the state's power should be limited to creating state police and enforcing martial powers.[57] Family and local communities should take charge of the rest of life's activities. The popular misconception of a "big-government Thomas Aquinas"—which came about in the last century[58]—is a complete and utter perversion of the truth.

To the contrary, Thomas regarded self-reliance and private-property ownership as vital to mankind: "It is lawful for a man to hold private property and it is also *necessary for the carrying on of human existence* [emphasis added]."[59]

Also indispensable for Thomas was personal financial-property ownership. In fact, he repeats Augustine's rule of thumb as to

---

of the father's personality; and speaking strictly, the child takes its place in civil society, not of its own right, but in its quality as a member of the family in which it is born. And for the very reason that 'the child belongs to the father' it is, as Saint Thomas Aquinas says, 'before it attains the use of free will, under the power and charge of its parents.' The Socialists therefore, in setting aside the parent, and setting up a state supervision, act against natural justice, and destroy the structure of the home." Leo XIII, Encyclical on Capital and Labor *Rerum Novarum* (May 15, 1891), no. 14.

57 Thomas Aquinas. *Summa Theologiae* II-II, 66, 8.
58 The Natural Law scholar John Finnis is probably partly responsible for this characterization of Thomas's philosophy, which poses that Thomas did not hold the view that is cited directly above from Thomas, *De Regimine Principum* 4, 9.
59 Thomas Aquinas, *Summa Theologiae* II-II, 66, 1.

the manner in which the state can so easily become a "robber"[60] if its laws restrict private-property rights. In *On Law, Morality, and Politics*, Thomas continues: "To take other people's property violently and against justice, in the exercise of public authority, is to act unlawfully and be guilty of robbery."[61] Of course, he offers the caveat that "if rulers exact from their subjects what is due them in justice in order to maintain the common good, there is no robbery."[62]

So, the key question is: What public roles would qualify for Thomas as satisfying "the common good" in present-day America? Not many. As noted above, the common good would seem to require *only* the martial and police powers of the state. Thomas writes: "Public authority is committed to rulers in order that they may safeguard justice. And so they are permitted to use force and coercion only in the course of justice, *whether in wars against enemies or in punishing civilian criminals* [emphasis added]."[63]

Whether it is popularly emphasized much or not, Catholic teaching in the famous encyclical *Rerum Novarum* by Pope Leo XIII tracks Thomas Aquinas's quote above very closely: "Private ownership, as we have seen, is the natural right of man, and to exercise that right, especially as members of society, is not only lawful, but absolutely necessary" (22). Immediately after this passage in *Rerum*, the famous encyclical repeats Thomas's above words.

---

[60] In his *Summa Theologiae* II-II, 66, Thomas Aquinas quotes Augustine (*City of God*): "If justice is taken away, what are kingdoms but massive robberies?"

[61] Thomas Aquinas *Summa Theologiae* II-II, 66, 8.

[62] Ibid.

[63] Ibid.

Taken together, all this underscores the Catholic call to public aid, not by heavy taxation but by private charity instead.

The same paragraph in *Rerum Novarum* refines this concept even further: "Whoever has received from the divine bounty a large share of temporal blessings, whether they be external and material, or gifts of the mind [which cannot be taxed!], has received them for the purpose of using them for the perfecting of his own nature, and at the same time, that he may employ them, as the steward of God's providence, for the benefit of others."

An individual holds his private property as his right, the Church affirms. Charity is man's duty, *Rerum* acknowledges, but it is religion's role to encourage it. And it is God's role to enforce it, not the state's: "There is no intermediary more powerful than religion (whereof the Church is the interpreter and guardian) in drawing the rich and the working class together, by reminding [not forcing!] each of its duties to the other, and especially of the obligations of justice" (19).

And to the *mere* two functions proper to central government that *cannot* be properly discharged by individual families—police and martial power—Thomas adds only one more power: a very limited basis for revenue collection. This is a simple tax owed to rulers for the civic job that they perform on behalf of the people they represent. But, once more, these "Thomistic taxes" are not a type of government-enforced charity; they are merely a method of compensating public servants. Churches and family fulfill the role, for Thomas, of charity dispensation.

So, Thomas Aquinas does *not*—as we've been led to think— view the state as the nanny-like enforcer of morals:

> Laws do not command regarding every action of every
> virtue. Rather they only command things that can be

ordained for the common good, whether immediately, as when things are done directly for that good, or mediately, as when lawmakers ordain things belonging to good training, which trains citizens to preserve the common good of justice and peace. Human laws do not by strict command prohibit every vicious action, just as they do not command every virtuous action.[64]

This Thomistic model leaves little or no room for the sort of statist, coercive, "public morality" comprised by twenty-first-century taxation. Nor does it leave room, for that matter, for *eminent domain*, discussed above. Both of these would almost always qualify for Thomas as state "robbery," as they rival the household father for his sacred role as provider.

And what does Thomas advise once the state becomes a robber of property or liberty?

Revolution.

Long before the American Revolution, Thomas Aquinas and his followers put forward an unequivocal right of revolution: "He who kills a tyrant to free his country is to be praised and rewarded."[65] About this particular passage, it has often been noted that "Thomas certainly does not go out of his way to differentiate between tyrannicide and less drastic forms of disobedience."[66] Thomas was not the peacenik that modernity

---

[64] Thomas Aquinas, *Summa Theologiae* I-II, 96.

[65] Thomas Aquinas, *Commentary on Lombard's Sentences* 44, 2, 2.

[66] "Thomas Aquinas on the Right to Resist," The Elfin Ethicist, July 6, 2006, http://www.shadowcouncil.org/wilson/archives/005614. html. This article also addresses the not negligible difficulty that Protestants face under the infamously anti-revolutionary scriptural admonition of Romans 13:1–7.

has made of him.[67] Spanish Jesuit Thomists Francisco Suárez and Juan de Mariana interpret Thomas by saying that there is little difference between life under a tyrant—a state that has turned to robbery—and being ravaged by a "ferocious and cruel beast."[68]

Thomas further distinguishes between permissible *insurrection* (tyrannicide meeting a few preconditions) and impermissible *sedition* (which does not pass those preconditions).[69] In fact, Thomas says that a king or lawgiver who exceeds his authorized power is the one who has committed sedition against his people, thereby triggering their right of revolution.

"If at any point," Thomas writes, "positive law defects from the Natural Law, a citizen may legitimately refuse to obey."[70]

Thomas cautions, however, that in order "to deserve this benefit from God, the people must desist from sin," and he later repeats that "sin must be done away with in order that the scourge of tyrants may cease."[71] Revolutionaries must always remember this caution, but few, except the American "Men of '76," seem to have done so.

---

[67] Aristotle, *EN* 1160b. Both Thomas and Aristotle favor quasi-political bodies or groups of overthrowers to individuals acting as lone assassins, but Thomas seems not to forbid it outright.

[68] Juan de Mariana, *Del Rey y de la Institucion Real*, vol. I, bk. I, chap. VI (Madrid, 1599), p. 109. The famous "School of Salamanca" of Spanish Jesuits was thornily Thomist, as seen here.

[69] Martin J. Littlejohn, *The Political Theory of the Schoolmen and Grotius: Submitted in Partial Fulfillment of the Requirements of Doctor of Philosophy in the University Faculty of Political Science* (Columbia, NY: Current Press, 1894), p. 155.

[70] Thomas Aquinas, *Summa Theologiae* I-II, 97, 3.

[71] Thomas Aquinas, *On Kingship: To the King of Cypress* (Aeterna Press), chap. 7. Thomas continues: "As the Lord says by the Prophet Hosea: 'I will give thee a king in my wrath,' and it is said in Job that he 'maketh a man that is a hypocrite to reign for the sins of the people.'"

Even with Thomas's condition that people must desist from sin in order to rebel or disobey authority justly, he is more extreme than Augustine in his support for forcible regime change. Even though Augustine holds that an unjust law is no law at all, he forbade tyrannicide by the citizens.

Regardless, we must remember that tyrannicide—condoned by Thomas and condemned by Augustine—is far more extreme than the particular revolt we call the American Revolution. Jefferson and company did not want to *kill* King George III. They did not need to. They simply wanted to secede from England, and it is a safe assumption that the political philosophy of Thomas Aquinas *certainly* (and that of Augustine *probably*) justified this.

What's most important for this chapter is the fact that Thomas *justified* the conditions of the American Revolution, whereas early Protestant thought could not. (Nor could the thought of the Enlightenment.)

The true story of the Prot-Enlight American Revolution contrasts starkly with the thought of Thomas Aquinas: as a response to intrusions into American liberty by the British government, some very confused Protestant colonists followed a set of doctrines known as "Whig Theory" set down in England during the prior century. Whig Theory represents a combination of Protestant and Enlightenment thought. Whig Theorists had begrudgingly, and secretly, followed the teachings of Thomas Aquinas and the Spanish Thomists in the area of natural rights (which, of course, included the right of revolution).

But, remember, both halves of Whig theory—"Prot" and "Enlight"—*rejected* Catholic Natural Law.

Therefore, colonists who followed the Whigs did so *against* their own Protestant and Enlightenment fundamentals regarding nature—which ran directly contrary to the three prongs of

Catholic Natural Law described in the introduction to this book. In so doing, they created a new, befuddled, self-contradictory sort of "Protestant Natural Law" theory in order to depose the so-called divine right of kings pushed by those loyal to the king.[72]

We have seen that the four natural rights (including the right of revolution) described in the Declaration of Independence hail back to Thomas Aquinas and his followers and the Aristotelian Catholic tradition. This has been kept an almost *total* secret in America.

After all, we've been taught that the rights described during the Revolutionary War emanated from the philosophy of John Locke and the Whigs, not from Thomas Aquinas or anyone earlier.[73]

---

[72] But, as one would expect, many Protestants still (more honestly) rejected Scholastic political theory as a "Romish" article of Catholicism and Natural Law theory. On the one hand, Anglican and royal-absolutist Robert Filmer wrote *Patriarcha* largely in response to Jesuits Suarez and Bellarmine. The Dutch Reformed theologian Jacobus Revius published his own response, *Suarez Repurgatus*. It suffices to say here that the Catholic tradition strongly affirms the right of revolution, whereas the early Protestant tradition rebuffed it ... that is, until certain Protestants — the Whigs — needed to borrow from it in order to respond to Filmer! Even today, the just revolution remains a difficult and obscure scriptural idea within Protestantism, which is really what this first chapter aims to show. Romans 13 seems to present much of this trouble. One notes as evidence of this schizophrenia the fact that some Lutheran universities even used works of Suarez as a textbook.

[73] At one point, Jefferson admitted that Aristotle was among the four most central figures, which stuck out like a sore thumb since "men of the Enlightenment" such as Jefferson had all but excised Aristotelianism and Scholasticism from the pages of history!

Let us now turn, as the American founders did, to the beliefs of the Whigs themselves, and assess whether their pseudo–Natural Law philosophy was truly independent of Thomas Aquinas or even whether it counts as a Natural Law philosophy at all.

"Protestant Natural Law" and "Enlightenment Natural Law" as Contradictions in Terms

At this point, the reader should understand from the introduction to this book that the English Whigs—and their American emulators—consolidated both halves of what I've called "Prot-Enlight." And we recognize today the effect: the total overturning of the rights regime that the founders established in 1776. What follows is further detail as to why neither half of Prot-Enlight could have possibly embraced (nor did embrace) Catholic Natural Law.

This portion of the book will not make sense without the introduction. But as a refresher before examining the Whigs, let's examine why both Prot-Enlight camps producing Whiggism *rejected* the truths of Catholic Natural Law (even as they relied on Thomas Aquinas's convenient conclusions for the purposes of the Declaration).

You may have heard the term "Protestant Natural Law." There should not be one. The concept represents a contradiction in terms. Neither the original Protestant Reformers nor their present-day American intellectual grandchildren, America's so-called religious Right, can affirm Catholic Natural Law.

Martin Luther held that the human will is "in bondage."[74] Without free will to choose right from wrong, ethical and political rights—products of liberty—make no sense. Luther's fellow

---

[74] Luther, *On the Bondage of the Will.*

Reformer John Calvin wrote that "as man is enclosed by the darkness of error, the Natural Law gives him scarce an inkling of the kind of service which is pleasing to God."[75]

One sees that although Luther and Calvin failed to reject the *term* "Natural Law," they did reject the *concept*.

Moreover, at the Synod of Dort in 1618 and 1619, very important early Protestant canons on this matter were laid out:

> There remain in man since the fall, the glimmerings of natural light, whereby he retains some knowledge of God, of natural things, and of the difference between good and evil, and shows some regard for virtue and for good outward behavior. But so far is this light of nature from being sufficient to bring him to a saving knowledge of God and to true conversion that he is *incapable of using it aright even in things natural and civil* [emphasis added].[76]

The last sentence says it all. For Protestants such as the American founders, if nature *cannot* tell us about civics — let alone about theology or ethics — then the efficacy of the Natural Law is destroyed. It must be one way or the other: nature is either intelligible or not. As Carl E. Braaten once famously wrote in *First Things*, Lutherans and Calvinists (i.e., the Protestants) "swing erratically between a position of utter rejection of Natural Law and one of conditional acceptance."[77] They can neither reconcile themselves with Catholic Natural Law nor do very well without it!

---

[75] *Calvini Institutio Christianae Religionis* (Geneva, 1559), II, 8, 1.

[76] *Canons of Dort* (1619).

[77] Carl E. Braaten, "Protestants and Natural Law," *First Things*, January 1992, https://www.firstthings.com/article/1992/01/002-protestants-and-natural-law.

Some modern Protestants who see the obvious practical value of Catholic Natural Law are quick to exaggerate the highly conditional ways in which Luther and Calvin *did* accept it. But this is not very convincing. To assert that Luther and Calvin were pro–Natural Law is, after all, to erase one of the very central foundations of the Protestant Reformation. The Protestant suppression of the Catholic Magisterium and Sacred Tradition wholly removed Catholic Natural Law from the practice of Protestant Christianity. Only the Bible (*sola scriptura*), one among three teaching pillars of the Catholic Church, remained available to Protestants.[78]

Wherever Luther and Calvin allegedly "embraced" Natural Law, they must not have been intending the Catholic version. For a coherent theory of republicanism, one needs the Catholic Natural Law described by Thomas.

Recall, to qualify as a Natural Law advocate, you need all three prongs of Catholic Natural Law detailed in the introduction.

Also, as mentioned above, if man's will is presumed to be "in bondage" or "predestined," as Luther and Calvin believed (respectively), then how can either thinker affirm even a limited Protestant sense of Natural Law? Ethics without freedom?

Impossible.

If man is "incapable of using [reason] aright even in things natural and civil,"[79] *how in the world* can citizens use

---

[78] The Reformation doctrine of *sola scriptura* excised two-thirds of the Catholic teaching voice, leaving "only" the Bible intact. The Magisterium and Holy Tradition were both severed. No surprise, these are the two pillars based upon the Natural Law. The Protestant cannot later recapture what the Reformation tossed aside simply because at some later point it became decidedly inconvenient not to have it!

[79] *Canons of Dort.*

their minds to take momentous political steps such as waging revolution? Or articulating constitutional rights in the processes of self-government?

They cannot.

Finally, by the early twentieth century, the Reformation developed (whether Luther and Calvin liked it or not) into a full repudiation of Catholic Natural Law. Protestantism culminated with the teachings of openly anti–Natural Law thinkers such as Karl Barth, who held it diabolical.[80] By our own day, such Protestant "development" included hyper-fragmentation into more than thirty-eight thousand Protestant sects.

Notwithstanding the impossibility of perfectly grouping all Protestants, it still makes sense to generalize *some* about the impossibility of a coherent "Protestant Natural Law" tradition. By its multifarious nature, Protestantism presents simply too many targets for a single arrow, but one can fairly generalize about Protestantism on the very basis upon which the Reformation was waged: fidelity to Scripture alone.

So much for "Protestant Natural Law."

We mustn't forget to reject the plausibility of "Enlightenment Natural Law." This oxymoron is a bit simpler to understand. Whereas the American grandchildren of the Reformation, the "religious Right," rejected Catholic Natural Law from *within* Christianity, the grandchildren of the Enlightenment, the "secular Left," rejected it from outside Christianity, or from total *secularism.*

---

[80] Otto Weber, *Karl Barth's Church Dogmatics*, trans. Arthur C. Cochrane (Philadelphia: Westminster Press, 1950), pp. 33–40.

In favor of "the new science," such Enlightenment thinkers[81] as Francis Bacon, Robert Boyle, Thomas Hobbes, David Hume, and John Locke rejected Catholic reasoning about nature (i.e., Aristotelianism-Thomism). Chapter 6 will deal with this new "scientism" specifically.[82]

The introduction to this book explained in far greater detail how and why the new Enlightenment view of nature in the late sixteenth and early seventeenth centuries included a rejection of Catholic Natural Law. The fine details are unimportant. Here, it suffices to repeat once more that such a rejection comprises three parts: *rejecting man's freedom within nature, rejecting nature's intelligibility, and rejecting nature's purpose.*

The reader should think about this in a general way: if nature is blind and random, as the Enlightenment (and in a different way, the Reformation) posited, *how could man and the rest of nature* be free, intelligible, or teleological? It cannot. And without these, Catholic Natural Law is implausible. Thus, "Enlightenment Natural Law" is also a contradiction in terms.

As we proceed into the next sections, it will become clear that most of the Enlightenment thinkers were *also* Protestant thinkers, which is probably why such a phenomenon as "Prot-Enlight" came about. And nowhere was this phenomenon more deeply rooted than within the Whig politics of England in the seventeenth century — the source to which the American founders looked for establishing their rights regime less than a century later.

---

[81] Prot-Enlight particularly denotes the English empiricists but also includes, to a lesser extent, some of the English rationalists.

[82] In most of these cases, this represented a new form of atomism, called by some "corpuscular reductionism," which openly embraced materialism, a view completely opposed to the intelligibility of Natural Law.

CATHOLIC REPUBLIC

It should now be clear that, in the sixteenth and seventeenth centuries, Reformation and Enlightenment thinkers agreed together about one primary proposition: that the Natural Law of the Catholic Church should be overturned in the modern world. For a whirlwind view of what happened in England the century before the American Revolution—the Whig or Glorious Revolution—see this very important footnote.[83]

---

[83] The Protestants rejected Natural Law from within Christianity; Enlightenment thinkers rejected it most often from outside Christianity. But the thought of both movements converged in the English political party called the Whigs in the middle of the seventeenth century. "Prot-Enlight," as I've called the phenomenon, lived and thrived among these early-Modern, anti-Royalist partisans of the English Parliament.

  Here's the gist of the Whigs' importance to America: the mostly Protestant American founders of 1776—"neo-Whigs" if you will—looked to the English Whig thinkers of the previous century. Most famous among these was John Locke. In fact, the principles of the American Revolution of 1776 largely *mimicked* the principles of the Glorious Revolution waged by the Whigs in England in 1688. Just as did the American revolutionaries subsequently, the theological politics of the Prot-Enlight Whigs set out the four natural rights we have discussed throughout this chapter! Yet, while the Whigs accepted such rights as intelligible conclusions taught by nature, the reader should now recognize that the Prot-Enlight philosophy they embraced actually *rejected* each of the Natural Law's premises (which produced the conclusions they wanted, natural rights). Catholic thought was thus secretly consulted—indirectly in some places and quite directly in others. And of course, the Catholic thinkers never received their due credit (until now!). As such, it is worth examining the writings leading up to and during the Glorious Revolution because such thinking was so closely examined and reproduced less than a century later by their American admirers. The bitter rivalry between Protestant Reformers and

Breaking the Old Regime

Catholic Counter-Reformers still burned white-hot in Europe and England in the middle and late seventeenth century. The reader must remember that the context of intra-Christendom religious rivalry was far starker in the 1600s and 1700s than it is today. The fervent anti-Catholicism of the American colonials ran back to English Whig politics between 1650 and 1750. This helps to explain why credit in America was stolen from the Catholic thinkers, without recognition, and given to the Protestant ones (who reified the nonsensical "Protestant-Enlightenment Natural Law" described just above).

Imagine a rival (Prot-Enlights) whose most loathed enemy (the Catholic Church) discovered and wielded something (Natural Law) that he himself absolutely needed for the struggle. Even more paradoxical, imagine that *that discovered thing* was the very source of their disagreement! So, imagine a person who, in a fight with his enemy, *takes from and uses against* that enemy the enemy's knife—all in the name of the rule that "knives should never be used in fights." This accurately mimics how both the Reformation and the Enlightenment related to the Catholic "knife" of Natural Law, especially in the English-speaking world.

For reasons hopefully now familiar to the reader, the concept of a "Protestant—or an Enlightenment—Natural Law" makes about as much sense as a circular square.

Now, the Whigs were English Parliamentarians who during the late seventeenth century opposed the English king on two firm grounds. First, as staunch opponents of all things Catholic, they opposed the hated line of Stuart kings, the "pretender" royals whom they viewed as secretly Catholic foreigners with non-English allegiances to "papist" countries. Second, as the political party first to elevate the legislative branch over the executive, Whigs forged a new political theory by assigning legislators "fiduciary" duties to the people they represented. The Whigs relegated the role of the executive branch—the king—to a secondary status in English government. Legislators, naturally close to the people, represent the popular interest in ways that kings, presidents, and judges cannot. The American recognizes this Constitutional concept well in his

CATHOLIC REPUBLIC

own Constitution. That is because it comes from the Whigs. During the 1640s the idea of parliamentary sovereignty was growing in England, whereby Parliament challenged the king at every turn. In 1649, Parliament put King Charles Stuart to death by the sword. Generally distrusted by the English people for his favoring of the "more Romish" Anglican Church over the "more Protestant" Presbyterian one and for his marriage to a Catholic French royal, King Charles saw his late monarchy give rise to two Civil Wars, culminating in his own beheading. With one swing of the sword, Parliament proved it *could* as much as that it *would*! In no small dose of irony, the notion that a king could be put to death by mandate of the people — via Parliament — should have been, but wasn't, ascribed to the Catholic Natural Law tradition discussed above. Instead, the Parliamentarians who went on to become the "Whig" party falsely claimed intellectual authorship over the doctrine of tyrannicide, even though their *sola scriptura* theology and their rejection of the inference of rights from nature seemed strongly to prohibit it.

In fact, most honest Protestants, to whom both the Natural Law tradition and its explanatory power remained unavailable, looked to chapters in the Bible such as 1 Peter and especially Romans 13 as admonitions against revolution and tyrannicide. *Thus, the reference by a very Protestant Parliament in 1649 to exclusively Catholic ideas in the execution of a Catholic king was both as secret and as ironic as the American Revolution turned out to be a century later.* Over the next three decades, the English idea of parliamentary sovereignty grew into a mature theory — notwithstanding its schizophrenic beginning. This meant that the tension between the Crown and Parliament would remain until the Glorious Revolution of 1688, by which time Parliament was widely recognized as the dominant reigning power in the English government. The very next year, 1689, John Locke's Second Treatise — the primary inspiration for the American revolutionaries nine decades later — extended the prior year's proposition to express that even *Parliament* is only conditionally sovereign. Parliament was to hold power only insofar as it represented the people, the true sovereigns. From that point,

The Whig Heroes of the Founders

Now you've seen why the American Prot-Enlight founders should have been unable *philosophically* to reason about Catholic Natural Law. Now we'll see how they were unable to do so *historically*. This involves something called "Whiggism."

The Whigs were the seventeenth-century English political party that first advocated parliamentary sovereignty, the overthrowing of kings, the ousting of crypto-Catholicism from English politics, and finally, the Glorious Revolution of 1688.

The English narrative in the century after the Reformation (the seventeenth) curves strongly toward "the enemy of my enemy is my friend."[84] In England, *Protestant* Whigs (Calvinists, to

---

"popular sovereignty" took such a firm hold over English politics that the Whigs essentially banished all Tories from all major governmental offices from 1715 until 1760, during the so-called Whig Supremacy. Lo and behold, who but the tyrant King George III would emerge in 1760 to break the Whig stranglehold! The fusty connection between the neo-Whig American colonials and King George's reintroduction of Tory politics into England was mostly accidental, if altogether fitting. Thomas Jefferson and John Adams were far more concerned with the ideas of the Whigs, rather than the personalities of the party itself.

[84] Since revolution-bulwarking "tyrannicidist" Catholic followers of Thomas Aquinas, Jesuits such as Francisco Suarez and Robert Bellarmine, had been firmly opposed by the Tory absolutists who defended the divine right of kings and the royal Oaths of (Protestant) Allegiance of 1606, 1643, and 1672, it is surprising that in England the first Whigs (who, like the Tories, were Protestant) willingly took such Catholic Jesuits as exemplars. Once again, "the enemy of my enemy is my friend" runs strong in politics.

For example, Whig archenemy Robert Filmer's *Patriarcha*—the crown gem of Royalist theory—was actually a response piece not to Whigs but rather to the forerunning arguments of the

be specific) began reading *Catholic* Natural Law philosophy to depose *Protestant*[85] Tories and Royalists. And they couldn't have been a bit happy about it. But indeed, sometimes the enemy of your enemy actually *is* your friend—temporarily. While the first of these Whigs were more bibliographically honest about the Catholic pedigree of their anti-Royalist ideas, their intellectual grandchildren in America a century later would not follow suit. Such Catholic pedigree was quickly—and perhaps intentionally—forgotten. Let's have a look.

Leading up to the thought of John Locke (1632–1704), the other originators of Whiggism on the Founding Fathers' reading lists sound like the title of a clown college, or a law firm: Hugo Grotius (1583–1645), Algernon Sidney (1623–1683), and Samuel von Pufendorf (1632–1694). Such thinkers, together with Locke, were the political names most often quoted from the West side of the Atlantic during the American founding.

And as you may have guessed, they were all *entirely* dependent on Catholic thought, which, from the Protestant perspective, was regarded as contraband.

Hugo Grotius, the earliest Whig hero, ranks as the fifteenth most cited author[86] by the American founders, according to a study by Donald S. Lutz. Grotius was the leading light among

---

Jesuits' Natural Law tyrannicide. This proves the point, more or less. The important thing is that the Whigs had a ready-made referent when they looked to rebuff the hated Royalists—fellow Protestants, but hated partisans. It is a strange plagiarism, although it is becoming familiar in this book.

[85] Anglicans and Gallicans, to remain specific.

[86] Donald S. Lutz, "The Relative Influence of European Writers on Late Eighteenth-Century American Political Thought," *American Political Science Review* 78, no. 1 (March 1984): 189–197. (Also, Lutz adds to these ideas his *Origins of American*

English Whigs until replaced by Locke sometime after the Glorious Revolution.[87] Also credited as having written the earliest Protestant apologetic handbook, he was a devoted Reformation thinker and a Dutch jurist who, like all the subsequent Whigs, felt curiously unashamed to articulate three natural rights that his theology could not account for. You know them as *life, liberty,* and *property.*

As Catholic apologist Father Robert Spitzer makes absolutely clear, the now famous short list of natural rights from Jefferson's Declaration came not from Grotius, but rather from a Jesuit Thomist *being read by* Grotius: "The principle of natural rights ... originated with a 17th century Spanish Jesuit named Francisco Suarez, in a 1610 tractate entitled *On the Law.*"[88] While Thomas Aquinas remains the "godfather" to these rights, the Thomist Suarez was certainly, as Spitzer points out, their direct "father." Grotius counts as neither of these.

While Grotius accepted the three natural rights (i.e., the basis for revolutions), which ought to have been offensive to his

---

Constitutionalism. Critique of Lutz published by Omohundro Institute of Early American History and Culture, 1990.)

[87] Michael Zuckert, *Natural Rights and the New Republicanism* (Princeton, NJ: Princeton University Press, 1994).

[88] Robert J. Spitzer, *Ten Universal Principles: A Brief Philosophy of the Life Issues* (San Francisco: Ignatius Press, 2011), p. 52. Spitzer continues the discussion on page 74: "We can see the faint outline of Jefferson's three inalienable rights ... Suarez's right to self-preservation corresponding to Jefferson's right to life, Suarez's right to the natural perfection of human nature corresponding to Jefferson's right to liberty, and Suarez's right to happiness corresponding to Jefferson's right to the pursuit of happiness. In another part of *De Legibus*, Suarez includes property within the notion of natural rights."

Protestantism, his shame kicked in regarding the right of revolution (a right he denied as an honest Protestant). It has been said that "those who seek in Grotius an intellectual ancestor of Locke or Jefferson, as a supporter of the right of revolution ... must look in vain."[89] This is because, as commentators have long noted, Grotius believed that "once [the people] had transferred their right of government to the ruler, they forfeited the right to control the ruler however bad their government was."[90]

Why pose three "natural" rights at all, if they are not guaranteed by a fourth—the right to defend them? Nevertheless, Grotius instituted a Whig theme that would be repeated frequently thereafter: "Protestant Natural Law" and "Protestant natural rights." At the very riverhead of Whig thought, Grotius borrowed *openly* from the Catholic thought of Thomas Aquinas and Francisco Suarez, even praising their works. But later Whigs would not be so transparent about their Catholic sources.

The first English Whig to make the American founders' reading list, ranking thirty-third most often cited,[91] was Algernon Sidney, a Protestant who, unlike Grotius, affirmed the right of revolution. It has been said that John Adams could not, without breaking into tears, read Sidney's fiery political philosophy. Thomas Jefferson, for his part, cited Sidney's *Discourses concerning*

---

[89] Stephen C. Neff, *Hugo Grotius on the Law of War and Peace*, student ed. (Cambridge: Cambridge University Press, 2012), p. xxxi.

[90] W. Friedmann, *Legal Theory* (Delhi, India: Universal Law Publishing, 1999), cited in Daudi Nyamaka's paper "Social Contract Theory of John Locke (1632–1704) in the Contemporary World," June 2011, available at Academia, https://www.academia.edu/1489291/Social_Contract_Theory_of_John_Locke_1932-1704_in_the_Contemporary_World.

[91] Lutz, "Relative Influence."

Government as "probably the best elementary book of the principles of government, as founded in natural right, which has ever been published in any language."[92] But the problem with Jefferson's claim is that Sidney himself acknowledged — perhaps by protesting too much — his intellectual debt to a Catholic called one "of the greatest of neo-Thomist Jesuits ... Robert Bellarmine."[93]

> I do not find any great matters in the passages taken out of Bellarmine.... I do not think myself obliged to examine all his works, to see whether they are rightly cited or not; however there is certainly nothing new in them.... But as he seems to have laid the foundation of his discourses in such common notions as were assented to by all mankind, those who follow the same method have no more regard to Jesuitism and popery, tho he was a Jesuit and a cardinal, than they who agree with Faber and other Jesuits in the principles of geometry which no sober man did ever deny.[94]

---

[92] Thomas Jefferson to John Trumbull, January 18, 1789, in *The Papers of Thomas Jefferson*, ed. Julian P. Boyd (Princeton, NJ: Princeton University Press, 1950), 14:467. Thomas Jefferson expressed related sentiments in a letter to Mason Locke Weems on December 13, 1804, in "Catalogue of the Library of Thomas Jefferson."

[93] Bradley J. Birzer, "Algernon Sidney and Yet One More Beautiful Founding Complication," *Imaginative Conservative*, March 24, 2014, https://theimaginativeconservative.org/2014/03/algernon-sidney-yet-one-beautiful-founding-complication.html.

[94] Algernon Sidney, *Discourses concerning Government*, ed. Thomas G. West (Indianapolis; Liberty Fund, 1996), p. 19.

Common notions? Why yes, Algernon, "common notions" means Catholic Natural Law, if that's what you mean!

Once more, Sidney was one of the first English Whigs who begrudgingly embraced his Catholic rivals.[95]

But even if Sidney had not directly referenced Bellarmine's work as he did, his admission that natural rights rank among the "common notions" of the world still means that he was engaging in a sort of commonsense, Catholic Natural Law reasoning. And, as we saw in the introduction, such reasoning should not have been available to a consistent Prot-Enlight thinker. Thankfully, for clarity's (and this book's) sake, he openly admits it!

Next we come to Samuel von Pufendorf, the tenth most often quoted source[96] of the American founders, and a famed German jurist. Pufendorf spent much of his academic life studying and writing on the works of Grotius. So obviously, any Grotian absorptions of Thomas (secret or admitted) would have trickled down to Pufendorf. Around the time when Sidney found a Catholic source to plagiarize in Bellarmine, Pufendorf conveniently "found" a right of revolution and even a "duty to overthrow tyranny" missed by Grotius.[97]

Subsequent to Pufendorf (and Sidney), the Whigs forgot their ideological hesitancy about revolution—even though none

---

[95] Because such Natural Law Catholic thinkers most effectively countered Sidney's Tory counterparts, like Robert Filmer in the Royalist *Patriarcha*, Sidney was certainly "picking between poisons." Ultimately, it is no surprise that Sidney's thought was thoroughly infused with a Catholic right of revolution, which Sidney would not have found in fellow Protestants like Grotius.

[96] Lutz, "Relative Influence."

[97] David B. Kopel, "The Scottish and English Religious Roots of the American Right to Arms," *Bridges* 12, nos. 3–4 (Fall–Winter 2005): 291.

of them could provide a non-Catholic basis for it! In this way, Pufendorf was a trailblazing Whig thinker—or at least a trailblazing plagiarist—along with Sidney.

Last in sequence, we come to John Locke, the American founders' Whig of choice. Locke is easily the best known of the *forefathers' forefathers*. He is the fourth most consulted source for the American founders (only the Bible and other nonpolitical sources outrank Locke). Also, the schizophrenia of Locke's philosophy is the most emblematic of America's so-called "Protestant Natural Law" and "Enlightenment Natural Law." By Locke's day, Whiggism had already completely plagiarized Catholic Natural Law, absorbed it entirely, and then conveniently forgotten about it. "Often classified as a Natural Law theorist but vigorously reject[ing] the Aristotelian metaphysics of the Scholastic [Catholic] tradition,"[98] Locke *cannot* belong under this classification. His thought stands unrivaled as the epitome of Prot-Enlight schizophrenia.

Locke's thought absorbed the natural rights but "forgot" their inconvenient justification: Catholic Natural Law.

Locke's entire philosophy was dedicated to proving how mechanistic and meaningless the universe is. The theme is utterly well-developed in the course of his writings. But suddenly, in his political discourses, Locke "flip-flops" by springing it on his reader that nature is *somehow* (not via Catholic Natural Law) the bearer of a meaningful message of God-given rights.

It's this simple: if a thinker rejects the central ideas of Thomas Aquinas, he *must be against* Catholic Natural Law. He must reject

---

[98] Edward Feser, "Classical Natural Law Theory, Property Rights, and Taxation," *Social Philosophy and Policy Foundation* 27 (2010): 21–52.

the concept of nature as moral, meaningful, and purposeful. Locke was doubly guilty of such a rejection of Catholic Natural Law, being both a practicing "Prot" and a practicing "Enlight."

The Bible counts as *supernatural* law; man's natural intellect and common sense (in relation to nature) equate to Catholic Natural Law.[99] In this vein, commentator Jeremy Waldron notes that "Locke was intensely interested in Christian doctrine, and in the *Reasonableness of Christianity* he insisted that most men could not hope to understand the detailed requirements of the law of nature without the assistance of the teachings and example of Jesus [i.e., the Bible]."[100] As Waldron points out, this would be denial, not acceptance, of Catholic Natural Law. Waldron continues, "Like the two other very influential [Prot-Enlight] Natural Law philosophers [being read by the founders], Hugo Grotius and Samuel von Pufendorf, Locke equated natural law [not with intelligible nature but] with the biblical revelation."[101]

---

[99] From very early in the Christian tradition—a millennium before Thomas Aquinas even—Natural Law thinkers such as Saint Augustine and the Patristics spoke about a "book of nature" (Natural Law) and a "book of Scripture" (supernatural law), as will be referenced in chapter 6. The latter is superior and more specific, of course, insofar as it memorializes inerrant revelation by God to man; but it is available only to believing Christians, lacking the universality of the Natural Law. As such, Locke's inclusion of Scripture as part and parcel of the Natural Law appears not only to be *new*, but also *tendentious* and *intellectually dishonest*.

[100] Jeremy Waldron, *God, Locke, and Equality: Christian Foundations in Locke's Political Thought* (Cambridge University Press, 2002). See also M. Elze, "Grotius, Hugo," *Die religion in geschichte und gegenwart* (in German); 3. Auflage, band II, col. 1885–1886, published 1958.

[101] Waldron, *God, Locke, and Equality*.

Natural Law *equals* Biblical revelation? "Natural Law," by its very definition, means deriving rights and duties from the intelligible world around us, *not* from Biblical revelation. Locke, however, was *forced* to proceed with that misdefinition. He rejected true Natural Law but supported the Whig revolution (in his *Two Treatises* [1689]) against the (ironically) Catholic tyrant in 1688's Glorious Revolution. In other words, he wanted the right of revolution even as he rejected its source. Similarly, a century later, the American founders, implementing Locke and calling themselves "neo-Whigs," wanted a right of revolution to overthrow "tyrant king" George III—also while rejecting the source.

In a nutshell, it is fair to repeat that Locke's "views show the shape of the new world that Luther helped create in proposing that each person should access God through prayer and Bible study"[102] (not through the three prongs of Catholic Natural Law[103] summarized in this book).

The simple fact is that if one's creed does not allow one to reason about rights or duties from nature alone—an ability both the Enlightenment and the Reformation dismissed—then he will have either *to rip off the Catholics* if he wants to turn revolutionary,

---

[102] Nicholas P. Miller, "America's Founding Protestant Philosophy," *Liberty* (January-February 2014), http://www.libertymagazine. org/article/americas-founding-protestant-philosophy. Nicholas Miller, Ph.D., is an attorney and associate professor of church history at Andrews University, Berrien Springs, Michigan.

[103] "Locke further shows that the law's obligatoriness can be no more established on the basis of reformulated Natural Law than it could be on the basis of immanent Natural Law." Michael Zuckert, *Natural Rights and the New Republicanism* (Princeton, NJ: Princeton University Press, 1994), p. 210.

or *to forebear under tyrannical regimes whenever they pop up*. There's no other way around it.

This is why each of the Whig thinkers or heroes bore such a tortured relation to Thomas Aquinas: like angry teens, they wildly craved independence (from both the Catholic Church *and* the Royalists), yet simultaneously they needed the vital "Romish" philosophy and patrimony to overthrow the Royalist yoke.

Whiggism was just crypto-Catholic political theory imported by English Protestants—many of whom were also Enlightenment empiricists—and turned directly against Catholics in the seventeenth century. Neo-Whigs continued the crusade against the Catholics (including the "more Romish" Protestants, such as Episcopalians) in eighteenth-century America. That is, Thomas Aquinas and Catholic Natural Law theorists were the secret heroes of the reluctant English Whigs (who were themselves the heroes of the later American neo-Whigs).

Neither the English Whigs nor the American founders could have waged revolution in 1688 or 1776 without secretly plagiarizing Catholic ideas. And this means that the American founding was unequivocally Catholic. Now how simple is that?

Breaking the Regime: First Phase in Any Republic

Thomas Jefferson wrote the Declaration of Independence, and fifty-six men signed it.

It should now be clear that only one man—the single Catholic signer of the Declaration—could have meant those Catholic Natural Law ideas *in full*, without modification, mitigation, or perversion. That man happened to be Charles Carroll of Carrollton. The main point of this chapter is that American rights first turned to pseudo rights *culturally*—because they were misunderstood by Protestants from the outset—and then *legally*.

Today, those rights are mere relics of the past.

But they can be returned to.

In other words, this chapter began by announcing that the four natural rights heralded by the Declaration have been replaced by cheap, functionally opposite substitutes. As such, government has grown to replace both religion and family. The religious Right (grandkids of the Protestant Reformation) blame "big government" in American politics, which they identify as the secular Left (grandkids of the Enlightenment).

The religious Right are *largely* correct: the natural rights of the Declaration were codified a decade later in the Constitution, albeit in an imperfect way. But this chapter has labored to show how *both* parts—Prot and Enlight—lent to the formation in the 1776 Declaration (and then in the 1788–1791 Constitution) of an American rights regime highly ambivalent about the source of those rights. And that ambivalence is precisely what has allowed the secular Left to pervert the American Constitution, replacing those prior Declaration rights with semi-forgeries.

America is the nation *wired Catholic, labeled Protestant, and currently functioning as secular*. This first chapter has argued that if America had been *honestly* labeled Catholic—following its wiring—then the initial understanding of rights would have been proper. In turn, those rights would not have been subject to perversion and to present-day secular functioning.

The final point of this chapter is also the biggest: the necessary Catholic wiring of our republic is not unique to America. All republics are by definition governments of self-rule, requiring Catholic Natural Law, which itself requires the "baptized Aristotelianism" of Thomas Aquinas. There is no other way to have a republic.

Interpretation: among would-be republics, America is not unique in its dependence on Natural Law Catholicism; all true republics are.

The principles of the Declaration of Independence represent not only the first step toward American independence, but the first phase of life *in any republic: breaking with the old regime.* You have just finished reading about this first phase as it must happen in any new republic.

Global geography is fixed: no undiscovered land exists where one can go and found his own new colony. As such, new republics must be begotten by breaking with old ones. As Jefferson wrote in the Declaration, borrowing from Natural Law Catholicism, America was founded by "dissolving political bands" with England and by clearly "declaring the causes impelling the separation."

So it must be for any new republic, not only the American one. There must be a document *breaking the former regime*, or at least breaking ties with it. Such a document must, as the Declaration did, list the reasons for the revolution. And as the reader now knows, those reasons must always be the same in any righteous (i.e., Catholic Natural Law) revolution: violations of life, liberty, and property. The right of revolution, a fourth right, is triggered by violations of those primary three. If the revolution succeeds, the former regime will be broken.

The ideas of Catholicism were absolutely necessary in the breaking of the English regime in America in 1776. Such ideas are indispensable to *any other* Natural Law revolution. After all, *anyone* who believes in the republican form of government actually borrows from Catholicism.[104]

---

[104] All this motivates a new "backdoor apologetics": instead of debating theology, backdoor apologetics wins converts through

Breaking the Old Regime

Now, after exploring the first republican phase — regime-breaking — we will go on to see how the second phase of all republics — *regime-making* — requires codifying into a Constitution those Catholic Natural Law rights recently won in revolution.

---

political science. Any secular or Protestant fan of limited government should be strongly persuaded by the requirements of republicanism to convert to the point of view that uniquely affirms it ... or else to abandon the position of limited government. And this should happen automatically after he sees that a republic can function only upon the corpus of Catholic presuppositions about the universe! It is time that Catholics, Protestants, and secularists in America affirm how republics and natural rights (along with chapter 2's subsidiarity, chapter 3's popular morality, chapter 4's humanism, chapter 5's political economy, and chapter 6's proper science) may only function from a certain point of view. And since proponents of limited government already embrace our conclusion, it is simply a matter of showing them that neither the post-Enlightenment nor the post-Reformation point of view can affirm these things with any internal consistency.

Chapter 2

Making the New Regime

The Crypto-Catholicism of the Subsidiarity in the U.S. Constitution

Liberty may be endangered by abuses of liberty as well as abuses of power.

—James Madison

The antifederalists have been called "men of little faith" in that they lacked faith in the safe future that the federalists foresaw under the Constitution. But in the context of the great mass of ratification documents, the antifederalists emerge as the ones who kept the faith—the ancient faith so fundamental a part of the ideological origins of the Revolution, from which, they argued, the Constitution departed.

—Bernard Bailyn, *The Ideological Origins of the American Revolution*, 331

If the role of the American government has grown dangerously large, as chapter 1 showed, it did so with Constitutional "permission." Many Constitution-loving conservatives seek to deny this fact (while liberals, of course, celebrate it). But it remains an indisputable fact: American liberals could not possibly have grown the central power of the state unless they had *some sort* of Constitutional sanction to do so.

To put this in the context of chapter 1: without a written English constitution, natural rights had never been codified for the American colonials of the early and middle 1700s, as they eventually would be under the American Constitution. Strangest of all is that American liberals were able to replace these codified natural rights entirely with pseudo rights — notwithstanding their "protection" after the ratification of the Constitution in 1788.

So, our present lack of natural rights in America is even more egregious than the colonists' lack thereof. Unlike theirs, which they never quite had a grasp on, our rights were *forfeited* to the federal government. And that gradual forfeiture shows that our country's descent into "big government" (established in chapter 1) involves the Prot-Enlight ideas woven into the Constitution itself,[105] as conceived by James Madison.

In the American republic, after all, we *have* a written and ratified Constitution, a Supreme law of the land, to invoke. By definition, all our laws have already passed Constitutional muster.

Thus, if the natural rights of life, liberty, and property are presently overlooked, that means they have been *legally* and *constitutionally* overlooked. How could (legally) protected rights be (legally) exposed to perversion and forfeiture? Shouldn't the people's Constitution have protected us against this?

This chapter will explain how and why such a Constitutional hijacking came to pass: the main idea behind the U.S.

---

[105] As with what was said of the Declaration in chapter 1, this chapter will focus on how the Prot-Enlight *general* misunderstanding of constitutionalism was incorporated into the *particular* U.S. Constitution.

Constitution, *federalism* (often called "states' rights"), involves local rule and the keeping of power at the community level. This was largely to the good, in early America. But federalism is supposed to yield small government; instead, it delivered the exact opposite by 2016. Here's why: federalism was incorporated incompletely into the Constitution. And this incompleteness stemmed from the Prot-Enlight misunderstanding of the fuller, Catholic version of federalism, called *subsidiarity, this book's second element of American crypto-Catholicism.*

Subsidiarity is "fuller" than federalism because *its* rendition of local rule operates on liberty, whereas *federalism's* version of local rule operates on license. Again, the misunderstood nature of American subsidiarity (i.e., federalism) codified within our Constitution (by Prot-Enlight) led to its eventual degradation and forfeiture: only Catholic Natural Law can sustain a *methodical* liberty that does not immediately disintegrate, like a counterfeit handbag.

So, this chapter will focus upon how Constitutional liberty and subsidiarity in America were perverted, culturally and legally, by the faulty interpretation of its Prot-Enlight framers. In assessing American federalism and subsidiarity, we shall examine the confounded Prot-Enlight sense of "liberty" actually guaranteed by the Constitution in 1788. (Recall how Prot-Enlight rejects the concept entirely, but thereafter seeks to benefit from American "liberties," through the unjustified and one-sided enjoyment of personal freedoms.) True liberty, unlike license, carries an onerous *burden* as well as an enjoyable *benefit:* i.e., true republics must arrange liberty such that household fathers and mothers shoulder the moral and religious enculturation of their children. This is the one true connection between Catholic Natural Law's liberty and subsidiarity.

To explain this concept, we must first ask what true constitutions actually accomplish.

By now, the reader should strongly suspect that our confusion about such a basic idea has something to do with the fact that America is the nation *wired Catholic, but labeled Protestant, and currently functioning as secular.*

Just as the act of founding was shown to be crypto-Catholic in chapter 1, we will see in this chapter that the act of framing followed suit. In both acts, crypto-Catholicism kept the Catholic ideas from transferring 100 percent, causing both to devolve more and more over time, the symptoms of which confront us even today.

We shall pick up right where chapter 1 left off, just as America's framers, or *makers* of the Constitution, picked up exactly where the founders — or *breakers* with the British constitution — left off. Most notable among these younger framers was James Madison, whose confused sense of subsidiarity crowns the Constitutional misunderstandings of liberty discussed in this chapter.

The founders acted, of course, in the late 1770s, whereas the framers acted in the late 1780s. That is, many founders *became* framers during the first few years after the close of the Revolutionary War. Because there was a continuity of purpose between the acts of founding and framing, one notes a continuity of personnel as well.

What Is a Constitution?

The best way to begin a chapter revealing the American Constitution to be a crypto-Catholic document is to ask, "What is a constitution?" The best way to answer this question is to connect the natural rights of the Constitution with those of the Declaration.

Making the New Regime

A Constitution is a type of document wherein the *natural rights*—unrecognized by tyrannical former regimes, e.g., Great Britain—transform into *political* rights, upon being recognized by a new regime.

Political rights are simply codified natural rights.

After the revolution (from chapter 1), the first order of business lies in codifying natural rights into law. Under our previous regime (e.g., Great Britain), natural rights went *uncodified*, unnamed, and unrecognized by the British law of the land. Most subjects of Great Britain only noted the chilly sting of their absence. Yet, leaders of the American Revolution, such as Thomas Jefferson, managed to claim them as genuinely natural rights—meaning they existed whether the regime recognized them or not. This is precisely what made Jefferson a leader, a founder.

But after those rights were recognized and then fought for in a revolution, they had to be guaranteed, going forward. Hence the drafting and ratifying in 1787 and 1788 of an American Constitution, and a Bill of Rights three years later. In *any* new republic, things must begin in approximately this fashion.

Constitutions accomplish *a couple of* things: (1) mentioning those few natural rights that were recently fought over and won; and (2) laying out the *procedures* guaranteeing the preservation of those rights, going forward.

The Constitutional watchword is governmental self-limitation. Just as Odysseus ordered his crew to tie him to his ship's mast to ensure that he'd avoid the alluring song of the Sirens, new legal regimes must limit themselves procedurally in the name of those newly won rights, lest the new government grow as tyrannical as the old.

Or even *more* tyrannical.

To further our maritime analogy, imagine a group of seafarers like the characters on *Gilligan's Island,* marooned on a desert isle. One or two years into their new life, such seafarers will have established rules in their small community. If Gilligan were to decide, by the dictates of the Natural Law, that the Skipper had violated Gilligan's natural rights (i.e., life, liberty, property), he would break with Skipper's old regime by declaring his independence, à la Jefferson via the Declaration of Independence. He would presumably move to another part of the island.

(Happily, Gilligan might be able to dispense with bloody revolution in this unique, "desert isle" context, where land is plentiful!)

All those acts in our Gilligan analogy constitute the Natural Law act of "founding" a new republic, as described in chapter 1.

But imagine further that Gilligan does not act alone. Several of the S.S. *Minnow's* other seafarers agree that the Skipper's regime has grown tyrannical. So they follow Gilligan. The very first thing Gilligan and his followers would tend to would be the drafting of a new document *framing* their violated rights. Most importantly, Gilligan's constitution would have to list the specific procedures needed to guarantee those rights to inhabitants of his new "republic" (i.e., his new area of the island).[106]

And the *procedural* aspect of the Constitution is precisely what this chapter will show to be the relevant subsidiarian part.

So you see, founding involves the Natural Law because it requires the discernment of "invisible," God-given, politically overlooked rights. Founding is, as the prior chapter showed, *step one* in

---

[106] Constitutional procedure turns out to be more important than listing specific rights (i.e., the Bill of Rights) themselves; as we will see, this procedural aspect is where subsidiarity (federalism) is most important.

the life cycle of any republic: breaking with the old regime. Framing accomplishes something further. Framing, *step two*, involves the procedure of textually preserving recently won rights in a new regime. Most importantly, it sets out procedures for maintaining them.

Founding and framing go together like a wink and a smile.

By the very role they play, both founders and framers presume Catholic thought by uniting the Natural Law with the governing apparatus of the new regime.[107]

The Catholic Position on Liberty: Subsidiarity

Remember from the introduction and chapter 1 that Catholicism, unlike Reformation or Enlightenment thought, embraces *genuine* human liberty. Liberty within a political community operates in a more delicate way than the hermit's liberty. In a community, liberty works only through the social principle that the Catholic Church calls *subsidiarity*.

What is subsidiarity? It is a relatively new term for a very old Catholic concept: "What individuals are able to do under

---

[107] As chapter 3 will make very plain, however, after the step-2 establishment of a new, moral constitution that duly recognizes natural rights, Catholic Natural Law must drop out of governing structures altogether. At that point, Natural Law governance over society must fall to the vigilant self-care of the republic's citizenry. This third step in republics (chapters 3 through 6) continues on, unless and until that new regime eventually becomes tyrannical in its own right, which occurs at the point when culture abandons the guard post of virtuous liberty. At that point, the republican cycle, beginning with yet another founding, starts anew: wash, rinse, repeat. Or: *break, make, stake* the republican regime. Nature shows that the life of all earthly republics is truly "cyclical." That is the sacred job served and preserved by republican culture.

their own power, society should not take over; similarly, what small societies can accomplish, larger societies should not take over." Besides being the Catholic social teaching *par excellence*, it is the only possible vehicle of true liberty within the political community.

The original U.S. Constitution, by a process called "federalism," left the overwhelming majority of governing functions to the individual states, whose laws would differ from one another. By our day, of course, this federalism (and its corresponding local rule) has broken down.

In America, subsidiarity was the principle at which the 1788 Constitution was aimed (in spite of the Prot-Enlight incapacities of the Constitution's framers). This much was true even though the term *subsidiarity* had not yet been used — not even within Catholicism — by the time of the American founding and framing. During the framing period, the term "federalism" was used instead. The Catholic *concept*, i.e., subsidiarity, was nevertheless there almost in full.

This chapter will show how the concept was operative long before the name.

Whatever you call it, the idea of subsidiarity entails forfeiting to government only those few powers that cannot be accomplished by individuals. The rest of the powers should be left for individuals in the form of family decision-making and local rule. (Not coincidentally, this was the central purported motive of the American framers.)

Pope Pius XI formally coined the term "subsidiarity" in 1931 in the encyclical *Quadragesimo Anno*. In that encyclical, Pius expresses that just as it is gravely wrong to take from individuals what they can accomplish by their own initiative and industry and give it to the community, so also it is an injustice and a grave evil and disturbance of right order to assign to a greater and higher association what lesser and subordinate organizations can do.[108]

Although it was Pope Pius XI who gave the concept of subsidiarity its *name*, it was Pope Leo XIII who, forty years earlier (*Quadragesimo Anno* means "forty years after"), had distilled Thomas Aquinas's political philosophy into the *concept* later known as subsidiarity. In fact, Pope Pius heavily quoted Pope Leo's earlier encyclical *Rerum Novarum*, which itself just paraphrased Thomas Aquinas: "the child belongs to the father" (14), not to the state. Upon those six short words rests the entire basis of Catholic subsidiarity. It establishes the *duty* of the parent to look after, provide for, educate, and nurture the child.

(One has liberties, according to the Catholic Natural Law, in order that he may discharge his duties. Benefits, or rights, always link back to burdens. Prot-Enlight "liberty" evolves into license precisely because it misses this major point.)

The *Oxford English Dictionary* puts it even more tersely: "Central authority should have a subsidiary function, performing *only* [emphasis added] tasks which cannot be performed effectively at a more immediate or local level."

The current American "nanny state" exemplifies the exact opposite of subsidiarity. The welfare state seeks to *surrogate for* fathers by providing sustenance for their families. For one shocking American example, *note that www.fatherhood.gov is an actual*

---

[108] Pius XI, Encyclical on the Reconstruction of the Social Order *Quadragesimo Anno* (May 15, 1931), no. 79. Properly understood, American Constitutional liberty equates to something very near Pope Pius XI's expression of subsidiarity.

website! This alone makes the point. If it weren't so sad, it would be hilarious![109]

Catholic Natural Law dictates that government should stay out of the way of the natural authority of the family (or of the neighborhood, one step up, or of local government, two steps up). The Church describes the family as the "original cell" of society (CCC 2207), which explains why the family finds itself at the center of true republics. Conversely, those who advocate *big government* attempt to place bureaucracy as the cell of society. This does not work out.

As will be shown below, the Catholic outlook does not and cannot simultaneously embrace these two competing cellular conceptions of society. Either one or the other is true, but not both.

---

[109] Wherever possible, citizens should decide vital questions for themselves, even in true republics. For one example, which we will revisit in chapter 5 — liberty of contract — Pope Leo XIII would have something surprising to say to today's Catholics: "Let the working man and the employer make free agreements, and in particular let them agree freely as to the wages; nevertheless, there underlies a dictate of natural justice more imperious and ancient than any bargain between man and man, namely, that wages ought not to be insufficient to support a frugal and well-behaved wage-earner" (*Rerum Novarum* 45). In other words, the principle later named "subsidiarity" demands that, in terms of republican liberty, while God's natural justice demands a certain morality, the state-sanctioned standards set by legality ought to be much less involved. Human law should not enforce every aspect of divine law; the latter will be enforced primarily in the next life. (Remember from chapter 1 how Thomas Aquinas explains in the *Summa* that "human laws do not by strict command prohibit every vicious action, just as they do not command every virtuous action." Chapter 3 will greatly expand upon this.)

And the *Catechism of the Catholic Church* has posed Pope Pius XI's words even more starkly against big government:

> Excessive intervention by the state can threaten personal freedom and initiative. The teaching of the Church has elaborated the principle of subsidiarity, according to which a community of a higher order should not interfere in the internal life of a community of a lower order, depriving the latter of its functions, but rather should support it in case of need, and help to co-ordinate its activity with the activities of the rest of society, always with a view to the common good. (1883)

But even with such Magisterial pronouncements clearly advocating governmental minimalism, there is widespread Catholic misunderstanding today regarding the requirements of subsidiarity.[110] Many Catholics in America and the West believe wrongly that central government ought to intervene *frequently* and *rigorously* in the private life of the family.

The cultural Catholic acceptance of "the nanny state" is strange because, according to Catholic doctrine, the central government is supposed to be the very *last* party involved in governing.

Remember from chapter 1 how Thomas Aquinas narrowed the sphere of governmental involvement to just *taxing, police,* and *martial* powers (which are anything but the only roles ascribed to government in today's America!).[111]

Local authority—family, church, neighborhood, and even city government—should be able to cover almost everything

---

[110] This may strike the reader as almost identical to the common American misunderstanding of federalism.

[111] Thomas Aquinas, *Summa Theologiae* II-II, 66, 8.

besides taxing, police, and martial powers.[112] Why? Because, as we shall see below, the basis for true authority lies in the ability to *teach morality and theology.*

Family and Church *can* teach; www.fatherhood.gov *cannot.*

Local authority—mostly the family—is the only means by which God's natural authority vested in the Church *to impart morality* may be closely imitated. In Thomas Aquinas's philosophy, "the highest form of life is not simply to contemplate [as it was for Aristotle], but to teach what is contemplated."[113] On this basis, almost every aspect of today's government violates liberty and subsidiarity, since the government mandates obedience without explication of its laws.

By the way, government should not be faulted for its inability to teach! Government legislation is simply not geared to explicate and teach the *moral justifications* for its laws. It lacks the capacity.

Once more, the moral basis for the Church's Natural Law focus on family authority is that family bears the unique capacity to *guide as it lets go* of developing youngsters. As the child matures morally, the father incrementally relinquishes power. Only this

---

[112] But even today's Catholics who advocate for wider governmental interference in private life, such as Joseph Pearce, often do so in an ambivalent fashion, admitting that subsidiarity "rests on the assumption that the rights of small communities—families or neighborhoods—should not be violated by the intervention of larger communities—the state or centralized bureaucracies." Joseph Pearce, "What Is Distributism?," *Imaginative Conservative,* June 12, 2014, https://theimaginativeconservative.org/2014/06/what-is-distributism.html. Often such Catholics advocate for both opposites—subsidiarian governmental minimalism and anti-subsidiarian governmental activism—within the same sentence!

[113] James V. Schall, "The Uniqueness of the Political Philosophy of Thomas Aquinas," *Perspectives in Political Science,* 26 (Spring 1997): 85–91.

act can be the genuine font of human authority, as modeled after the superhuman teaching voice of the Church. The father rewards or punishes not by *coercing the child* but by increasingly *appealing to the child's burgeoning free will and intellect.*

Thus, Catholic Natural Law advances the father, and not the government, as the earthly example of man's Heavenly Father. Proper motivation for the use of a growing child's freedom comes from understanding that morality is *reasonable*; conversely, it cannot stem from the very low, unexplained standards of behavior set by the criminal law. Again, government and laws cannot bring a developing child to a moral understanding of the world. It is for this reason that the child belongs to the father, not to the state.[114] In *The God of Jesus Christ*, Pope Benedict XVI beautifully expounds upon this topic:

> If human existence is to be complete, we need a father, in the true meaning of fatherhood that our faith discloses, namely a responsibility for one's child that does not dominate him but permits him to become his own self. This fatherhood is a love that avoids two traps: the total subjugation of the child to the father's own priorities and goals, on the one hand, and the unquestioning acceptance of the child as he is, under the pretext that this is the expression of freedom, on the other. Responsibility for one's child means the desire that he realize his own innermost truth, which lies in his Creator.[115]

By the time he reaches adulthood, the good man need be restrained only by himself. And a society full of such men requires

---

[114] Leo XIII, *Rerum Novarum* 14.
[115] Benedict XVI (Joseph Ratzinger). *The God of Jesus Christ: Meditations on the Triune God* (San Francisco: Ignatius Press, 2008).

little or no government, as James Madison once famously re-marked.[116] This is why the family must be conceived as the central unit of society: self-control cannot be taught in any other fashion. This is also why the advocates of big government do not *want* a society of self-controlled, religious men: it would abolish their only means of acquiring and maintaining power.

Recall that neither the Prots nor the Enlights even confirm the existence of human free will (i.e., liberty), meaning that subsidiarity is unavailable to them. Liberty is the goal and the object of subsidiarity. Moreover, if human beings are neither moral nor sufficiently intelligent — yet another incapacity posed by Prot-Enlight — then the closest approximation of subsidiarity will be a sort of amoral, mechanistic subsidiarity. In America, this is called *federalism.*

So, in review: the state cannot cultivate the maturing, liberty-prone human mind. The state bears only the power of rote *coercion.* From afar, it can only force or dominate. Aristotle wrote that, at best, abiding by laws engenders only "accidental virtue,"[117] since the state cannot motivate the individual with moral understanding or freely electable virtue.

The father guides; the state compels.[118] True virtue, the goal of our liberty, should therefore be seen as a product of the home, never of the state.

---

[116] "But what is government itself, but the greatest of all reflections on human nature. If men were angels, no government would be necessary. If angels were to govern men, neither external nor internal controls on government would be necessary." James Madison, *Federalist* No. 51.

[117] Aristotle's entire *Nicomachean Ethics* (*EN*), but especially chapter 3, deals with this Aristotelian admonition very specifically.

[118] But in twenty-first-century Prot-Enlight America, "family" has become a hollow concept. Even most political conservatives today utter the word in a de-moralized, secular context, with

Liberty versus License: A Quick Review

Recall from chapter 1 the substitution of license for liberty, stemming directly from Prot-Enlight and its rejection of Catholic Natural Law before and during the American founding and framing periods.[119]

---

little understanding of the term's sacramental theology (i.e., its crypto-Catholicism). In our day, even most decent conservative families fall into one of Pope Benedict XVI's two parenting "traps"—mindless absolutism on the one hand or aimless relativism on the other—because the Prot-Enlight conceptions of "liberty" and "family" that came to dominate American life have nothing to do with moral goodness. Chapters 4 and 5 will explain this in further detail.

[119] On the basis of subsidiarity described here, the Natural Law proves indispensable in framing constitutions, generally and specifically. Generally, Catholic Natural Law is required anywhere on the globe, anytime after a true republic springs righteously from a just revolution to make a new regime. Specifically, just such an example was the historical case in America in the 1780s when our framers sat down to construct a Constitution. While the American Constitution names all three of the now-familiar natural rights in its two due process clauses appearing in the Fifth and the Fourteenth Amendments, let's keep our focus on just one of these rights, as the overarching one: liberty. Focusing on the other two will be unnecessary. Why should we think of liberty as "overarching"?

Liberty equals the "tell" for healthy constitutional republics. In every case where liberty can truly be said to exist, a constitution has successfully guaranteed and secured a "republican form of government," enabling the other two, life and private-property rights. Conversely, the primary symptom of a republic in name only is a lack of liberty.

Liberty is rarely if ever removed openly and notoriously in places with a deeply entrenched historical commitment to natural rights, such as England or America. In such places, when tyranny is on the ascent, tyrants must subtly and gradually

Recall also the *symptoms* of widespread license in society: the Constitutional "freedom" to murder babies in all fifty states; the common assumption that our freedom of speech should be unbounded; the invincibility that a politically illiterate electorate is invited to attach to its own uninformed opinions at the ballot box;[120] the shameless practice of total sexual license—homosexuality, contraception, pornography, sodomy, fornication, abortion. All these are *openly advanced* by governmental "public service" programs (e.g., www.fatherhood.gov) seeking to regularize the ill use of human freedom.

In a republic that denies true liberty and Catholic Natural Law, one sees the omnipresence of the federal government in daily life. This entails the shrinking of the family's authority over developing its own private land, running its own family business, burning its own firewood, selling its own wheat, or even choosing its own light-bulb wattage!

In other words, we have freedoms we should lack, and we lack freedoms we should have!

Something is definitely up. The Constitution has failed to safeguard liberty in the fashion in which it was wired—or *should*

---

replace liberty with its opposite, license. Remember Indy and the bag of sand from chapter 1.

Before the people's liberty can be taken by tyrants, the popular understanding of this right itself must be sufficiently perverted into its deceptive shade, license. Otherwise, the citizens would "get wise" to the skullduggery afoot. Even as would-be statists may be aided by man's concupiscent nature, the subtle perversion of natural rights by such tyrants takes time and hard—if diabolical—work. In America today, of course, all of the above seems clearly to be a *fait accompli*.

[120] Pope Benedict XVI famously wrote of this phenomenon: "Truth is not determined by a majority vote."

have been—back in 1788. The big question is: *Was America truly and soundly wired in 1788 such as to guard true liberty?* After all, if it was, how could the perversion of liberty have happened on such a large scale?

A few of our genius founders and framers possessed astounding prescience (even as they espoused a blinding Prot-Enlight philosophy). Massachusetts's Son of Liberty and founding firebrand Samuel Adams noted:

> A general dissolution of principles and manners will more surely overthrow the liberties of America than the whole force of the common enemy. While the people are virtuous they cannot be subdued; but when once they lose their virtue they will be ready to surrender their liberties to the first external or internal invader.[121]

Adams was, without knowing it, espousing the Catholic Natural Law principle of liberty, eerily similar to an idea of James Madison quoted at the beginning of this chapter: "Liberty may be endangered by abuses of liberty as well as abuses of power. There are numerous instances of the former as well as of the latter; and the former rather than the latter is apparently most to be apprehended by the United States."[122]

Think of the connection between these two founders' quotes: ultimately, it is the connection between the previous chapter and this one. In other words, the two passages together maintain that *only by embracing vice and abandoning virtue will American liberty be surrendered.* After all, true liberty must repudiate vice, or else it does not count as true liberty.

---

[121] Samuel Adams, letter to James Warren, February 12, 1779, par. 4.

[122] James Madison, *Federalist* No. 63.

Given the opportunity, liberty's opposite, license, will take up its name and even its form. Liberty renders the individual generally independent of the state; license renders him utterly dependent upon it.

This notion is a bit counterintuitive.

Imagine a large family happily and self-sufficiently operating on its own land. They mind their own business, literally and figuratively. They work hard. According to the first social principle of the Catholic Natural Law, subsidiarity, the governance of this family farm comes from the head of this household. Thus, the concept of "government" remains a vague abstraction to this family. Because they use their resources and their freedom to pursue what is natural, or good, they will be happy in their self-reliant liberty. Note how this family goes above and beyond the low moral standard set by the law.

On the other hand, the practice of license entails thorough dependence on the state: individual decisions are systematically transferred to the government. This is the opposite of subsidiarity. Imagine a single woman who has embraced the diabolical message of the government (via the popular culture and the mainstream media): she is sexually "liberated." Whenever her sexual license eventuates in an "unwanted" pregnancy, she acts upon what she has been told: a young woman should not be "punished with a baby,"[123] the natural consequence of sex. This single woman believes, as politicians have had her believe, that the taxpayer should subsidize her continuing bacchanalian lifestyle (a "right,"

[123] Barack Hussein Obama, town hall meeting in Johnstown, Pennsylvania. The full extent of the demented assumptions about life resound in a stultifying manner, when sex is fully divorced from its *telos*, life: "If [my two daughters] make a mistake, I don't want them *punished with* a baby [emphasis added]."

as discussed in chapter 1) in the form of welfare entitlements, "free" contraception, and then taxpayer-funded abortion or—if she doesn't exercise her pseudo right to death—taxpayer-funded daycare. Her only goal appears to be material pleasure, which is all that her reliance upon government offers her—for a time. But in the end, even her licentious pleasure will fade. All that will remain will be the dominion of the government, which won its power by substituting license for liberty.

As defined above, these two examples show that liberty will "sink" or "swim" based on whether it conforms to subsidiarity. Mass liberty must operate upon morally motivated, local self-rule; mass license will always assume the form of dominion by a large, central, faraway government enabling a sin-distracted people to continue to sin. Recall from *Pinocchio* Lampwick's license and eventual servility on Pleasure Island. It is no coincidence that Walt Disney conceived of Lampwick's licentiousness as eventuating in his transformation into a *beast of burden*, subject to the yoke of evil.

Big government always begins its takeover by encouraging the popular distraction of sin. (License is no form of freedom at all, recall, but is rather complete slavery.) What begins as the governmental subsidy of vice and governmental shelter from the *natural* moral consequences of such vice ends as outright tyranny. Ruminating on the slavish dominion of license, Saint Augustine wrote that "the good man is free even if he is a slave; the wicked man is a slave even if he is king."[124]

America retains a weak, crypto-Catholic orientation toward true liberty. But such an orientation is now heavily admixed with Prot-Enlight license. We have seen why this is the case culturally. Let's now examine why it is the case historically and

[124] Augustine, *City of God* 4, 3.

constitutionally. The "father of the American Constitution," Prot-Enlight James Madison, was highly ambivalent (but ultimately dismissive) about the writings of the father of modern subsidiarity: Baron de Montesquieu.

Federalism as Prot-Enlight Subsidiarity

In America, as noted above, subsidiarity is far better known in its de-moralized, Prot-Enlight form. Americans call it "federalism" or "states' rights." While each of these terms expresses a basically salutary idea about how liberty and authority should be allocated within republics, each term still represents a secularized version of subsidiarity. Whether called "federalism" or "states' rights," the concept remains incomplete without the moralistic goal of freedom.

And in this purposeless version, "Prot-Enlight subsidiarity" (i.e., federalism) lost most of its potency in America throughout the years. What exactly happened?

In America in 1786 through 1788, statesmen throughout the thirteen states deliberated about getting rid of its original Constitution. As compared with the new Constitution, in retrospect, this original Constitution, called the Articles of Confederation, operated on a truer version of subsidiarity.

The Articles were jettisoned in favor of a more "energetic" new Constitution, which would allocate slightly more power to the central government. Not advocates of big government, the framers wished to forfeit to the central government *only the powers most necessary and none more*. Their aim was, famously, "energetic but [still] limited government."[125]

---

[125] Colleen A. Sheehan and Gary L. McDowell, *Friends of the Constitution: Writings of the "Other" Federalists, 1787–1788* (Carmel, IN: Liberty Fund, 1998).

Though they didn't say it, their goal was to preserve their de-moralized "Prot-Enlight subsidiarity"—local control—won from Great Britain ten years prior in the Revolutionary War, while adding a few limited but (as they saw it) necessary powers to the central government.

Technically, from 1776 until the Constitution's ratification in 1788, the thirteen states operated as their own separate countries, meaning that they enjoyed local rule in the fullest sense!

In the next sections, we will examine what the framers, particularly the *lead* framer, James Madison, had in mind. In spite of Madison's frequent dalliances with subsidiarity through his enthusiasm for the philosophy of Montesquieu, fans of small government should nevertheless expect to be disappointed: Madison was a notorious ditherer.

By today, after all, we know how the story played out. The American Constitution of 1788 was fated eventually to forfeit all semblance of American subsidiarity to the central government. On the basis of his unfaithful discipleship to Montesquieu, Madison's innovations overwhelmed the formerly subsidiarian *spirit* of the Articles, leaving us with a new Constitution.

We've already seen how the American substitution of license for liberty stemmed from the Prot-Enlight founding in the Declaration. We are about to see specifically how the influence of Prot-Enlight pervaded the framing era and the ensuing Constitution. Under Madison's watch, subsidiarity was to devolve into its secularized version, mere federalism (which would further devolve by our day).

Whatever moderate dose of license was substituted for liberty during the founding and framing, by our day, license has come to be the *primary* Constitutional "right," on the popular view.

However imperfectly the secular concept of states' rights originally resembled the fuller, Catholic concept of subsidiarity, by our day, even the secular version of local rule has died completely away. Again, recall www.fatherhood.gov, supreme testimony of all!

One might be tempted to wring one's hands over this sad fact. But in any republic *not* founded upon Catholic Natural Law, things are fated to shake out that way.[126]

In a Prot-Enlight republic such as America, we should expect to see *precisely* the sort of constitutional problems with liberty and subsidiarity that we do. These problems arise from an all-consuming American ambivalence with regard to such

Catholic doctrines. We have spent much time in these first two chapters demonstrating that freedom is the Prot-Enlight *Achilles heel*, rendering true subsidiarity impossible.

James Madison as Prot-Enlight Framer

What Jefferson was to the Declaration, Madison is to the Constitution. For the purpose of analyzing Prot-Enlight in the *1770s*, Thomas Jefferson, the primary author of the Declaration, was the most illuminating American founder. Similarly, for analyzing Prot-Enlight in the *1780s*, James Madison, the "father of the Constitution," is the most instructive American framer. Just as, in chapter 1, we looked at Jefferson's philosophical influences in drafting the Declaration, so, in this chapter, shall we look at Madison's philosophical influences in drafting the Constitution.

[126] After all, "Prot-Enlight liberty" is as *implausible* (perhaps even *impossible*) a phenomenon as "Prot-Enlight popular morality" or as "Prot-Enlight just revolution." Each of these proves to be as self-contradictory as "Prot-Enlight Natural Law." The ideas are paradoxes, "circular squares," contradictions in terms.

In chapter 1, we saw that founder Jefferson *truly* imported into the Declaration a *pseudo* Natural Law thinker, John Locke (and Locke's fellow Whigs). Here in chapter 2, we will see that framer Madison did just the opposite: he *pseudo*-imported into the Constitution a *true* Natural Law thinker, Montesquieu. As different as Jefferson's and Madison's influences may have been, the effect was the *very same*. Each respective thinker's final document took on a pseudo–Natural Law characteristic, a germ that grew more and more potent over time.[127]

American poet Robert Frost once wrote this of James Madison: "Now I know ... what Madison's dream was. It was just a dream of a new land to fulfill with people in *self-control* [emphasis added]. That is all through his thinking ... to fulfill this new land ... with people in *self-control*."[128]

In fact, "self-control" is perhaps the best word yet for distinguishing liberty from license. Liberty requires internal control, whereas license requires no control exerted whatsoever. Although it is easy to agree with Frost's apt redefinition of "liberty," it is far less easy to agree, ultimately, that Madison's true aim was to enshrine such a concept within the Constitution.

The remainder of this chapter will show that during the framing period, James Madison proved to be a thoroughly Prot-Enlight thinker. True liberty, as derived from Catholic Natural Law, cannot have been at the center of his work — the Constitution. Ultimately, Madison's Prot-Enlight versions of liberty and subsidiarity were *pragmatic* instead of *moral* principles. This

---

[127] This turns out to be the most efficient way to summarize chapters 1 and 2.

[128] Robert Frost, speech given at the twenty-eighth annual commencement at Sarah Lawrence College, Bronxville, New York, June 7, 1956.

unhappy substitution is the heart of Madison's secret modifications of the Catholic Natural Law philosophy of Montesquieu.

Thus, subsidiarity was only *incompletely* wired into the American Constitution. This means that the document's crypto-Catholic wiring for Natural Law was partial at best. Madison, we
will see, attempted to set up the American system to be able to
function on the basis of *de-moralized* freedom.

But the Baron de Montesquieu, Madison's most frequent cita-
tion, described human freedom and locally ruled republics in a
fashion *far* more consistent with Catholic Natural Law.[129] During
the great Constitutional ratification contest of the late 1780s, only
true Montesquieuians were faithful proponents of the Natural Law.

Montesquieu stated clearly, as we shall see, that de-moralized
versions of liberty and subsidiarity would not work in republics.
He articulated three cardinal rules for framing republics,[130] stemming
from Catholic Natural Law. Quite explicitly, Madison rejected
each of these three rules of classical subsidiarity for true republics (remember that Robert Frost would later rebrand liberty as
"self-control"):

1. Subsidiarity as restraint against religious diversity in
   republics
2. Subsidiarity as restraint against geographical expansion
   of republics

---

[129] So, the danger exists that one might take Madison too literally
by assuming that he meant to incorporate into the Constitution
the Catholic Natural Law propositions of Montesquieu. Such
an assumption would be against the plain facts.

[130] Thomas L. Pangle, *The Great Debate: Advocates and Opponents
of the American Constitution* (Chantilly, VA: The Teaching Company, 2003). Pangle's insightful analysis is absolutely *crucial* to
my commentary on Montesquieu and the Anti-Federalists.

3. Subsidiarity as restraint against the sharing of powers
   by governmental branches

Madison's deliberate modifications during the late 1780s of Montesquieu's three cardinal rules for republics show that Madison was not any sort of Natural Law thinker, even if the former was a role he often played.[131] In these three specific ways (described in the next sections in greater detail), Madison modified the classical characteristics of republics, creating a prototype for the *modern, Prot-Enlight "republic."*

During the intense, late 1780s debates between Madison's pro-Constitution Federalists and the anti-Constitution Anti-Federalists over the adoption of the newly proposed Constitution, both sides cited Montesquieu as the unquestionable authority. But modern history shows that only the Anti-Federalists were Montesquieu's — or Catholic Natural Law's — true disciples.

The Federalists, on the other hand, proved to be only superficial admirers. James Madison's abject lack of devotion to true Montesquieuianism[132] typified the Federalist approach. His competing conception of local rule did *not* center on Montesquieuian subsidiarity.

---

[131] If all this sounds a little bit "inside baseball," as it may on first blush, the reader should remember the general argument put forth by this book: in formation, Prot-Enlight America gleaned Catholic Natural Law's benefits, natural rights, without the foundation for those benefits. The Declaration and the Constitution stripped the political "goodies" from the Natural Law — local rule, natural rights, and revolution — without their proper Catholic context and without giving due credit to their source. Such plagiarism eventuated in our failed republic, unable to conceive honestly of the concepts it regularly invoked, and able to celebrate only deceptive shades thereof.

[132] Pangle, *The Great Debate.*

Deliberately so.

Madison, a notorious waffler, whose final words were, "Nothing more than a change of mind, my dear,"[133] paid heed to esteeming republican virtue, the Natural Law, and civic self-restraint. But his big three modifications of Montesquieu showed definitively that he couldn't have meant it.

While Madison would go on to "flip-flop" parties and ideologies throughout the 1790s and early 1800s, his camp during the ratification period remained that of the central-government-supporting Federalists. The Federalists "showed themselves to be thoroughly modern in insisting that if there was a problem in their society, reform of *political institutions* [rather than cultural mores or a recurrence to the principles of Christianity] must be the solution."[134]

Ultimately, Madison would favor a Whiggish, amoral, mechanistic way of keeping the new Constitutional regime locally ruled by state governments. Neither he nor his Federalists ever gave up on local rule, but the problem was in their anti–Natural Law methods. It is generally *true* that Madison wanted local rule; it is generally *untrue* that his method of achieving it was through true liberty or subsidiarity. And such an attempt at "having your cake and eating it too" eventuated in the republic of our day *not* being locally ruled at all.

Nowadays, an identical Catholic version of this critique of America holds that "with the weakening of the internal restraints

---

[133] As quoted in Ralph Ketcham, *James Madison: A Biography* (Charlottesville: University Press of Virginia, 1990), p. 670.

[134] Kevin R. C. Gutzman, "Did the Federalist Papers Really Matter?" *Imaginative Conservative*, April 30, 2104, https://theimaginativeconservative.org/2014/04/versions-of-the-federalist-papers.html.

that healthy family life teaches, the state will need to impose more and more external restraints on everyone's activities."[135]

While Madison and the Federalists cannot be blamed for *intending this outcome*, they can at least be blamed for opposing the Anti-Federalists who articulated surprisingly well the incipient danger. In other words, Federalist urgings to reform *political* institutions stands opposed to Anti-Federalist emphasis on the reform of *cultural* morality. Notwithstanding their Prot-Enlight biases, Anti-Federalists were followers of Montesquieu (and implicitly, the Catholic Natural Law tradition), who unwittingly incorporated corresponding assumptions about man and nature.

If Madison's Prot-Enlight view was that humans were unable to restrain themselves, one might ask of Madison: *How could they rule themselves?*[136]

Like Jefferson's crypto-Catholic founding, Madison's crypto-Catholic framing is what caused the young republic to be *incompletely* — instead of *not at all* — Catholic. So, we have that much to be grateful for.

Thomas Jefferson had moments of truth. He squinted at Catholic Natural Law by saying that, at times, "it becomes necessary

---

[135] George, "A Tale of Two Churches."

[136] It follows naturally, then, that Prot-Enlight framers such as Madison sought to keep society crime-free and vice-free with amoral means that did not depend upon the scruples of individuals. And in this vein, Madison's radical departures from Montesquieu's Catholic Natural Law recipe for subsidiarity tend to make a fair amount of sense, as do the unintended degradations in local rule. Madison, however, like Jefferson, preferred rather schizophrenically to *sound* classical. To this end, Madison and other Federalists frequently cited Montesquieu as if they were true believers in something like Catholic Natural Law.

for one people to … assume among the powers of the earth, the separate and equal station to which the laws of nature and nature's God entitle them."[137]

Likewise, James Madison had his own shining moments. During the Constitutional ratification period, Madison made a famous plea: "Is there no virtue among us? If there be not, we are in a wretched situation. No theoretical checks, no form of government can render us secure. To suppose that any form of government will secure liberty or happiness without any virtue in the people, is a chimerical idea."[138] Sadly, neither Jefferson nor Madison made the necessary connection between these ideas and their undeniable source: the Catholic Natural Law.

Jefferson's prevailing Prot-Enlight sympathies are best shown by his affinity for John Locke, Madison's by his *lack of genuine affinity* for the Baron de Montesquieu.

Shortly, we will examine Montesquieu's three cardinal rules for republics. But before we look at the teachings of Montesquieu, let's first get to know the man.

Baron de Montesquieu

You might know the Baron de Montesquieu (1689–1755) as the *creator-discoverer* of the three branches of government: legislative, executive, and judicial. But his significance is much greater. The importance of the three branches to the concept of subsidiarity is considerably vaster than we've all been taught.

Before examining how Montesquieu's political philosophy formed a set of Catholic Natural Law guidelines for republics

---

[137] Thomas Jefferson, *Declaration of Independence*.
[138] James Madison, speech at Richmond during the Virginia Ratifying Convention, June 20, 1788.

in the (very anti–Natural Law) eighteenth century, let's look at who this influential French thinker and three-branch innovator was.

His life itself was that of a very lapsed Catholic. Obviously, his "lapsed" status renders his classification as a Catholic political thinker a little tricky. But on a close inspection, he was a profound and even detailed affirmer of Catholic Natural Law.

Upon her death, Montesquieu's mother secured his Catholic education at the Oratorian College of Juilly, where he would be educated in classical Catholic thought. From the age of eleven until twenty-two, he was taught ancient Greek through medieval renditions of the Natural Law. Even as the young Montesquieu fell into apostasy for most of his life, his classical education in the Catholic Natural Law influenced his political philosophy for all his life.

Montesquieu was *not* a religious thinker, however. He would not return "home" to his mother's Catholicism until very shortly before his death. And some of his less important ideas were regarded as heretical by the Church, earning his book *Spirit of the Laws* a place on the dreaded Roman *Index* of forbidden texts.

Nevertheless, Montesquieu's political thought must be seen as nothing other than true subsidiarity. Even in *Rerum Novarum*, Pope Leo XIII "recognized the benefits of organizing government around the three powers of legislative, executive, and judicial branches."[139] This was quite a specific Catholic nod to the importance of one of Montesquieu's contributions to Catholic Natural Law political philosophy.

---

[139] *Foundations of Catholic Social Teaching: Living as a Disciple of Christ* (Notre Dame, IN: Ave Maria Press, 2015), p. 152.

In fact, it has been remarked that "if one comprehends classical political philosophy well enough, one sees in the subject of Natural Law an intimate relationship between the thought of Montesquieu and that of the classicists."[140] Montesquieu is the best and perhaps the only representative of genuine subsidiarity during the early modern period (at which time all the other political thinkers assumed Whiggish properties of the Prot-Enlight). For at least a century before or after him — even if it wasn't recognized at the time — Montesquieu's was a lone voice articulating truly Catholic Natural Law politics.[141]

Even during his almost lifelong Catholic lapse, Montesquieu affirmed the *civic* importance of religion and morality in republics. (As demonstrated by Jefferson and Madison, Prot-Enlight thinkers often emphasized religion and morality superficially, but later contradicted such an emphasis.)

Thus, the popular but superficial conception of Montesquieu among conservatives today is that he was a sort of intellectual hero to Madison and those in favor of the new Constitution of 1788.

Ultimately, nothing could be falser! As the Anti-Federalists volubly pointed out at the time, just the opposite turns out to be the case.

---

[140] J. Loubet, "The Ethics of Montesquieu and the Natural Laws," trans. of "L'Ethique de Montesquieu: Principe de la Fondation de la Democratie Americane," published in *Actes* of the Academe Montesquieu, vol. 2 (1986), pp. 95–128.

[141] This concept entails, if we recall our definition in the introduction, a (1) morally informed politics situating political institutions as both naturally (2) intelligible and (3) teleological. And that much remains true even if Montesquieu didn't consider himself a Catholic moralist in the fashion of Thomas Aquinas.

James Madison and fellow Federalists cited Montesquieu in order to borrow authority from his wild popularity during the time. But most of these citations were either camouflaged perversions or outright rejections of Montesquieu's proclamations about the Catholic Natural Law. Madison and company thereby worked cryptically *against* Montesquieu's project while claiming his banner. (The Anti-Federalists were the true devotees of Montesquieu.)

Without a whit of exaggeration, one can fairly say that the entirety of the Constitutional ratification contest between the Federalists and Anti-Federalists[142] played out in Montesquieuian terms. Whereas Locke was most often quoted by the founders in the 1770s, Montesquieu was most often quoted by the framers in the late 1780s.

As eventual losers of the debate, the Anti-Federalists grounded their rejection of the proposed Constitution upon its failure to comport with Montesquieu's philosophy. They bemoaned how Madison wrongly presumed to *improve upon* Montesquieu in three ways.

---

[142] Flustered, Montesquieu's true American disciples, the Anti-federalists—who also failed to understand the deep, Catholic subsidiarity inherent in his thought—screamed against the walls of the convention hall this obvious but overlooked fact. A Natural Law republic (the only true sort of republic, as the reader now knows) must center on Catholic subsidiarity. Although both Montesquieu and the Antifederalists failed to use the term, both parties managed to describe subsidiarity's requirements perfectly. The shrewd reader of Montesquieu notes that "morality is indeed the basis of the entire political conception of Montesquieu, and *Spirit of the Laws* represents a return to the cradle of right, conforming to nature." Loubet, "The Ethics of Montesquieu."

CATHOLIC REPUBLIC

Madison and the Three Montesquieuian
Requirements of a True Republic

Subsidiarity as Restraint of Religious Diversity in Republics

Montesquieu consistently held, along with the Catholic Natural Law tradition, that in creating *and* sustaining republics, the citizenry must be universally virtuous. For Montesquieu, morality was an absolute necessity. A republic simply could not survive popular licentiousness or even moral mediocrity. He writes: "Virtue in a republic is a most simple thing: it is a love of the republic.... The love of our country is conducive to a purity of morals, and the latter is again conducive to the former."[143]

To that end, Montesquieu reasoned, republican self-rule could work only if citizens shared and practiced a common religion, which would render them commonly virtuous. Under a single religion, all citizens would together pursue and avoid the same things.

And this is precisely what the long-standing Catholic Natural Law tradition, from the Patristic age (A.D. 100–450) through the late medieval period (1250–1500), had meant by a *res-publica*: a "citizen's ideal" or a "shared goal." Montesquieu identified that republican ideal, binding society together, as Christianity,[144] and

---

[143] Montesquieu, *The Spirit of the Laws* (1748), bk. 5.

[144] Judging historically — not philosophically — Montesquieu noted the counterintuitive phenomenon (as this book does) that Protestantism, not Catholicism, had usually corresponded with the republican spirit. But for Montesquieu, the teachings shared by all Christian sects sufficed to bind a people together: "The Christian religion is a stranger to mere despotic power. The mildness so frequently recommended in the Gospel is incompatible with the despotic rage with which a prince punishes his subjects, and exercises himself in cruelty.

he did not advise admixing Christianity and other faiths in a republic. He advised *against* diversity, in other words.

A morally restrained, Christian people, Montesquieu reasoned, would not put their own good ahead of others' or engage in sinful self-serving. (James Madison would call such self-serving "faction.") And he would point out that only such a selfless people could be *truly* republican citizens.

The American Anti-Federalists wanted to follow Montesquieu's insistence upon universal Christian virtue among the citizenry. But they did not win the debate.

James Madison, on the other hand, sought to "outsmart" Montesquieu by figuring a way to maintain a republic peopled by economically selfish, or morally mediocre, citizens. And fellow Federalists followed Madison, not Montesquieu. It's not that Madison *wanted* citizens to be bad Christians or that he *prized* moral mediocrity; rather, Madison attempted to calculate how low the bar could be set in a republic and still thrive. In the famous *Federalist* No. 10, for example, Madison considers how a republic might weather having a diverse mixture of moral and immoral people, with the latter making up the vast majority and consequently having an interest "averse to the common good."

As this religion forbids the plurality of wives, its princes are less confined, less concealed from their subjects, and consequently have more humanity: they are more disposed to be directed by laws, and more capable of perceiving that they cannot do whatever they please" (*The Spirit of Laws*, bk. 5). Montesquieu did not sufficiently understand the distinction between Catholic and Protestant theology to conclude what this book has regarding Prot-Enlight's incapacity to maintain republics. Nevertheless, his distinctions were all Catholic in nature.

Note the striking similarity between Madison's definition of faction and the Christian definition of sin.

Remember, for Montesquieu and the Catholic Natural Law tradition, such moral and religious diversity—bad mixed with good—would render a true republic impossible! Republics require universally virtuous citizens, lest they *factionalize themselves*—i.e., group themselves according to competing interests, identities, and creeds.

Madison asserts that this republican obstacle (as seen from the Montesquieuian perspective) might be avoided by "either controlling the effects or removing the cause [of faction]"[145]—either (1) tolerate faction but downplay its defects; or (2) remove the grounds for faction: *diversity* (of religious and moral sentiment, including competing sects of pious Christian worshippers—or even those with no religious faith at all).

Madison and his Federalist disciples wanted the first option; Montesquieu's Anti-Federalist followers in the colonies wanted the second.

Ultimately, being a Prot-Enlight thinker, as opposed to a Catholic Natural Law thinker, Madison goes on in *Federalist* No. 10 to argue *against* Montesquieu—who advised "removing the cause" of faction. In other words, Madison decided that the Catholic Natural Law approach to faction was too restrictive to apply to the type of large, diverse "republic" that he envisioned.

That is to say, ensuring that the republic was peopled with a universally *moral* citizenry of Christians was ultimately too exclusive a standard for Madison, who wanted America to be big and inclusive. Thus, Madison tried to dream up a system for maintaining an amoral republic: the effect of religious and

---

[145] James Madison, *Federalist* No. 10.

moral diversity (i.e., faction) would be not *removed*, but rather *controlled*. And his proposed way of controlling faction was … more faction: Madison wanted to have so many squabbling, selfish factions, in other words, that they drowned out one another's competing interests.

This is the famous content of *Federalist* No. 10. It is condemning evidence of Madison's Prot-Enlight skepticism (which characterized the Catholic Natural Law view of politics as naïvely optimistic). It rather clearly shows Madison's preference for cynical Enlightenment political philosophy over that of the "naïve" Catholic Natural Law, and his Protestant (Episcopalian) bias for depraved views of the human will over Catholic Natural Law ones.

Now compare this to Madison's (schizophrenic-sounding) words from the same period: June 20, 1788, at the Virginia Ratifying Convention. There, he sounded *just like* Montesquieu: "To suppose that any form of government will secure liberty or happiness without any virtue in the people, is a chimerical idea."

But remember, James Madison was one of history's greatest wafflers! Ultimately, the Father of the Constitution prevailed in defense of the opposite notion: a large, commercial republic that would bear, by design, *lots and lots* of faction (meaning popular diversity and vice).

Montesquieu be damned. On Madison's model, a large number of competing amoral interests would drown out any one faction's ability to take control. *Don't insist on morality or unity.*

Madison figured that this way would be more effective and far easier than Montesquieu's high bar of one religion (Christianity) and one set of moral guidelines.

We recall the words of the *only* American founder who could possibly have meant the Declaration fully—the Catholic Charles Carroll of Carrollton: "Without morals a republic cannot subsist any length of time; they therefore who are decrying the Christian religion, whose morality is so sublime and pure … are undermining the solid foundation of morals, the best security for the duration of free governments."[146] Only a *Catholic* could truly articulate the Montesquieuian importance of unity in morality and religion within a republic. This tees up our discussion in the next sections.

Subsidiarity as Restraint against Geographical Expansion of Republics

Montesquieu held that *in order to be kept morally exclusive, any club must also be kept small.* He held the same for republics. James Madison rejected Montesquieu's geographic restraint of republics. As stated above, Madison wanted the new American republic to be expansive. But a pseudonymous Anti-Federalist writer who called himself Cato countered the geographically expansive hopes of Madison and the Federalists by citing Montesquieu: "It is natural, says Montesquieu, to a republic to have only a small territory; otherwise it cannot long subsist."[147]

Cato was correct. This second Montesquieuian condition—against vast republics—goes hand in hand with the first cardinal rule above.

In that passage, Cato correctly highlights Montesquieu's view of republics as literally and figuratively diminutive. Because, as we saw above, faction and diversity are averse to republican unity, both the population and the perimeter of republics should be reduced. In still more specific words, Montesquieu thought that

---

[146] Charles Carroll, Letter of November 4, 1800.
[147] Cato, *Third Letter*, Fall 1787.

republics must be kept geographically small in order to retain their characteristic of religious-moral unity.

Contrary to the popular mantra of our day, a true republic must be oriented toward what the framers called "fellow feeling," the opposite of diversity or pluralism.[148] Fourteen centuries prior to the American ratification debates, into which Anti-Federalist Cato insinuated himself, Saint Augustine defined a republican people as a "multitudinous assemblage of rational beings united by concord regarding *loved things held in common* [emphasis added]."[149] His definition was perfect. A republican citizenry, in other words, may be called a "people" only if they stand for one and the *same* thing.

This can be done only within a tight group of like-minded republicans. Cato continues, narrowing the principle he learned from Montesquieu:

> Whoever seriously considers the immense extent of territory within the limits of the United States, together with the variety of climates ... the dissimilitude of interest, morals, and policies, will receive it as an intuitive truth, that a consolidated republican form of government therein can never form a perfect union.[150]

To combine Cato's geographical insight with the principle expressed in the foregoing section: republics must be small enough to be peopled by only one *kind* of citizen: a Christian affirmer of Catholic Natural Law.

---

[148] Most people are familiar with *E pluribus unum*, or "out of the many, one."

[149] Paul Rahe, *Republics, Ancient and Modern*, vol. 2 (Chapel Hill, NC: University of North Carolina Press, 1994), p. 62.

[150] Cato, *Third Letter*.

Remember, whether or not he used the term, Montesquieu's goal (and that of the Anti-Federalists who followed him) was to lay out the conditions needed for subsidiarity.

Montesquieu's point was that big countries of diverse peoples will not be governable locally. Along similar lines, they cannot remain morally unified. Big countries require a "nerve center" like Washington, D.C., where all decisions shall be made. Think of the Roman Empire as it grew and grew. This model of large state authority is the perfect *opposite* of family authority: when decisions are made from afar, then local rule, moral justification for law, and family autonomy perish.

James Madison outright rejected Montesquieu's teaching about geographic restraint. Madison wanted America to become a giant country, and in this, he sought to "outsmart" Montesquieu. With the ratification of the new Constitution of 1788, he got his way, especially after the United States subsequently went from thirteen states (which was *already* too big for Montesquieu, the Anti-Federalists argued) to fifty.

Madison honestly, if wrongly, thought that the United States could be both vast and pluralistic, without the consequent troubles of faction and tyranny forecast by Montesquieu. He wrote in *Federalist* No. 10:

> The smaller the society, the fewer probably will be the distinct parties and interests composing it; the fewer the distinct parties and interests, the more frequently will a majority be found of the same party; and the smaller the number of individuals composing a majority, and the smaller the compass within which they are placed, the more easily will they concert and execute their plans of oppression. Extend the sphere and you take in a greater variety of parties and interests.

Clearly, this excerpt is an extension of Madison's Prot-Enlight reasoning about how to control faction: through mechanical factors such as vastness and pluralism, rather than through moral or geographical restraint. Once more: faction should be countered with more faction. This, Madison knew, required size. And yet Madison's geographical "correction" of Montesquieu served only to damage American subsidiarity and to hasten the American march toward big government.

Subsidiarity as Restraint against the Sharing of Powers by Governmental Branches

Montesquieu's third admonition for subsidiarity and republics was that the three branches of republican government (legislative, executive, judicial) should *never* share or overlap powers:

> Nor is there liberty if the power of judging is not separated from legislative power and from executive power. If it [the power of judging] were joined to legislative power, the power over life and liberty of the citizens would be arbitrary, for the judge would be the legislator. If it were joined to the executive power, the judge would have the force of an oppressor. All would be lost if the same ... body of principal men ... exercised these three powers.[151]

Unlike the first two cardinal rules of Montesquieu, which concerned *cultural* dimensions of subsidiarity, this third one represents a *governmental* aspect. It further establishes Madison's willful overturning of Montesquieuian subsidiarity.

Think of what you learned in grade school: the Constitution installs "checks and balances" in the three branches of the federal

---

[151] Montesquieu, *The Spirit of the Laws*, bk. 5.

government. Few people anymore recall that checks and balances are *opposites*. Checks are overlaps or shared powers among the three branches; balances are the different powers specific to each branch—*making, enforcing,* and *interpreting* law. Montesquieu argued that there ought to be no checks within good government, only balances. He correctly predicted that allowing checks would lead to collusion among the branches, whereas the goal of good constitutions was to engender rivalry between the three. Each branch should do only that which is proper to it: that is—to *make* (*legislative*), *enforce* (*executive*), or *interpret* (*judicial*) the law.[152]

One of Madison's famous Anti-Federalist rivals, calling himself Brutus, exercised a Montesquieuian impulse by advising Madison against "the dangerous and premature union of the President and the Senate, and the mixture of legislative, executive, and judicial powers."[153]

Brutus went on more broadly to lament "such an intimate connection between the several branches in whom the different species of authority is lodged"[154] in the proposed Constitution.

Madison seems to have understood the importance of Brutus's Montesquieuian message, even if he decided against it. How do we know this? Well, as a preface to his unsuccessful first-proposed (but rejected) Bill of Rights, Madison demonstrated a view far more compatible with that of Brutus and Montesquieu (than of his own Federalist partisans) by writing:

---

[152] "For the Lord is our *judge*, the Lord is our *lawgiver*, the Lord is our *king*" (Isa. 33:22, emphasis added). While Montesquieu pioneered the political philosophy relevant here, Scripture acknowledges such a tripartite set of distinctions within authority itself.

[153] Brutus, *Fifth Letter*.

[154] Ibid.

The powers delegated by this Constitution are appropriated to the departments to which they are respectively distributed: so that the Legislative Department shall never exercise the powers vested in the Executive or the Judicial, nor the Executive exercise the powers vested in the Legislative or Judicial, nor the Judicial exercise the powers vested in the Legislative or Executive Departments.[155]

But Madison the waffler eventually went against all his sensible Montesquieuian impulses, in this realm as well. He willfully did the opposite, evidencing his disbelief in Catholic Natural Law.

If Madison had listened to the wisdom of Montesquieu, then the Constitution would not have enshrined such things as an executive veto — wherein the president acts as a legislator; or a Senatorial ratification of executive treaties — wherein legislators act like the president; or a doctrine like "judicial review" — wherein judges act as legislators (to name only a few).

Conclusion

At this point, the skeptical reader might say to himself: "Okay, if I've followed chapter 2 correctly":

- Current American Constitutional liberty, as popularly understood, is just license (just as chapter 1 said it is in the Declaration of Independence).
- American doctrines of federalism, states' rights, and local rule turn out to be a Prot-Enlight form of de-moralized, secularized subsidiarity.

---

[155] Madison's failed proposal before Congress for a preamble to the *Preamble to the Bill of Rights*, June 8, 1789.

- James Madison modified three Montesquieuian cardinal rules (for establishing what later would be called "subsidiarity") in a way that contradicted the Catholic Natural Law at the center of Montesquieu's work.
- The translation of these Catholic concepts (liberty, subsidiarity) into Prot-Enlight versions (license, federalism) explains their eventual failure in the context of unfolding American history.

"This is all great and highly convenient *theory*," the skeptical reader may say, "but if it's all true, wouldn't the American Catholic Church have been making similar arguments at the time?"

Well, I am glad you asked.

The Church at the time said so, as boldly as it could from within a largely anti-Catholic republic. In 1791, the year in which James Madison's Bill of Rights (which he had so fervently opposed only three years earlier) was ratified, the first archbishop of the United States answered this question.

He was, fittingly, John "Jacky" Carroll of Baltimore, the cousin of Charles Carroll, the only Catholic signer of the Declaration of Independence. Archbishop Carroll wrote "A Prayer for Government" and had the prayer recited in all the diocesan parishes he oversaw.

It is "enlightening"[156] that Archbishop Carroll's prayer addresses both how the Church viewed the specific principles of the new American Constitution and also "what the Church teaches that all government should be."[157] The archbishop knew

[156] Scott P. Richert, "A New Declaration of Independence" *Crisis Magazine* July 4, 2014, https://www.crisismagazine.com/2014/new-declaration-independence.
[157] Ibid.

that Catholic Natural Law principles would work not only for America, but for all republics. Also, the archbishop seemed to have the vague sense that in spite of the young republic's fervent anti-Catholicism, Rome's invisible principles were already indispensable to it:

A *Prayer for Government*
We pray Thee, O God of might, wisdom, and justice, through whom authority is rightly administered, laws are enacted, and judgment decreed, assist with Thy Holy Spirit of counsel and fortitude the President of these United States, that his administration may be conducted in righteousness, and be eminently useful to Thy people over whom he presides; by encouraging due respect for virtue and religion; by a faithful execution of the laws in justice and mercy; and by restraining vice and immorality. Let the light of Thy divine wisdom direct the deliberations of Congress, and shine forth in all the proceedings and laws framed for our rule and government, so that they may tend to the preservation of peace, the promotion of national happiness, the increase of industry, sobriety, and useful knowledge; and may perpetuate to us the blessing of equal liberty.

In this single, ambitious paragraph, Archbishop Carroll makes mention of each of chapter 2's now-familiar main ideas: three distinct branches of governing, the basis of all authority as divine, and the goal of liberty as virtue.

Now the archbishop's prayer, of course, was not infinitely ambitious. Archbishop Carroll did not "connect the dots" for his partly Prot-Enlight audience, which would have been to articulate to a young, anti-Catholic nation that neither a Protestant- nor an Enlightenment-guided republic could serve its purported goal. No, this would have been a suicide mission! Archbishop Carroll, certainly out of a healthy fear for his own "papist" neck, stopped short of saying specifically that *only* Catholicism can accomplish all this. But the idea is there for an astute reader.

Fortunately, it has taken some 225 years for all the Prot-Enlight shortcomings to show up in full force.

Yet even now within Catholicism's orthodox ranks, there is much misunderstanding regarding the relation between our Church and the state. (Chapters 3, 4, and 5 pick up on this point where this chapter leaves off.)

On the topic of Catholic republicanism, even today's faithful Catholics divide into two camps, neither one acknowledging that republics *require* Catholicism: on one side are the *compatibilists* who view Catholicism as *somewhat* fitting with republics; on the other are those *non-compatibilists* who hold them *outright* irreconcilable.[158]

This chapter opened by showing what a constitution is: any government that brands itself as *constitutional* requires Catholic Natural Law. We will conclude by noting that the "non-compat-ibilists" are flat-out wrong and that the "compatibilists" haven't gone far enough (to say that they are "compatible" is to understate the needfulness of the connection between republicanism and Catholicism).

Both the founding and the framing steps in a republic's life require Catholic Natural Law, and thereby, Catholicism. In other words, republicanism needs the ideas of Catholicism

---

[158] Patrick J. Deneen "A Catholic Showdown Worth Watching," *The American Conservative*, February 6, 2014, https://www. theamericanconservative.com/2014/02/06/a-catholic-show down-worth-watching/.

more desperately than either side of the debate has been willing to acknowledge.[159]

And with that, we conclude our analysis of the framing of republics — i.e., the second life phase constituted by *making* the new regime. Just as the British regime was broken with on the basis of Catholic Natural Law, the new American regime was made on that same basis. During America's first republican life phase (founding), Jefferson *genuinely* imported the thought of *pseudo*–Natural Law Whigs such as Locke (who plagiarized Catholic thinkers); during America's second republican life phase (framing), conversely, Madison *pseudo*-incorporated the ideas of a *genuine* Natural Law thinker (who represented Catholic political theory accurately).

Jefferson's and Madison's respective results were the same, however: in each phase, America was wired to be crypto-Catholic. And that is why I've referred to both of the first phases as inauthentic, or partial, Catholic Natural Law.

The remaining four chapters describe the staking of the regime *within the citizenry or culture*, the third and final republican life phase. This phase spans from immediately after the ratification of the Constitution until the end of the republic's life, whenever that may occur. Recall, a republic's life is described as a "phase" precisely because it is cyclical.

The cultural symptoms of decline discussed in those chapters will be more recognizable to the modern reader. Although *breaking* and *making* the regime took place within the purview of our

[159] Here's the problem with both sides of this intra-Catholic debate. Too often, republics are thought of as a species of democracy. But democracy, like monarchy, does not require a constitution at all. Without requiring a constitution, a government fails to require Catholic Natural Law principles, as republics do.

CATHOLIC REPUBLIC

young republic's leadership (i.e., its Revolution-era government), the third phase takes place at the level of the country's citizenry.

While a good constitution is indispensable, in a republic, popular morality must be sought and enforced by the people's culture, not by the government.

Chapter 3

Staking the New Regime in the American Culture

The Crypto-Catholicism of American Morality

Our Constitution was written for a moral and religious people. It is wholly inadequate to the governance of any other.

—John Adams

Without morals a republic cannot subsist any length of time; they therefore who are decrying the Christian religion, whose morality is so sublime and pure . . . are undermining the solid foundation of morals, the best security for the duration of free governments.

—Charles Carroll, letter to James McHenry, November 4, 1800

Chapter 2 showed that the Prot-Enlight American founders and framers harbored deeply conflicted expectations about the moral, cultural, and political dimensions of republics. In the Declaration of Independence and the Constitution, they denied yet shamefully borrowed key elements from Catholic Natural Law.

CATHOLIC REPUBLIC

When it comes to the popular morality of republican culture, Catholic Natural Law demands a very high standard. In fact, a republic cannot work without such a high standard.

Accordingly, early American leaders paid no small amount of lip service to the necessity of (Catholic) private virtue as the central *cultural* fixture of republicanism. But their Prot-Enlight philosophy precluded, on paper anyway, the possibility thereof. Recall from the introduction the three prongs of the Catholic Natural Law denied by both Prot-Enlight camps.

The third element of crypto-Catholicism in our Prot-Enlight republic is *individual and popular morality*. In America, Catholic morality, like the other elements of Catholic Natural Law republicanism, was partially and secretly wired into the system but has never been labeled Catholic, and so gradually ceased to function.

The third, final, and lengthiest republican phase, *staking the new regime in the citizenry*, is covered in chapters 3 through 6. This phase comprises the passing of the baton of leadership from the framers to the people after the Constitution has been set up. Beginning (in this chapter) with the element of individual and popular morality, we will discuss America's *culture*, not its *government*. In other words, the people of any republic must choose morality freely and independently of declarations, constitutions, and as we will see, even laws. Only the *noncoerced* choice by citizens for morality counts as the cultural "staking" of the principles of the Declaration and the Constitution within the republic's heart.

In American history, this indispensable cultural staking simply did not happen sufficiently in the eighteenth and nineteenth centuries. But such a staking must be perfected in our day, if America is to restore its republican status and survive the widespread cultural apostasy in our midst.

Unlike republican life phases one (*breaking the old regime: founding*) and two (*making the new regime: framing*), as discussed above, this last phase must be accomplished by the people, not by the government. The idea is worth repeating. This third phase entails the trickiest requirement of republicanism: authentic *self-rule* by the citizens. In fostering true republicanism, leadership by founders and framers — regime-breakers and -makers — goes only so far. If a republic is to thrive rather than devolve into a republic in name only, then the people must take the reins at the beginning of this critical phase (*staking the new regime in the heart of the citizenry*).

As the saying goes: "You can lead a horse to water, but you cannot make him drink." As it were, the "horse" (i.e., the republic's people), must choose for itself to drink of republican culture's lifegiving "water," in this case, true Christian morality. Founders and framers can only lead the horse up to that point.

True Christian morality is best represented by the Catholic Natural Law's "virtue ethics." As will be discussed below, virtue ethics focuses on the behavior and character that each *individual* should choose for himself, rather than reliance on external laws and customs of his culture. Virtue ethics comes directly from the tradition of Aristotle and Thomas Aquinas.

If anything, today's American moral culture seems to be moving backward, toward paganism. True morality requires not *crypto*, but *outright* Catholic Natural Law: since America's moral wiring was misunderstood by most Americans, its eventual "backsliding" was predictable from the very beginning.

As the reader now knows, American Prot-Enlight thought remained well outside the philosophical boundaries of the Catholic Natural Law, rejecting man's free will and the possibility of his virtue. A Catholic can, without contradiction, view "moral theology [as] the science of imitating God,"[160] as Monsignor Garrigou-Lagrange once wrote. But a Protestant (or especially a secularist) cannot. Thus, the Prot-Enlight founders' and framers' references to *necessary* republican virtue, cited throughout chapters 1 and 2, obliquely invoke the Catholic Natural Law in a shamefully plagiaristic way — and in a way that should not have been available to them (given their staunch anti-Catholicism).

Because American morality drew water from an off-limits well, with an undersized and leaky Prot-Enlight pail, they were able to take only little sips from the water (i.e., the comprehensive Catholic Natural Law). Besides, the incompatibility between the pail and the water within it tainted the latter with rust.

That "rust" was moral relativism.

The Tainted Waters of Moral Relativism

Moral relativism is the assumption that all global ethical systems are equally valid. For example, cannibalism is practiced in some parts of the world and rejected in others. According to moral relativism, both practices are equally valid. We know this is absurd.

Yet this toxic philosophy gained a foothold in America on account of our nation's highly insufficient adaptation of the Catholic Natural Law morality (i.e., virtue ethics). In our day, we have seen relativism for what it really is — not just a toxin, but a *neurotoxin* — which has gained momentum and grown rampant. Only Catholicism's virtue ethics can restore to America its focus on the unique republican role of virtue.

[160] Réginald Garrigou-Lagrange, *Beatitude: A Commentary on Saint Thomas's Theological Summa, Ia-IIae, qq. 1–54* (CreateSpace Independent Publishing, 2016).

Breaking down Christian ethics was one of the Enlightenment's foremost goals. On the other hand, the Reformation's
regard for ethics was far more complicated: breaking down virtue
ethics was a *mostly unintended* consequence of the Protestant
Reformation. Given the Protestant rejection of prongs one, two,
and three of Catholic Natural Law (from this book's introduction), mankind had, for the Protestant, neither a free will nor a
sufficiently enlightened intellect to participate in ethics, aside
from reading commands appearing in the Bible.

This makes the Protestant breakdown of ethics seem mostly
unintentional.

On the other hand, the earliest Protestant Reformers disdained
the Aristotelianism within Catholicism; they had an even more
particular dislike for Aristotle's virtue ethics. Protestants today look
back and wonder whether, on the whole, "Luther's Reformation
was a response to Aristotle's *Ethics* since, "for Luther, [the bondage
of the will] is the 'hinge' on which everything else turns"[161] and
since Aristotle's ethics represents the diametrical opposite of this.

This makes the Protestant breakdown of ethics seem quite a
bit more intentional. This tension within Protestantism should
be borne in mind, as we segue into discussing moral relativism.

Just after Benedict XVI became pope, he was asked to identify the greatest danger in the modern world. His response was:
"the dictatorship of relativism."[162] Only weeks before this, when
celebrating what turned out to be his final Mass before becoming

---

[161] Paul Louis Metzger, "Aristotle and Luther on Justice, Virtue,
and the Reformation," Patheos, October 11, 2014, https://www.
patheos.com/blogs/uncommongodcommongood/2014/10/aristo-
tle-and-luther-on-justice-virtue-and-the-reformation-of-values/.
[162] Benjamin Wiker, "Benedict vs. the Dictatorship of Relativism,"
National Catholic Register, February 25, 2013, www.ncregister.

pope, he put it in an even more specific way: "A dictatorship of relativism is being formed, one that recognizes nothing as definitive and that has as its measure only the self and its desires."[163]

What did the pope mean? And, for our purposes, what does moral relativism have to do with the American phenomenon of Prot-Enlight? How does moral relativism in America today influence the legal system under which we live?

Just like the rest of the West, the American mainstream has embraced the relativist view that each individual may *validly* choose for himself which morality, if any, will guide his life.[164] No ethical systems really matter for the relativist, because none of them are *actually, objectively* true. So, any choice will basically do.

"Rigorous Christian morality may work *for you,*" today's moral relativist is often heard to say to the non-relativist, "but not for me. It is not *my* truth. Each of us has his own, and all truths are equally valid." As the Straussians often say, if all values are relative, then cannibalism is a matter of taste.

Moral relativism represents an utter rejection of virtue ethics. The denial of the existence of virtue is the telltale symptom of the moral crisis in America today. Moral relativism grew from a once-small niche at the academic and anti-intellectual fringes of society into the dominant corner occupied by the popular culture in the West today.

Make no mistake, moral relativism has always existed, from before even Aristotle's day. Almost four centuries before Christ,

com/blog/benjamin-wiker/benedict-vs.-the-dictatorship-of-relativism.

[163] Benedict XVI, opening homily at the 2005 papal conclave.

[164] It is, of course, unproblematic to acknowledge that people really do choose a system of ethics—as long as one maintains the logically necessary conclusion that all systems but one must be errant.

Socrates's street-debating rival Gorgias expressed surprisingly modern-sounding views on moral relativism. Two millennia later, the Enlightenment would transform moral relativism from a minority worldview (comprising either too *much* intellectualism or too *little*[165]), into a startlingly popular way of life, embraced by most. An early Enlightenment philosopher, Thomas Hobbes, gave voice to the view that the next five centuries would adopt regarding morality in nature: "the notions of right and wrong, justice and injustice, have [in nature] no place. Where there is no common power, there is no law; where no law, no injustice."[166]

Virtually all the American founders and framers agreed—or thought they agreed—with Catholic founder Charles Carroll's statement at the beginning of this chapter: "Without morals a republic cannot subsist."[167] Universal *Christian* morality among the citizenry, they would often repeat, is absolutely necessary for the survival of any republic. This is unquestionably correct. But what they did not admit was that the *type* of Christian morality matters.

Self-rule requires moral rulers who are *not* legislators, judges, or governors, but citizens!

Citizen leaders.

Self-rule.

Only that is republicanism.

---

[165] In a certain sense, relativism was the martial currency of the ancient world, the conqueror's world—that of the Egyptians, Babylonians, Persians, Greeks, Carthaginians, Franks, Angles, Huns, Romans, Visigoths. But prior to the Enlightenment, relativism did not bear the intellectual potency or the popularity that it would assume in the sixteenth century. After the Enlightenment, it has become the moral worldview of the pedant—in civil times of peace, not war.

[166] Thomas Hobbes, *Leviathan* 1, 13.

[167] Charles Carroll, letter to James McHenry, November 4, 1800.

But all the non-Catholic American founders and framers — every one of them except Carroll — simply could not explain, given their anti–Catholic Natural Law background, *why* or *how* morality operates. Nor could they explain *how* their Protestant and/or Enlightenment versions of morality could be thought of as universal (as could the Catholic version). The Protestant viewpoint, after all, held both human liberty and human morality to be impossibilities for fallen mankind. So did the Enlightenment viewpoint, for opposite reasons: man is simply a complex organism, a meat machine, and nothing more. (Chapters 1 and 2 thoroughly demonstrated this Prot-Enlight dilemma in the realm of *political* principles. Henceforth, we will talk about it in the context of *cultural* principles.)

It is therefore no wonder at all that popular conceptions of crypto-Catholic morality grew perverted over time in America.[168]

While big-government regimes will always encourage relativist license and renounce genuine liberty in order to grow their own power (as chapter 2 showed), here in chapter 3 we will look at the other side of the coin: popular culpability. In other words, even though chapters 1 and 2 discussed the government's share of the blame when liberty gives way to tyranny, there exists a more onerous moral burden upon the citizenry, for establishing a sense of true liberty. Chapter 2 showed that widespread immorality always grows government power; chapter 3 will now show how widespread Catholic morality — virtue ethics — produces the self-reliance that *rebuffs* that governmental growth.

---

[168] There is one and only one solution to moral relativism: morality must be universally disclosed and recognized within nature. The American idea of liberty (which is available, as a function of Catholic Natural Law, even to non-Christians) must at its core connect to Catholic moral theology, if American popular morality is to be redeemable at all.

Even in its definition, true virtue requires self-reliance. We will see just how.

But since Protestants embrace the same Ten Commandments and the same Sermon on the Mount as Catholics do, *why* is the Reformation sense of morality any less likely to supply republicanism its cultural lifeblood, liberty?

American Confusion about Free Will

As stated in the introduction, chapter 1, and especially chapter 2, any genuine reflection of American liberty originally vested in the U.S. Declaration or Constitution must have hailed from the single worldview capable of affirming free will: Catholic Natural Law. By definition, one can engage in virtue only if he is accountable for his actions. And a person is accountable for his actions only if he possesses a will that is free. The *Catechism of the Catholic Church* states that such freedom "makes man responsible for his acts to the extent that they are voluntary" (1734).

But by way of quick review, neither camp of Prot-Enlight ever accepted that the human will was free. Therefore, man's actions can *never* please God (i.e., for the Protestant). So why try? As Louis Bouyer says:

> In the light of numerous Protestant accounts, from the sixteenth century to the present day, this doctrine [of Protestant free-will rejection] may be summed up by saying that it is impossible to affirm and uphold the sovereignty of God without a corresponding annihilation of the creature, especially man. To recognize any worth at all in man ... while maintaining his close dependence upon God, would seem an infringement of the divine majesty, by the very fact of this dependence. In particular, to suppose that man,

as the result of God's grace, has the power to do acts good in themselves, even granted his total dependence upon God, would be to destroy the gratuitousness of grace and so to deny the sovereign freedom of God's action. And to say that man, as the recipient of saving grace, could be himself pleasing to God is to be guilty of blasphemy. Finally, it would be a relapse into idolatry to suppose that man, even when regenerated and recreated, in St. Paul's words, in holiness and justice, could possess any value and still worse to attribute to him the power to "merit" anything, in any sense of the word. Affirmations of this sort occur frequently in Luther and even more in Calvin. As for Barth, his entire system turns on them.[169]

Catholic morality in America continued to be ridiculed as "Romish," as it had been since the Reformation, but it was evidently worthy of plagiarism all the same. In spite of themselves, Jefferson and the founders made never-ending reference to the necessity of virtue in the citizenry. Even libertarian-leaning founders such as Jefferson knew that a strong separation of religion and the state would mean an eventual breakdown in morality: "In a society in which it was widely accepted that civil government depended upon religion and upon the morality it inculcated, any hint that dissenters aimed to separate religion from government ... insinuated that dissenters desired to undermine the moral foundations of government."[170]

But this didn't mean that just any *open* Catholic morality could be tolerated. In America's case, any Catholic Natural Law

[169] Louis Bouyer, *The Spirit and Forms of Protestantism* (London: Harvill Press, 1956), p. 176.
[170] Phillip Hamburger, *Separation of Church and State* (Cambridge, MA: Harvard University Press, 2009), p. 66.

morality that managed to squeeze through our borders must have been crypto-Catholic.

According to Catholic Natural Law, moral goodness is the purpose of liberty. We are left free in order to do right, to discharge our duties.[171] This is why virtue is so important in republics! According to Catholic Natural Law, man can be free in the political sense only if he is first free in the theological sense. All liberty is theological; all liberty is political. There cannot exist different "types" of it at all. To discover (and, as we will see below, to habituate) the moral good is the very reason God gave liberty to human beings in the first place.

For Catholics, all human beings share the divine gifts of *free will*, a *natural intellect*, and *moral prudence*. Free will is the Catholic view of the state of the soul: unlike the Protestant view, Catholics see the human will as free from the blinding nature of sin.[172] Man is not predestined for sin, as in the Protestant sense. The human intellect, on the Catholic view, naturally governs the will. As such, it must be considered a trait universal to all humans, not only to Christian converts or to "the Elect." This means that, even in man's sinful state of nature — prior to his Christian conversion — Catholic Natural Law holds that the human mind *can* discern right and wrong. Thereafter, it is possible for the person to pursue morality through his chosen behavior.

---

[171] Pope John XXIII's encyclical *Pacem in Terris* (April 11, 1963) discusses this at length.

[172] Man is only *partly* free from sin to the extent that God has given him a "prime liberty" in the form of his intellect. To allege that man is wholly free from sin would be to posit the heresy of Pelagianism — the very existence of which ought to prove to Protestants that the Catholic view of sin is not as "pagan" as many of their luminaries have assumed.

This ability is something that Aristotle and the Catholic thinkers who followed him would call "prudence."

Life involves choices made in real time. Most decisions of a moral nature in daily life are *split decisions*, "taking account of particular facts"[173] and needing to be made off the cuff. Aristotle explains that this is the role of prudence, the ability to deliberate instantaneously about "what is advantageous as a means to the good life in general."[174] To this end, prudence is real-time moral judging in the real world, wherein action must be chosen without lengthy amounts of study.

In review, Catholicism enshrines one and only one type of liberty—the sort that unites free will, natural intellect, and moral prudence. As such, political liberty is not ultimately distinguishable from theological liberty. How can man be free individually, but unfree collectively (i.e., politically), or vice versa? It is impossible: human freedom is a pale, but real, reflection of God's completely free, intelligent creation of the universe.[175]

Strangely, however, both halves of Prot-Enlight attempted to affirm man's political liberty while denying his theological liberty. Human will is taken to be either *wicked* (Prot) or *animalian* (Enlight); human intellect is seen as either *fully darkened by Original Sin* (Prot) or *wholly reducible to the function of the organs* (Enlight); the Prot-Enlight version of prudence is received as something like *blind animal instinct* (by both halves of Prot-Enlight). Accordingly, neither camp sees that the world bears the possibility

---

[173] Aristotle, *EN* VI, vii, 7.

[174] Aristotle, *EN* VI, v, 1.

[175] For the Catholic, man's imperfect (but real) liberty emanates directly from God's perfect freedom. All good human choices are part of God's creation. Thus, mankind's freedom is not an illusion, as it is for both Protestants and Enlightenment secularists.

of freedom—except, of course, when either one borrows secretly from Catholicism.[176]

On the Protestant side, one encounters "theological determinism": the total rejection of human freedom and morality following mankind's fall from grace. For every shade of Protestant—over thirty-eight thousand sects and counting—man's will is hopelessly enslaved to sin. Remember, Luther deemed the human will to be "in bondage." Calvin, more extreme in his view of man's utter predestination, wrote that "Natural Law gives [man] scarce an inkling of the kind of service which is pleasing to God."[177]

---

[176] As the Declaration of Independence reminds us, liberty is a pre-governmental, divine heirloom possessed by every last human being. In every non-tyrannical society on the globe, citizens are furnished one opportunity after another to discharge their duties in their private lives. The state should not act as their conscience. For obvious reasons, then, Catholicism's free will, natural intellect, and moral prudence are absolutely indispensable if republican self-rule and morality are to exist.

[177] John Calvin, *Institutes of the Christian Religion* II, 8, 1. But remember, Calvin was deeply confused as to whether man's conscience could intelligibly discern morality. In certain other places, he wrote as if he were a Catholic affirmer of the Natural Law: "As a seed of religious awareness is implanted in the heart of man so that he may recognize and honor his Lord, so conscience is given him that he may sufficiently distinguish between right and wrong. The activity and insights of conscience are the language in which the law of nature is couched." *Institutes* II, 2, 22. Wilhelm Niesel writes that, for Calvin, "The law of nature has only one purpose: namely, to make man inexcusable before God." *The Theology of Calvin* (Cambridge, England: James Clarke, 1956), p. 102. In other words, to Calvin, man's conscience is oriented toward recognizing his inevitable moral failure rather than discerning actions that may lead to his eventual moral conversion, a proposition that falls short of affirming what is meant on any construction of the free-will component of

The ungoverned will blindly chooses sin, for the Protestant, without fail.[178] Early Reformers such as Calvin and "Luther took an opposing stance [to Aristotle, in holding that] we become good by *being made good* ... [since] the fallen will is not free to choose the good."[179] Even from the outset, Protestants took the position that only God, not free will, makes a previously selected few good enough to be "saved."

On the Enlightenment side, one encounters a complete, atheistic rejection of morality.[180] Unlike the Protestant rejection, the atheistic mockery of morality lacks subtlety. Atheists pose a

---

the Natural Law. Contrast this Calvinist view sharply with the *Catechism*'s statement that "[freedom] makes man responsible for his acts to the extent that they are voluntary" (1734).

[178] The rejoinder commonly offered by the Puritans and other Protestants is flatly insufficient: as noted above, they spuriously divide liberty into *political* and *theological* sorts. According to this bizarre rejoinder, man somehow deserves relative freedom from the dominion of other men, even though, Protestantism insists, man can never enjoy bona fide liberty or know what to do ultimately with his political liberty! At the early Reformation Council of Dort, recall, it was agreed that mankind is incapable of governing even day-to-day affairs, let alone important theological ones. Because the Protestants suggest a political freedom not in conformity with an orientation to the good—true liberty—freedom must logically be, at bottom, license, which is completely disconnected from the *goal* of human life.

[179] Metzger, "Aristotle and Luther."

[180] Enlightenment epistemology, varied as it was, severed the human intellect from knowing anything lasting about reality. In the eighteenth and nineteenth centuries, Kant became the favored philosopher on the continent of Europe; Locke was already the favored philosopher in England and America. In the West, these Prot-Enlight philosophers had a tremendous influence on views against the intelligibility of nature morally, scientifically, and metaphysically.

stark determinism whereby individuals lack souls and intellects. As such, humans are nakedly unfree animals, living by instincts alone. Humans, mere animals, simply do *what* their bodies tell them to do *when* their bodies tell them to do it. Such a description excludes morality altogether. Urges and instincts are the sovereigns of everyday human life. Human beings are no more than complex, amoral beasts. On this Enlightenment model, man is no more capable of free moral choice than animals, plants, or even inanimate objects.[181]

So in the final analysis, while some distinctions may well be warranted, the atheistic rejection of free will is not substantially different from the Protestant rejection. In either regard — Protestant or Enlightenment — one recalls the caution of Boethius: "Man towers above the rest of Creation so long as he realizes his own [free, rational] nature, and when he forgets it, he sinks lower than the beasts. For other living things, to be ignorant of themselves is natural; but for man, it is a defect."[182]

---

[181] Recall from the introduction and chapter 1 how the Enlightenment men, heroes of the American founders, strove to defend their position. Thinkers such as Locke, Newton, Hobbes, and Bacon subscribed to a strange and utterly false view of metaphysics called "corpuscular reductionism," or "atomism," which reduced human activities to physical principles. According to these paradoxical materialist principles, all human activities reduce to the observable, material appetites that man manifests in his basest state. Accordingly, for these Enlightenment thinkers, human choice is a mere illusion of the human brain — just as it was in a slightly different sense, for the Protestants. Man, being a mere animal, does not choose between two options; he simply and mechanistically defers to that which is more compelling to his senses.

[182] Anicius Manlius Severinus Boethius, *The Consolation of Philosophy*, trans. W. V. Cooper (N.p.: Ex-Classics Project, 2009), https://www.exclassics.com/consol/consol.pdf.

Now, let us return to the context of *morality within republics*.

Thomas Jefferson admitted, in 1825, that Aristotle was one of the primary four influences on the American republic.[183] This rare nod to Aristotle might or might not have included the Aristotelian *virtue ethics* that grounded the Aristotelian politics (after all, Jefferson was certainly not referring to Aristotle's *Metaphysics*, *Physics*, *Logic*, *Poetics*, etc.). Now, recall that both the Reformation and the Enlightenment considered Aristotle to be public enemy number one.[184]

These two facts clearly do not make sense together unless there was some plagiarism of Aristotle's virtue ethics at work.

We have spent time above showing that a certain strain of moral relativism springs to life in the Protestant view of sin and the Enlightenment view of instinct. Both fly in the face of the virtue that Jefferson implicitly endorsed for republicanism. In other words, Jefferson and the founders seemed to take the commonsense, virtue-ethics view (with Aristotle) that "by doing just

---

[183] "In another, his famous letter of 1825 to Henry Lee, [Jefferson] claims the ideas of the Declaration to be from Aristotle, Cicero, Locke, and Sidney [that is, two legitimate Natural Law thinkers and two phony ones]." Bradley J. Birzer, "Happiness: Did the Greeks and the Founders Share a Definition?" *Imaginative Conservative*, September 18, 2012, https://theimaginativeconservative.org/2012/09/happiness-aristotle-and-the-american-founding.html. Dr. Bradley Birzer mainly points in the opposite direction in this article — that Jefferson did *not* openly recur to Aristotle in the Declaration. This Jefferson letter of 1825 seems as puzzling to him as to me, and he does insinuate that the founders couldn't avoid indirect reference to Aristotle.

[184] This was especially the case on account of the Aristotelian system of ethics and causation.

things we become just."[185] But they did so in a muddled sense, since, of course, the young Prot-Enlight republic would not willingly endorse that view. This crypto-Catholic American incorporation of Aristotle's ethics has much to do with the eventual growth of American moral relativism.

Moral Relativism in America

Everything appearing above leads to the conclusion that in America, we live among competing subcultures that profess either *no human morality whatsoever* (Enlight) or a *fatalistic morality, doomed by mankind's Fall* (Prot). Protestants want, but deny, the possibility of a moral world, while secularists deny even the existence of morality! Indeed, Prot-Enlight leaves the morally inclined American virtually nothing to offer other than complete silence ... or conversion to Catholicism.

All the same, today's American immorality and amorality grab the attention of all but the least sensible.

Regarding this obvious moral decline, the Catholic will commiserate with his secular and especially his Protestant friends (the sensible ones, anyway). But he needs to have another look at what his friends *believe*. (Thereafter, he will not express such surprise as to the state of our country!)[186]

---

[185] Aristotle, *EN* 1103b.

[186] And his secular and Protestant friends should harbor nothing but a confounded sense of satisfaction that, indeed, the world "works" as their philosophies have calculated. Of course, the truth is that their twin philosophies are self-fulfilling: when humans are encouraged to allow their will to guide their intellect — instead of vice versa — they will happily oblige. The order of virtue ethics that is or was at work will break down. Relativism will then abide.

Since no Enlightenment thinker ever succeeded in doing away with *how one objectively ought to live*,[187] only the fatalist Protestant option would seem to remain. That is, Protestants admit that the Ten Commandments are real but deny that such morality is attainable in the "fallen" world!

But, judging by America's current popular culture, it appears that some perverse bargain has been struck between crypto-Catholic virtue ethics (tacitly endorsed by Jefferson) and Prot-Enlight fatalism (both halves of which, for very different reasons, reduce to "Why try at all?").

And whoever operates on such a bizarre moral basis will inevitably conclude that either: *no moral claims are true* or *all moral claims are true*. This is moral relativism.

Go ask any state university student if human morality is objective. You will be confidently assured that it is not! Follow up by asking, "So, slavery is not wrong?" Hilarity ensues. You've never seen someone "backtrack" or squirm as your new friend will.

Sometimes, moral relativism is expressed in the language of all-permissiveness. At other times, it appears conversely as all-consuming skepticism: i.e., that *nothing* is really true. (Yet, even this skepticism most often seems, at least initially, to embrace all systems of morality at once: "Well, if I can't say which answer is correct, then I don't dare call any of the options incorrect. *They are all equally valid, then*.")

And this insecure embrace of everything seems to be the doom of our age, to which Pope Benedict XVI referred as the

---

[187] Friedrich Nietzsche, for one famous example, arrived at a sort of *morality of aesthetics*, in spite of his announcement that objective morality is dead, along with God. He could not shake all traces of morality, however he tried. It is impossible.

"dictatorship of relativism." It furnishes the best reason why the faithful appear so very *odd* to the unfaithful: the faithful alone enjoy moral certainty, while all others toil in uncertainty and fear. Accordingly, the faithful are persecuted for their fervent, religious high standards, which aggravate the "inferiority complex" already afflicting the unfaithful who fall short. Sooner or later, relativist *affirmers of everything* will become *affirmers of only what is easiest, most pleasurable, and most popular* (which are all the same thing). Not long thereafter, these same moral relativists who once denounced all denouncing will denounce only the good.

As the Old Testament says: "Woe to those who call evil good and good evil, who put darkness for light and light for darkness, who put bitter for sweet and sweet for bitter!" (Isa. 5:20, RSVCE). Prot-Enlight America today—once squinted at by Jefferson as a "virtue ethics" society, if secretly—is morally upside down. Now we know how, what, and why: moral relativism.[188]

---

[188] It is technically impossible to believe what the cultural mainstream claims to believe—that all and no moral positions are simultaneously correct. The default position has become one of accepting first-world freedom, without freedom's purpose. Today, for the first time in human history, this relativist contradiction seems to be the globally preponderant point of view. From chapter 2, the reader already knows the alternate name of the relativist situation: license. By chapter 3, this is already our third approach to the doctrine of license, "freedom for its own sake" (rather than for the specific sake of pursuing the good). One abuses his freedom, of course, the very moment he presumes it to be a self-justifying end, a good in itself. A relativist society will always brainwash its people—in schools and through its entertainment culture—to believe that any "absolutist" form of moral freedom presented by the Catholic Church, which insists upon its own universal correctness, must

be injurious to true freedom. Paradoxically, this couldn't be any more erroneous. Relativism, a neurotoxin gradually concocted over the last several centuries, puts forth the proposition that all debaters can "agree to disagree" about the moral truths of the universe, with neither side needing correction. In order for something to be called "true," however, it must be exclusive of all other positions. If two uncles were to argue over whether the lights in the basement are on or off, one man must be correct and the other incorrect. By and large, even the relativist world still accepts simple logical propositions such as this. Conversely, in the field of ethics, the world has turned against realism, root and branch. If an argument springs up between those two uncles, playing ping-pong in the same basement, as to whether the American bombing of Hiroshima and Nagasaki was morally permissible, few in the West would still assert that one of them must be absolutely wrong and the other must be absolutely right. "They are both right ... in their own way." Today, the world refuses to account for its insane disparity of responses in these respective situations: Why is the light switch "certainly" on or off, but bombing innocents can somehow be "in between" right and wrong—or both? This is because Prot-Enlight (predominantly post-Enlightenment thought) has successfully popularized its rejection of Catholic Natural Law in the field of ethics. The effects of such a popularization, while insane, have engendered a politically correct comfort enjoyed by the people, unlikely to be abandoned by the cultural mainstream anytime soon. The milieu remains quite pleasant when nobody has to be corrected. No one is ever deemed to be wrong. Few are ever called "dumb," or even "uneducated." People are rarely condemned (excluding, ironically, truly religious people, who are ridiculed) as immoral. Pleasure-seeking vices are lauded as "individualistic" in the fashion of a Nike commercial, held on par with the narrower path of virtue. "Don't judge me" is everywhere received as an impenetrable defense for sinners seeking not to repent but to continue unabated in their sin. The great majority of young adults, beginning in the university, judge that it is sufficient to be "spiritual, but not religious." And

But here is the good news: truth will out. Relativism is false, however temporarily convenient it may be for the forces of vice and evil. As is the case with all Catholic Natural Law principles, our knowledge of virtue ethics is inborn. All humans intuitively—on account of the universality of Catholic Natural Law—know it. Supreme Court Justice Anthony Kennedy's *Planned Parenthood* remark that "at the heart of liberty is the right to define one's own concept of existence, of meaning, of the universe, and of the mystery of human life" is ultimately a laughable expression that no one really believes, however much they may claim otherwise.

Natural Law Catholicism has been the great opponent of moral relativism since Pontius Pilate rhetorically asked Christ, "What is truth?" (John 18:38).

Aristotle's ethical system and pre-Christian monotheism required a few key modifications in order to avoid vestiges of pagan contradiction (for example, the perennial trap of "spiritual, but not religious"[189] which has returned to society so popularly today). Thomas Aquinas furnished just such modifications. Since America still *claims* to be a nation committed to religious tolerance, however, let's assess virtue ethics as it originally appeared in the writings of pre-Christian Aristotle—with a little fine-tuning by Thomas.

Virtue Ethics: Habit and the Golden Mean

Acquiring the virtues is both simple and natural, on the Aristotelian view supplemented by Catholic Natural Law. Moreover,

---

such a position presents a comfortable, if fictive, "middle way" between theism and atheism.

[189] Although today's university students may think they invented "I'm spiritual, but not religious," it goes back at least as far as Gnosticism (which the Catholic Church rebuffed then, too!).

there is no way to acquire virtue except by the simple methods first described by Aristotle. In fact, Aristotle's *Nicomachean Ethics*, which antedated Christ by three and a half centuries, might well be seen as Natural Law's "coming out party."

Aristotle's commonsense doctrine says that cultivating virtue is a gradual process, marked by two main features: *moderation* and *habit*. Thomas Aquinas and his followers, with minimal modification, incorporated into Catholic Natural Law these two crucial aspects of Aristotelian ethics.

Centuries later, the American founders would insist on the necessity of virtue for the creation, maintenance, and survival of the republic (which required plagiarism from Catholic Natural Law).

First, let us consider what Aristotle says about the doctrine of moderation: "moral qualities are so constituted as to be destroyed by excess and by deficiency."[190] Or, more simply, moderation is the golden mean. It is the middling behavior chosen between two extremes, both of which turn out to be vices. For example, Aristotle names "courage" as the moral middle between the two extremes cowardice (deficiency) and rashness (excess): "Let us first take courage. We have already seen that courage is the observance of the mean in respect of fear and confidence."[191] Aristotle explains that the ethical, courageous man will stand and fight a reasonable battle in which he is evenly matched; the unethical, cowardly man will not fight even a fair battle; the unethical, overconfident man will rashly fight single-handedly against ten or even ten thousand opponents. Only the middle way (which Aristotle applies to all other virtues as well) denotes courage.

[190] Aristotle, *EN* II, ii, 6.
[191] Aristotle, *EN* III, vi, 1.

Thomas Aquinas approves the above passage, since Aristotle deftly "shows by what actions virtue is [actually] caused":[192] moderate behaviors falling between two opposite vices. The Natural Law inherent in Catholic ethics involves this golden mean.

So moderation explains *what* a virtue is, but one still wonders *how* virtue is cultivated. While nature does not produce in man something like *inevitable virtue*—for Aristotle, as for the Catholic thinkers who followed him, virtue can be opted *against*—nature does instill in man the capacity to cultivate virtue. This capacity is filled by habit.

Aristotelian habit is not a term of art: it means precisely what you think it does. For Aristotle and the Catholic Natural Law ethical theorists, we are what we repeatedly do, not what we do just once or twice: "Moral excellence is not an act, but a habit."[193] Virtue is accomplished through a consistent sequence of freely willed acts. Once a virtue becomes habitual, it continues to become embedded deeper within a person's character.[194]

Again, approvingly, Thomas Aquinas writes that Aristotle "proposes that moral virtue originates in us from the habit of acting."[195] Character is built through the repetition of virtuous acts, Aquinas affirms.

---

[192] Thomas Aquinas, *Commentary on the Nicomachean Ethics* 2, 2, 2.

[193] Will Durant, *The Story of Philosophy: The Lives and Opinions of the World's Greatest Philosophers* (New York: Simon and Schuster, 1926), pt. VII. Durant is summing up Aristotle's virtue ethics from the *Nicomachean Ethics*.

[194] That is to say, virtue is exercised—and eventually perfected—in the action by which it was formed (to borrow a famous Aristotelian phrase).

[195] Thomas Aquinas, *Commentary on the Nicomachean Ethics* 2, 1, 1.

This means that one must use the intellect to train the will. Aristotle gives the example that *we become just by doing just acts*, as men become builders by building houses. And we measure the development of such virtue "in relation to pleasures and pains"[196] felt during and after the act. We know we have acquired a virtue only when its performance no longer feels painful. In fact, Thomas Aquinas emphasizes the great detail in which Aristotle "explains how we may recognize virtue already produced":[197] not only by a lack of pain, but even by the sensation of pleasure in the virtuous act!

For example, let's examine the New Year's resolution of committing to a daily jog. During the first few weeks of the year, the jogger finds the aspirational virtue (i.e., fitness by jogging) to be unpleasant and difficult. In fact, the new jogger finds his resolution so difficult that he is initially motivated through intellect alone: he *knows* he needs to lose weight but is *pained by* his jog.

So, he is not yet truly virtuous, even after his first few daily jogs.

But as the jogger stays the course, his daily perseverance gradually makes jogging easier. By the time jogging has become a habit, this virtue has been mastered. This is the key for Aristotle and Thomas Aquinas. Once mastered, such a virtue is embedded, as Archbishop Fulton Sheen would say, in the jogger's "character."[198] It no longer exists abstractly in his intellect, as something potential and desired. It is now second nature to him. And Aristotle's system of virtue ethics serves to explain why keeping New Year's

---

[196] Aristotle, *EN* II, iii, 6.
[197] Thomas Aquinas, *Commentary on the Nicomachean Ethics*, 2, 3, 3.
[198] Fulton Sheen said this so regularly that it is unnecessary to cite any one source.

resolutions becomes easy after a while. The jogger will even miss his daily jog, initially so loathed by him, if he were to skip it.

On the other hand, just going through the motions (as the jogger does on the first day of his resolution) is what Aristotle calls "accidental virtue."[199] Only after our jogger experiences pleasure during his jog will he have achieved *true virtue*: "An action is just or temperate as long as it is an action such as a just man would do, but the agent of the action is just or temperate only when he does it the way a just or temperate man would."[200] For Aristotle, accidental virtue is incomplete. It does not count as true virtue.

This is key to our examination of the relation between morality and legality in republics. According to Catholic Natural Law, true morality (virtue ethics) *cannot* be cultivated in the citizenry through laws alone; that would merely create accidental virtue. True morality cannot be legislated.

Does the Law Make the Citizen Moral? The Positivism-Originalism-Activism Spectrum

Here's the point of the above discussion of the basics of virtue ethics: neither law nor any motivation besides free, individually-imposed moral choice and habit can truly or fully make men morally good.[201] But in various corners of the "American experiment,"

---

[199] Aristotle, *EN* V, ix, 15.

[200] Aristotle, *EN* II, iv, 4.

[201] Thomas Aquinas took the Aristotelian idea even further when he interpreted this passage in Augustine: "Therefore [on account of Augustine's rationale], human laws, by not prohibiting some sins, rightly permit them" (*Summa Theologiae* I-II, 93, 2). Thomas then places the idea beyond any doubt: "Human laws do not by strict command prohibit every vicious action, just as

CATHOLIC REPUBLIC

even many Catholic commentators often say otherwise. They imply that law, because it aligns with morality in many undeniable ways, makes citizens morally good. Such commentators, along with most of today's legislators and judges in America, have not taken seriously the Aristotelian distinction between accidental virtue and true virtue. This means that they draw together too closely the relation between jurisprudence and ethics, and thereby suggest a *contradiction* of Aristotle: that "actions prescribed by law make citizens truly moral." These commentators, judges, or legislators err on the side of virtually no distinction between legality and morality, advocating *activism* (i.e., *"legislating morality"*); and conversely, they err on the opposite side, proposing that

---

they do not command every virtuous action" (ibid.). In other words, Thomas rejects activism. On the other hand, (along with Aristotle and Augustine) he rejects activism's opposite, positivism, which denies all interaction between legality and morality. If the citizens, rather than judges or legislators, were the true sovereigns in republics, then morality must influence legality *partially*, but not *completely*. This requires originalism. The American founders and framers would draw on this idea in order to keep the role of each branch of the new American government small. In spite of the clear position of medieval and ancient Catholic Natural Law thinkers, the disciples of twentieth-century philosopher Leo Strauss asserted that positivism and presumably even originalism were born during the Enlightenment (specifically, in Machiavelli's philosophy). This is incorrect. Nevertheless, the Straussians have been exceedingly effective at popularizing this view—called the "modern divide"—which held that up to, but not after, the beginning of the Enlightenment, activism was the only point of view. Non-Catholics and Catholics alike in Prot-Enlight America have been deeply influenced by the false notion of this modern divide. As such, the Prot-Enlight mainstream in America equivocates violently between the two extremes, activism and positivism.

152

there is virtually no morality in the law, which is *positivism* (i.e., *"separation of church and state"*). Now the reader sees that, for the Catholic Natural Law tradition, the individual citizen must choose virtue *apart* from the law, even if he happens accidentally to be following a law when he acts rightly:[202]

> To observe an understood and fair law is not to be coerced by it. Coercion only arises for Aquinas when someone acts unreasonably in a situation that seriously endangers others or the common good. Thus, a free and just society will be one primarily run by free obedience to law on the part of those who understand it and will to be just or fair according to its stipulations. A society that requires a constant and heavy dose of coercion is one rapidly deviating from the norms of reason and free adhesion to what is understood to be required. [203]

---

[202] Aristotle's distinction confirms that true virtue can be attained only by individuals who act morally by their own choice and habituation, not by government compulsion. Thomas Aquinas's philosophy of law carried this even further. When we apply Aristotle's and Thomas's words to our laws and Constitution, it becomes clear that there must be a middle way between *too strong a connection between morality and law* and *too loose a connection*. If the Constitution or law was properly made, and the republic is peopled by moral citizens, then the framework of laws will ultimately be *moral* when interpreted strictly. But judges should not substitute for a plain, "original" reading of the Constitution, because the original Constitution should already be sufficiently moral. Judges' moral interpretation of law represents a radical departure from the inherent morality of republican rule by a moral people.

[203] James V. Schall, "The Uniqueness of the Political Philosophy of Thomas Aquinas," *Perspectives in Political Science* 26 (Spring 1997): 85–91.

Aristotle addressed positivism as all too easy a pitfall, saying that "some people [falsely] think all the rules of justice are merely conventional, because whereas a [physical] law of nature is immutable and has the same validity everywhere, as fire burns both here and in Persia, rules of justice are seen to vary."[204]

But many American Catholics,[205] who rightly fear this complete divorce of legality and morality, seem to have overcompensated. By saying that there ought to be *little or no conceptual separation* between legality and morality, they go to the opposite extreme: activism. But such Catholic proponents of activism do

---

[204] Aristotle, *EN* V, vii, 2.

[205] Even fellow Catholics and good-faith affirmers of the Natural Law such as Dr. Hadley Arkes and Dr. Robert P. George seem to assume that the jurisprudence proper to the Catholic Natural Law is some form or another of judicial activism—known by their own loaded branding as the "Natural Law Jurisprudence." For example, take Dr. Arkes's "Natural Law Manifesto," as appearing in the *Claremont Review of Books* 11, no. 4 (Fall 2011), where he writes: "Our allies on the conservative side retreat to some safe formula of positive law, a focus on the text of the Constitution, or a commitment to 'Originalism' and tradition. But with that move they transmute the question; they turn jurisprudence into legislative history." Aristotle, Augustine, and Thomas Aquinas all beg to differ with good Dr. Arkes, who appears to be genuinely unaware of the longstanding Aristotelian tradition, consisting mainly of Catholics, who would reject Arkes's "Natural Law jurisprudence." They would reject it not for the Enlightenment's positivism, but rather in favor of a jurisprudence that acknowledges the composite (objective-subjective) nature of human law and the incomplete nature of the overlap between legality and morality. Dr. Arkes's implicit endorsement of the view of a "living Constitution" is at odds with a text-based approach to the nation's laws; this opposition, falsely taking the name of the Natural Law, would have staggered Aristotle or Thomas.

so without consulting the very experts whose caution against positivism they've heeded!

We are hardly left to speculate. Aristotle specifically noted that "actions prescribed by law are only accidentally just"![206] And Thomas Aquinas seems strongly inclined to accept Aristotle's distinction, holding that "human laws do not by strict command prohibit every vicious action, just as they do not command every virtuous action."[207] *So, the accidentally virtuous man follows the law in a fundamentally different way than the truly virtuous man does:* the former is motivated to obey laws only by the force of the law, the latter by his well-formed character. It's like the difference between night and day.

Originalism (i.e., strict interpretation of the Constitution), posing a *modicum* of overlap between morality and legality, represents the jurisprudence of the Catholic Natural Law, foreshadowed by Aristotle and Thomas. As we saw in the last chapter, there is *just enough* morality in the U.S. Constitution—so it should be strictly interpreted. Consider originalism the golden mean between activism and positivism. Originalism acknowledges the small dose of Natural Law morality at work in the supreme law

---

[206] Aristotle, *EN* V, ix, 15.

[207] Thomas Aquinas. *Summa Theologiae* I-II, 93, 2. To apply Thomas's reasoning here to our present-day republic, one notes that what legal scholars and theorists call *strict textualism* (a type of originalism)—judicial review by close scrutiny of and obedience to the text of laws and constitutions—is a far more Thomistic template than a jurisprudence composed of the judges' own conception of morality, which ends up being mostly or wholly divorced from the text of a law. While Thomas's notion seems to us to be self-evident, it was not always so. Early on in the Catholic Natural Law tradition, this exception needed to be explained. Most scholars have missed Thomas's position.

of the land, the Constitution, but accepts the reality that day-to-day lawmaking in republics is done on a mostly amoral basis.

As long as the original text of the (moral) Constitution is interpreted strictly, strictly interpreted laws made in accordance with the Constitution will not violate the Natural Law.

This Catholic Natural Law principle aligns with our common sense: good men do the right thing for the right reason. Mediocre men will usually do the right thing for wrong reasons. In other words, the citizens must be virtuous in order to want, make, and obey good laws. On the other hand, immoral citizens will resist, dislike, and sometimes disobey good laws.

Neither a republic's legislators—through *passing* law—nor its judges—through activist *interpreting* of law—can make an immoral nation morally good. This is crucial. The mistrust and restraint of activism was one of the fundamental American principles of the founding. Jefferson wrote, "The Constitution, on this hypothesis [that judges can decide, independent of plain text, whatever *they think* is morally good], is a mere thing of wax in the hands of the judiciary, which they may twist and shape into any form they please."[208]

---

[208] Thomas Jefferson, letter to Judge Spencer Roane, September 6, 1819. In other words, the intuitive mistrust of the judiciary by Thomas Jefferson and the Jeffersonians stemmed indirectly from a crypto-Catholic hunch that virtue ethics requires (in terms of the relation of morality to legality) individualism, not collectivism. Individualism requires the strict interpretation of law. Jefferson and his disciples were right, if accidentally. In other places, Jefferson stated similarly: "Our judges are as honest as other men, and not more so ... and their power is the more dangerous, as they are in office for life and not responsible, as the other functionaries are, to the elective control" (letter to William Jarvis, September 28, 1820); "A judiciary independent

Founding and framing documents such as declarations and constitutions can (and, in our case, mostly did) set a nation off on the correct moral foot. But the only way citizens may become truly moral is through individual, voluntary virtue.[209] This truth

---

of a king or executive alone, is a good thing; but independence of the will of the nation is a solecism, at least in a republican government" (letter to Thomas Ritchie, December 25, 1820); "The great object of my fear is the federal judiciary" (letter to Judge Spencer Roane, 1821).

[209] As concerns the early American republic, it is very clear that most American founders and framers wanted just such originalism. Even Alexander Hamilton, one of the Federalists who argued most fervently for a strong judiciary, mocked activism, to some extent. In *Federalist* No. 84, he calls bills of rights "aphoristic," quipping that they would "sound much better in a treatise of ethics than in a constitution of government." Yet, in Dr. Hadley Arkes's "Natural Law Manifesto," he imputes to a line by Hamilton in *Federalist* No. 84 ("here in strictness, the people surrender nothing ...") its perfectly opposite meaning. Dr. Arkes seeks to make the point that good government regimes should comprise treatises of ethics; Hamilton says precisely the opposite. If, as Aristotle posits, "to be a good man is not in every case to be a good citizen" (*EN* 1130b29), then judges would have no basis for the anti-originalist jurisprudence that Dr. Arkes urges. In other words, even the judiciary-loving Alexander Hamilton distinguished between a judge's proper role as interpreter of law and a moral role not properly judicial at all. Deriving from the English common law, there exist terminological nuances at the heart of American law involving two distinct types of illegality: laws against *malum prohibitum* and those against *malum in se*. Law involving *malum prohibitum* infractions is generally independent of morality. The evil being proscribed by this type is "evil" only in a contingent or circumstantial way. Think, for instance, about traffic laws in England and in America: the English drive on the left side of the road, whereas Americans drive on the right. The great majority of

was not by any means *deeply understood* during the ancient and the medieval periods, in which Aristotle and Thomas wrote, but the seeds were certainly present in both thinkers' moral philosophy.[210]

But Catholic Natural Law's truth does not depend upon our accepting it, of course. It exists above and beyond human laws, indirectly informing them. Therefore, certain elements of Natural Law automatically operate within decently made laws.[211]

Conclusion

The whole point of this third chapter has been to emphasize that a culture of mostly moral individuals is as necessary to republics

---

American laws, regulations, and ordinances are considered *malum prohibitum* laws. Law involving *malum in se* infractions, on the other hand, is generally dependent on morality. The evil being outlawed by this type of law may be called genuine moral evil: think of murder, for example, even if good men refrain from murder for moral and not legal reasons. Not coincidentally, the legal concept of *malum in se* is almost identical to the Catholic *Catechism*'s concept of innate moral evil.

[210] Prot-Enlight America today wrongly assumes that the distinguishability between morality and legality came from the Enlightenment. (Specifically, I mean the Straussians, who believe the claim that the distinction was engendered by Machiavelli.)

[211] In this chapter, I've argued against activism, which some wise, yet mistaken, commentators have called "Natural Law jurisprudence," a misnomer whereby judges ignore the text of the Constitution and laws in favor of their private interpretation of morality. (You can't just stick the words "natural law" into a phrase! Even though activism often claims the Catholic Natural Law in its title, it is opposed to the moral presumptions underlying self-rule.) In reality, activism, or "Natural Law jurisprudence," attempts to force one highly fallible judge's morality upon citizens unwilling to accept it.

as a correct founding and framing are.[212] In other words, there exists a spectrum on the issue of whether (and to what degree) morality influences legality: at one extreme is the position of no influence, called *positivism*, and at the other extreme is the position of total influence, called *activism*.[213] Between these two positions is a golden mean called *originalism*, holding that the Supreme Law of the Land (i.e., the Constitution) has a strong

---

[212] This is the essence of originalism: whatever is "legal" should be considered as it was originally written. And for the most part, whatever is popular should be — if you live in a true republic — what is morally right. Judges should not attempt to render laws "moral" after they've been validly passed by the legislature. As America declined from being mostly Protestant to mostly secular, judges began feeling that they had to, in their rulings, "make up for" the lack of cultural morality.

[213] Activism is doubly wrong, because (1) activist judges are frequently incorrect in their "correction" of fairly made law (think of pro-gay-marriage judges!), and (2) even if they are correct, they cannot by intentional misinterpretation force morality upon an utterly immoral citizenry that has willfully legalized immorality. In a true republic, if founded and framed correctly, the greatest driver of morale and morality should be a robust, Catholic Natural Law popular culture. The people should insist on laws that are consistent with a Constitution consisting of the crypto-Catholic rights of life, liberty, and property (thereby enabling the citizens to discharge their duties in private life). Look at the tale of the declining U.S. Constitution: within two centuries of its inception, an increasingly relativist populace reversed its cursory subsidiarity and inverted the meaning of the life, liberty, and property rights that it guaranteed. Here and there, progressive judges accelerated the process of moral devolution. But it is plainly evident by the people's gradual acceptance of such judicial tyranny that they were not as opposed to it as they originally seemed.

basis in morality, but that its text should be strictly interpreted. Catholic Natural Law requires originalism.

The idea that human laws do not make human beings truly moral crept up in Aristotle and Augustine but became well-developed in the writings of Thomas Aquinas. The idea of virtue ethics—with its originalist leanings—came first from Aristotle.[214] Originalism was further nuanced by Natural Law Catholic thinkers such as Augustine and Thomas Aquinas before being passed on to Montesquieu (and even to some of the nineteenth- and twentieth-century popes) and finally—in a crypto-Catholic, Prot-Enlight way—to Madison, Jefferson, and the American framers.

We have seen how Aristotle began it all (what we are calling originalism).[215] From there, Augustine put this notion into the helpful Christian context of sin, which Aristotle (in his pagan

---

[214] Famous commentators such as W. D. Ross have long noted Aristotle's developing and somewhat ambivalent position on the relation between legality and morality throughout the *Nicomachean Ethics*. But Aristotle's final position definitely equated to something much like originalism, rather than the activism with which he begins the treatise.

[215] Aristotle asked pointedly whether it is possible through law, compact, or threat to force another person to become good. It is not, he concludes. Virtue becomes the true sort only when acquired by an individual in the fashion of the truly moral man: this requires free and intentional self-habituation by the individual's will. But even more subtly, Aristotle goes on in other places of the *Nicomachean Ethics* to develop the finer contours of the doctrine, saying that "to be a good man is not in every case to be a good citizen" (*EN* V, ii, 11). This concept proves utterly novel in the history of political philosophy. W. D. Ross even remarked on this highly prescient, but confusing, turn in the history of political thought to the effect that Aristotle's understanding of his own ethical-political project expanded as he worked his way from book 1 to book 10 of the *Nicomachean*

context) would have mislabeled *vice*: "Laws written for the people's governance rightly permit [venial sins], and [only] God's Providence punishes them."[216] Let us remember, not all sin should be forbidden by human law as "illegal." Augustine is certainly not saying that *none* of society's laws should reflect morality, which would be idiotic (such a claim would be that erroneous idea of positivism, which would later come from the Enlightenment). Augustine is saying, rather, that *some* of a republic's laws should not outlaw all immorality. In the Constitutional context, this is originalism.

This grossly restricts the jobs of legislators and judges in republics. But many intelligent and faithful Catholic commentators do not seem to understand why. They fail to see how the legal compulsion of judges and legislators that attempts to "legislate morality" actually *violates* rather than honors the Aristotelian virtue ethics of the Natural Law.[217] *As shown above, the connection is quite simple: true virtue must be habituated voluntarily.*

Ethics. Ross comments that Aristotle moves from a statist to an individualist emphasis within the importance of morality.

[216] Augustine, *On Free Choice* I, 5, 13.

[217] The true jurisprudence corresponding with the Natural Law is originalism, not so-called Natural Law Jurisprudence. And this distinction is key for what eventually became, during the 1780s, the American founders' basic conception that whatever interrelation between morality and legality would come to exist should do so from the cultural "bottom" up, rather than from judges and lawmakers down. Jefferson wrote: "the germ of dissolution of our federal government is in the constitution of the federal judiciary ... working like gravity by night and by day, gaining a little today and a little tomorrow, and advancing its noiseless step like a thief over the field of jurisdiction, until all shall be usurped from the states, and the government of all be consolidated into one." Thomas Jefferson, letter to Charles Hammond, August 18, 1821.

So, what does this all mean for the third and final phase of republicanism — the staking of Catholic Natural Law in the American culture? Here in chapter 3 we have asked how, morally speaking, the popular culture must maintain the republic. The answer is: *through virtues freely chosen by individual citizens.* If, and only if, the citizens are (mostly) moral, then the system works. Without mostly virtuous citizens, there is no republic.

Moving right along, chapter 4 will show how and why the related concept of "separation of church and state" was radically exaggerated by anti-Catholic secularists in America during the nineteenth and twentieth centuries (and how this negatively influenced the ensuing outlook on what a human being is).

Chapter 4 (along with chapters 5 and 6) considers the remaining four elements of culture necessary for maintaining the proper Catholic Natural Law morality of republics. In each of those cases, it was Protestant collusion with Enlightenment thought that caused the damage, and perhaps even delivered the death blow, to the American republic.

Chapter 4

Staking the New Regime in the American Culture

The Crypto-Catholicism of Church and Personhood

The Church, in fact, is not a place of confusion and anarchy, where one can do what one likes all the time: each one in this organism, with an articulated structure, exercises his ministry in accordance with the vocation he has received. . . . The Church is above all a gift of God and not something we ourselves created; consequently, this sacramental structure does not only guarantee the common order but also this precedence of God's gift which we all need.

— Pope Benedict XVI[218]

But for Catholicism, there is no fully authentic Christian spirituality without the realization of an equal co-presence of our fellow-believers with Christ and ourselves, in the Church.

— Louis Bouyer, *Introduction to Spirituality*

---

[218] Benedict XVI, *The Fathers* (Huntington, IN: Our Sunday Visitor, 2008), pp. 10, 11.

To its everlasting shame, from its founding through the present, America has struggled badly with the definition of "person." From the outset and from slavery to infanticide, the Prot-Enlight misdefinition of personhood in the popular culture has caused unspeakable moral catastrophe in America. A government seeking to strip the rights of a certain group (e.g., fetuses) can simply redefine that group as "nonpersons," and has often done so.

Sound familiar? It should. This misdefinition, its application, and its ill effects are together the fourth symptom of our American republic's decay.

Prot-Enlight America misdefines personhood because it relies on one or two faulty brands—the Biblicist or the secularist, or both—of what is called *humanism*: a given worldview's teaching on what a human being is. For Catholicism, following Aristotle and Boethius, "humanism" means understanding mankind as body and soul, intellect and will. As we will see below, Catholic Natural Law requires of its definition of "humanism" an intimate connection to the supernatural in our day-to-day lives. This means the sacraments of the Catholic Church.

Conversely, each respective camp of "Prot-Enlight" famously sought in the sixteenth century to "demystify," to *expose as superstitious*, Church- and sacrament-based Catholic humanism. The effect of this de-mystification was surprisingly literal. In places like America where Reformation or Enlightenment philosophy became popular, the seven most fundamental aspects of being human, the sacraments (or in Greek, *musterion*, "mystery"), were robbed of their import in day-to-day life. These sacraments are central to the full definition of "Church," the institution that consecrates and distributes them.

Desacralization, de-mustification: whether in English or Greek, the Prot-Enlight forfeiture of the seven keys to daily life "teed up" a view of humanity that was drastically less *humane*. It turns out the Catholic concept of the Church is as necessary to republicanism as is the Catholic concept of the person. Again, by excluding Catholicism and its sacramental concept of "Church," America cut off the only true path to correctly defining "person-hood" and "humanism."

The fourth element of crypto-Catholicism[219] in Prot-Enlight America is *humanism*, which, if properly construed, must be based upon the definitions of "Church" and "personhood" according to Catholic Natural Law.

Our previous chapter invited the reader to imagine the American republic without the aid of Christian — specifically Catholic — virtue ethics. It was indeed an ugly picture. This chapter will show how all the essential dimensions of republican culture noted in previous chapters can coexist only with the definition of "Church" put forward by the Catholic Natural Law tradition.

For American survival, not every American needs to become Catholic, but he does need to understand and accept natural rights, subsidiarity, and citizen's morality as uniquely Catholic ideas. These are ideas that prove utterly unacceptable from a Protestant or Enlightenment perspective. Although these two things — *understanding Catholic ideas for what they are* and *being or becoming a practicing Catholic* — are frequently the same thing in republics, they do not need to be. It is quite feasible that they can

---

[219] In other words, what is "Church"? Ultimately, it is a riddle that will also end up answering just what a human person is. When "Church" and "personhood" are understood outside their Catholic context, they dissolve into cheap copies. As a result, society turns to eugenics and collectivism. Think slavery. Think abortion.

be separated: a non-Catholic can understand and even appreciate the Catholic ideas of true republicanism for what they really are.

But here in chapter 4, the crypto-Catholic element of humanism changes the story a bit. Unlike the elements we have looked at so far, Catholic humanism requires religious *participation* rather than mere acknowledgment of its Catholicity.[220] Humanism entails a series of "mysteries" (*musterion*) that demonstrate not only what a human being is, but what a human being *should* practice and *could* become. These mysteries are sacraments, which sum up human existence. And, of course, only a Catholic can receive the sacraments. In this sense, this chapter begins to sound as if it *does* require all the republican citizenry to be Catholic and thereby comes the closest to outright apologetics. In that way, it is unique among this book's chapters.

Long story short: to entertain the *proper* view of what a human being is, the American citizen must have at hand the Christ-instituted sacraments, which means that the American citizen must have a proper conception of Church (the only institution capable

---

[220] Chapter 4's second aspect of republican culture (within *staking the regime*), will be referred to as "humanism" when it appears in a philosophical or theological context, and as "personhood" when it appears in a popular context. Throughout the introduction and chapters 1, 2, and 3, I've described the Catholic Natural Law as indispensable for republics. But, as those chapters made clear, none of those formulations *required* that republics comprise exclusively practitioners of the Catholic Faith. Instead, natural rights (chapter 1), subsidiarity (chapter 2), and a moral citizenry (chapter 3) were described as most legitimately secured when openly understood in their proper Catholic, Natural Law iterations. But chapter 4's proper humanism requires something a step closer to *actual participation* in the Faith by republican citizens and thereby comes nearer to qualifying as outright apologetics.

of bestowing those sacraments). In both republics and churches, Christians must be seen as "members of one another;"[221] meaning, nothing can serve as a surrogate for the unifying sacraments.[222]

---

[221] Clement (third successor of Peter), *Adversus Haereses* 46, 6–7.

[222] The present rise of centralized state power in America betrays the Prot-Enlight perversions of not only natural rights, subsidiarity, and morality but also of a faulty Prot-Enlight stab at humanism. The twentieth century bore witness to no small amount of such collectivist tragedy around the globe. In each instance, individuals were first asked, then told, then forced to sacrifice their lives, liberties, and properties to the collective. In the most noteworthy twentieth-century cases—against the communists and the fascists—America bailed Europe out. According to the *Catechism*: "The Church has rejected the totalitarian and atheistic ideologies associated in modern times with 'communism' or 'socialism.'. . . Regulating the economy solely by centralized planning perverts the basis of social bonds." Communism, socialism, National Socialism, fascism, distributism, and all other types of "central planning" or statism contemplate a faulty, collectivistic tableau of humanity. Individual persons are employed merely as means to some state-controlled end. In far greater detail, chapter 5 explores the common economic flaw in these systems—a radical departure from Natural Law.

But today, Prot-Enlight America faces its own crisis of humanism. Chapter 4 "tees up" chapter 5 in the humanist sense. And no one is going to bail us out. We must act for ourselves, as the reader now knows, or else perish. This chapter deals with the most spiritual (and ecclesiastical) dimension of our republic's road to reparation. Insofar as true Christian humanism rejects collectivism outright, it values (without idolizing) the individual. In this capacity, Christian humanism may also be called "Christian individualism," yet one more product of the Natural Law. But a hefty word of caution is warranted as to individualism: both of the false, Prot-Enlight humanisms to which this chapter will respond also congratulated themselves as competing sorts of individualism. They aimed, initially, to

CATHOLIC REPUBLIC

What Is "Proper Humanism"?

Proper, or Catholic Natural Law, humanism requires something supernatural: the seven sacraments. Christ distilled *how to be human* down to seven ways of living. The natural is revealed through the supernatural.[223]

Being an *individual within Christ's body* (the Catholic Church) is the best definition of "Christian humanism," which cannot be achieved through individualist means such as *sola scriptura*: reading the Bible on your own.

Genuine Christian humanism must be marked by the Christian's active participation in sacramental unity with other Christians. Christ exists within His *Mystical Body*, the Church. He is the literal and figurative head; the Church is His literal and figurative body. As the eminent theologian Louis Bouyer has written: "The Word of Christ, which is One with Himself, with His

---

avoid sacrificing the individual to the collective, but gradually came to do so on the basis of uncorrected faults in their view of individualism. The *Catechism* reads: "[The Church] has likewise refused to accept, in the practice of 'capitalism,' individualism and the absolute primacy of the law of the marketplace over human labor." Thus, it becomes clear that there exist *improper* individualisms, represented by either facet of Prot-Enlight, which eventually lead back to statism. This seems to be a truism denied by most political conservatives of our day. In the last analysis, we will see how such improper humanism turns right back into worship of the collective (derided by conservatives and all lovers of liberty). In far greater detail, chapter 5 deals with this.

[223] Christ revealed Himself to man. This means true humanism. Such was a central teaching of the Second Vatican Council's Constitution on the Church in the Modern World, entitled *Gaudium et Spes*. From that document, Pope Saint John Paul II vastly absorbed the teaching and enlarged it.

living presence, remains always present in the Church inasmuch as the Church is founded on the apostles."[224]

So, on the basis of Christ's temporal and spatial presence in the Church, all Protestant renditions of humanism (which deny such presence) should be ruled out; they are not genuine forms of "participation." Nonsacramental and nonliturgical approaches to the Scriptures get "stuck in the past" and lack *anything* to do with the present.

And, when considering proper humanism, don't even mention the new secular vision of humanity inaugurated by the Enlightenment! Infinitely more problematic than even the Protestant conceptions, secular humanism is based on moral relativism, as we saw in the previous chapter. Relativism led directly to the big-government restriction of religion and to the genocide of the twentieth century.

Sadly, that seems to be America's current path, the path of "separation of church and state." And yet even in this Prot-Enlight nation, as secular as things have become, everywhere in America one still hears about "going to church."

In other words, the fourth symptom of the secret plagiarism of Catholic Natural Law was crypto-Catholic usage of the word "Church" by Protestant America. Few have noted how strange and obvious this appropriation was (and remains). American

---

[224] Bouyer, *Introduction to Spirituality*, 26. Near this passage, Bouyer expands on this principle: "It is, therefore, into the Church, the true body of Christ, that we must be incorporated in order to participate in the Spirit of Christ, and as a consequence, to receive His words, not as a mere dead letter, but as words which remain always life-giving because here they remain always living, always uttered by the very Word of God."

Protestants usually refer to themselves as belonging to a church, after so virulently rebuking the Catholic idea before and during the colonial age of the Puritans.

Even in our secular age, the sense of *belonging to a body of Christian believers* seems to remain the most important dimension of humanism within Protestant American culture. "Selecting a church" is important to American Protestants.

But as this chapter will show, "Church," in its communal aspect — as the Mystical Body of Christ — and in its individual aspect — as Catholic "personhood" — must go together *sacramentally*. Already quoted above, Catholic liturgist Louis Bouyer shows that "this [sacramental life of the Church] ... is where we are to find the Mystery of Christ as the life of 'Christ in us, the hope of glory.'"[225]

When the individual and the communal aspects of "Church" get separated (or in other words when "Church" is conceptually stripped of its capital C, as in Protestant cultures) both aspects break down. *Consequently, the definition of the human being breaks down: slavery and abortion begin happening to selected "nonpersons."*

It is here that one notes the impasse between America's Catholic wiring (i.e., embracing some confused sense of "church" instead of "Church") — and its Protestant labeling and secular functioning.

Thus, the Protestant communities must not be referred to as "churches," but as "congregations," as Pope Benedict XVI reminded us in the 2007 document "Responses to Some Questions regarding Certain Aspects of the Doctrine on the Church." The Protestant denominations, he writes, "cannot be called 'churches'

[225] Bouyer, *Introduction to Spirituality*, p. 39.

in the proper sense."[226] Such a label cannot apply to them because they lack apostolic succession and the "many elements of sanctification,"[227] especially the seven sacraments.

So, an effective way to think about this chapter is that American Protestant (and Enlightenment) culture forfeited not only the Natural Law of the Catholic Church, as we've seen in the first three chapters, but also the *supernatural* sacraments that proceed from the Catholic Church. And doing so had profound political implications for the outlook on the individual[228] human being and on separation of church and state.

[226] "Pope: Other Denominations Not True Churches," NBCNews. com, July 10, 2007, http://www.nbcnews.com/id/19692094/ ns/world_news-europe/t/pope-other-denominations-not-true-churches/#.VRwzZo7fLYg.

[227] Ibid.

[228] The individual's sense of belonging to a body of Christ (i.e., to the Church, humanism) is therefore the second, crypto-Catholic aspect of republican culture in the third phase (out of three) that I identify in the republican life cycle. Such a sense of belonging to the Church is *wired*, but neither *labeled* nor *functioning* properly in America today. And this second necessary aspect of republican culture is Christian humanism: a proper, natural view of human existence.

Smarmy campaign slogans aside, human beings prove to be any republic's most important single natural resource. Yes, this sounds like a bad campaign speech. But, as the *Catechism* teaches, the citizens' moral happiness is the single end of good government. As such, no republic can thrive without a proper public conception of what human beings are and what they need in order to thrive. And that definition cannot be separated from the definition of "Church." As the reader can probably guess, I will show how early American culture admixed improper Prot-Enlight humanism with some healthy elements of crypto-Catholicism. Thus, one confronts in America today a mix of the healthy and unhealthy brands.

The Natural Communities

Unlike the other five elements of crypto-Catholicism discussed in this book, the Church's sacraments are *higher than* Natural Law. Even as they are revealed in the three prongs of the Catholic Natural Law, they equal Christ's revealed *supernatural* law.

Catholic humanism correctly identifies the *natural communities* that nature provides for every person.[229] Because nature provides them, they assume priority over the comparatively meaningless elective communities that man chooses for himself (e.g., political free associations, workplace friendships, or business cooperations).

Think of natural communities as Jefferson correctly spoke of natural rights: both are "unalienable." Membership is not optional. As any political candidate running for office with a "black sheep" family member knows, natural communities, like family, cannot simply be "gotten rid of," the way that politically inconvenient friends can be. Church and family are nature-provided societies—bearing a "closeness to home" that involves the subsidiarity explained in chapter 2.

The reader should recall chapter 2's teachings about the divine, fatherly, local model for human authority. It is infinitely more natural to obey an authority who lives in your home than it is to obey a faceless authority who lives three thousand miles away. Similarly, humanism must be very closely connected to the concept of locality, or community. What it is to be properly human is learned naturally, parentally, and at (or near) home.

To learn our human nature is to learn our proper *function*, as Aristotle and Thomas Aquinas taught. Mankind, the political animal, cannot function properly apart from his natural communities.

---

[229] "Natural community" is a term of art for "*community* meeting the standard of Catholic Natural Law."

The natural communities besides *Church*, are *family* and *neighborhood*. This chapter will deal with America's Prot-Enlight ambivalence about the concept of *Church*, while the following chapter will concern the indirect Protestant and the direct Enlightenment inversions of *family* (and, to a much lesser extent, *neighborhood*).

The Enlightenment (the secular Left) set out to rid mankind of all nonelective duty. This required allowing him — the secular Left falsely reasons — to "opt out" of all three natural communities.

Although the Protestant Reformation genuinely sought to retain Christ, America's modern religious Right severed ties with the natural, sacramental community of Church. Although the religious Right attempted (unsuccessfully) to hang on to the other two natural communities, family and neighborhood, we will see in the next chapter how the forfeiture of Church indirectly led to a Protestant degradation of the view of family.

Jesus' True Humanism: Sacramental Theology

More than *neighborhood* (or, in some ways, even *family*) the natural community of *Church* shows us the perfect example of humanity, Jesus Christ. The Catholic Church reveals how to be human through the beatific daily mystery of the sacraments.

Louis Bouyer pointed out the unexpected truth that Christ's humanity (i.e., His personhood) was *most*, not *least*, developed among all humans: "The Christian ... tends to the full development of a life which is wholly human and at the same time wholly personal, in the discovery of a God who is not only Himself a person, but the personal being *par excellence*."[230] The last five words of that sentence are key. Jesus was the most human person

---

[230] Bouyer, *Introduction to Spirituality*, p. 18.

ever to live. As such, he left us an "imprint" as to how best to undertake our lives. This imprint is the idea of sacrament.

Going about his earthly life, man naturally craves daily grace. Every last human appetite corresponds with a natural function, according to Thomas Aquinas. His claim addresses the concern that man, left to his own devices, will become too estranged from grace and would begin to prefer this world to the next, worshipping created things instead of the Creator.

The sacraments remedy such a concern.

Remember that we are admonished as Christians to be "in the world, but not of it."[231] The errant Biblicist (Prot) and secular (Enlight) humanisms were both guilty of being too much "of the world."

As daily reminders and the ultimate implementation of God's grace, the sacraments embody the Church teaching on the *possibility* of truly human life in Christ. This is the connection between the natural and the supernatural: *what life could be.* The Catholic humanism of the sacraments prompts us to both aspects of Christ's fully divine and fully human life. As such, the two-dimensional sacraments ought to be at the center of Christian living and of our definition of "human being."

In short, Catholic Natural Law humanism revolves around its sacramental theology. Briefly discussing two distinctions at this point will further clarify why the Catholic brand of humanism is uniquely indispensable to republics.

Distinction 1: The Sacraments, the High and the Low

Obviously, there is a "high," otherworldly aspect to all seven sacraments. There is a "low," worldly aspect to them as well.

---

[231] While this famous Christian aphorism is not properly scriptural, see John 15:19; 17:14; 1 John 2:15; James 1:27; 4:4.

Ironically, the latter is far subtler and less appreciated among Catholics than the former—which is taught clearly in most Catholic grade school textbooks.

The high (otherworldly) aspect of the sacraments culminates in the Transubstantiation of the Eucharist, which makes possible Christ's *continuing* real presence with us on Earth. The Second Person of the Trinity, Jesus, assumed mortal form. He was flesh and bone. Even during His thirty-three years on earth, however, He was God. This is called the *hypostatic union*: Jesus was fully man and fully God.

And His physical presence among us lives on exclusively in His real presence in the Eucharist, celebrated by the Church.

By receiving the divine *Body* and *Blood* (with *soul* and *divinity*) of Jesus in the Eucharist, man consummates his relationship with Christ. Eucharistic Communion gives us unique life and grace. As such, the *Catechism of the Catholic Church* calls the Eucharist the "source and the summit of the Church's life" (1407). None of the other six sacraments is referred to in this way. From Jesus' death in A.D. 33 onward, the Eucharist became man's most important remaining physical link with the Trinity. The life of the Son lives and abides within the (individual) communicant, just as the grace-infused communicant comes to dwell (communally) in the Body of Christ.

This means that the six lesser sacraments are there primarily to serve and make possible the Eucharist. Just as Catholic humanism culminates in the Eucharist, its evergreen promise is renewed through the sacrament of Confession, which allows the sinner to "renew" his ability to receive Eucharistic Communion. Just as Confession subserves the Eucharist, so also do the other five sacraments. There can be no genuine Christian humanism outside of Christ with us (i.e., the Eucharist), which is to say, outside the interplay of Confession and the other lesser sacraments with it.

Ironically, on the other hand, the "low" (worldly) aspect of the sacraments bears more subtly on our view of human existence. The worldly sense of the sacraments instructs us how to live, day by day. As in Edgar Allan Poe's "The Purloined Letter," the most obvious truths often evade us the most wholly. In other words, putting the Eucharist and the other sacraments into their *daily* context heightens their nuance.

In fact, when calling to mind the grace of the sacraments, we recall that the Greek word for "sacrament" is *musterion* (or *mysterion*), "mystery." All but one chapter of the New Testament was originally written in Greek, a more philosophical and holistic mode of thinking than the Latin translations.[232] And upon translation of the former into the latter, the concept of *musterion* became the coarser and less holistic Latin version, *sacramentum* (see CCC 774).

The Romans were like the "jocks" of the Ancient world, struggling to translate the Greeks' "brainiac" language into a simpler context that the Romans would recognize. This was especially the case when it came to the concept of sacrament. In Latin, *sacramentum* (being translated from Greek) had secular and "pre-Christian origins,"[233] borrowed from the initiation rite through which a soldier was incorporated into the Roman army.

---

[232] Tertullian is credited with the first equation of *musterion* and *sacramentum*, with Jerome following close behind him. Think of sacrament in these two senses: both the narrower, less philosophical, and more secular Latin initiation (*sacramentum*) and the more holistic, Greek, daily mystery of re-initiation (*musterion*).

[233] Monsignor Maurice V. O'Connell and Joseph Stoutzenberger, *The Church through History* (Boston: Harcourt Religion Publishers, 2007), p. 50.

The present task is to put both the Greek and the Latin into the context of Catholic Natural Law humanism.

Mysterious in their simplicity, the sacraments teach Catholics everything we need to know about daily life in the *image of God*. Remember in chapter 2 when the teaching role of the natural community (Church and family) was introduced as the natural community's most important distinguishing feature? It is especially in this daily, holistic sense of the sacraments that the *instructive* role of the Church emerges: the Church is the bestower of the *musterion*, which, among other things, *instructs*. And it is precisely this sacramental, mysterious grace freely given to man by God—through the natural community of the *Church*—that gives us the structure of authentic Christian humanism.

For example, we see that the Eucharist is not only the (otherworldly) transubstantiation of bread and wine into Christ's divine flesh and blood, instituted at the Last Supper, but at the same time, it is Christ's humble model of (worldly) breaking daily bread with friends and family in simple prayer, joy, and fellowship. It is not the soul alone that requires sustenance, after all, but the body as well. For man, the uniquely rational and social animal, this sustenance includes and even requires human fellowship at mealtimes.

The sacrament of the Eucharist instructs mankind how to take meals. Pope Benedict XVI has written:

> Eucharist originates in the love of Jesus Christ, who gave his life for us. In the Eucharist, he evermore shares himself with us; he places himself in our hands. Through the Eucharist he fulfills evermore his promise that from the Cross he will draw us into his open arms. In Christ's embrace we are led *to one another* [emphasis added]. We are

taken into the one Christ, and thereby we now also belong reciprocally together. I can no longer consider anyone a stranger who stands in the same contact with Christ."[234]

Each of the lesser six sacraments, as well, is susceptible of both an otherworldly and a worldly application.

Confession is not only the (otherworldly) act of contrition between sinner and confessor acting as Christ. It also involves and influences apologies between laypersons in (worldly) day-to-day life. This is a most central, load-bearing pillar of culture: the contrasting notion that "love means never having to say you're sorry" is an idiotic creature of a relativist, narcissist, Enlightenment culture. It is utterly untrue, and it's the stuff of declining republics.

Baptism and Confirmation, instituted by Christ through His baptism in the Jordan and through the descent of the Holy Spirit at Pentecost, are (otherworldly) one-time initiations or affirmations of Christian fellowship within the community of the Church. On the other hand, they also remind us of the Holy Spirit's daily presence in our (worldly) lives, especially during our "trials by fire." During Christ's life, He provided support to His friends and followers. After His death, He sent "the Helper."

Holy Matrimony too is a binding (otherworldly) covenant between man, woman, and God, instituted by Christ at the wedding feast of Cana. But it is also a prominent (worldly) aspect of day-to-day romance. The natural community of the family, as the next chapter will expound upon in great detail, rests upon a sacramental conception of Matrimony. It suffices at present

---

[234] Joseph Cardinal Ratzinger, *Images of Hope* (San Francisco: Ignatius Press, 2010).

to say plainly that marriage, when properly Christ-centered (as a sacrament), grows holier with each passing day. When not viewed properly, marriage and the family, which rests upon it, are like a house built upon sand. And a whole society of such nonsacramental marriages—remember that Martin Luther was the first on record to call marriage a "worldly thing"[235]—is like a *second story* built upon a house built upon sand.

A Catholic priest under Holy Orders is analogous to a spouse under matrimonial vows: priesthood bears a worldly aspect, where the father interacts with his flock, and an otherworldly aspect, where the father interacts through prayer and consecration with his own Heavenly Father.[236]

---

[235] Martin Luther, *Weimar*, vol. 12. p. 131. Luther "argued that marriage cannot be a sacrament for the simple reason that it is not exclusive to Christians.... If you have a friend who is a Muslim, a Jew, or a Hindu, they will not ask you what marriage is, and you do not have to explain it to them in Christian terms." Ken Collins, "What Is a Sacrament," Rev. Ken Collins' Website, http://www.kencollins.com/sacraments/sacrament-02.htm.

[236] Holy Orders is perhaps the most obvious vocational alternative to Holy Matrimony. A Catholic man's choice, then, is between becoming a father or becoming a Father. The existence of Holy Orders helps even the laity to put into context its call to holiness: procreation and family.

Too often, even faithful Catholics conceive of the vocational "fork in the road" as that between Holy Orders and *labor*, or between priesthood and *productivity*. But the true decision dichotomizes priesthood and parenthood (not material productivity or success). As Mother Teresa of Calcutta often said: "Not everyone is called to be successful, but everyone is called to be faithful." And this is accomplished in one of two ways: parenthood or priesthood. Family life is the content of chapter 5.

Last Rites not only constitute the final (worldly) living act of the Catholic but also stand as a daily reminder of the utter necessity and the chastening (otherworldly) holiness of our death, like the last sentence in the Hail Mary. This reminder should be present not only at the funeral or the grave, but rather every day from the cradle thereto. "In the midst of life, we are among death,"[237] and the early Christians understood this chastening proposition far better — more on a daily basis — than we do.

In short, the Christ-instituted and scripturally derived sacraments constitute the most central stuff of real Christian humanism. The seven sacraments *are* the full experience of man in his humanity. They are our worldly path to the otherworldly. Daily, they show us how to live in this world. Without them, there can be no such doctrine as Christian humanism at all. As we are about to see, both the Reformation and the Enlightenment attempted unsuccessfully to make from whole cloth a view of humanity that all but precluded the Catholic conception of "Church," built around the seven sacraments.

Distinction 2: Pre-Sacramental, Sacramental, and Post-Sacramental Theology

As *Christians*, we acknowledge that our Judeo-Christian faith harkens ceaselessly back to a parent religion, Judaism. But we also profess a specific belief that, through Christ, we have moved beyond Judaism's "old law" of sacrifice. As *Catholic* Christians, we acknowledge the sad truth that, following up on the Reformation, Protestant Christians miscalculated that they had "corrected" Catholicism's sacramental view of Church, in roughly the same fashion that Christianity perfected Judaism's sacrificial view of it.

---

[237] "The Committal," in the Book of Common Prayer.

In this section, we will examine the error in this Protestant assumption.

The most clarifying way to think about the spectrum between Judaism, Catholicism, and Protestantism is this: Judaism is *pre-sacramental* theology; Catholicism is *sacramental* theology; Protestantism is *post-sacramental* theology.

On these three members of the religion spectrum, Louis Bouyer has written:

> The specific characteristic of a Catholic spiritual life is the additional and basic distinction that God not only actually does speak to us (as the Jews have believed since the Old Covenant), that he not only has already spoken to us in a definitive way in his Christ (as the Protestants believe together with us), but also that he continues to speak to us, and to speak to us in his Christ, by and in the Church. Here it becomes evident that Catholicism is not only one form of Christianity among others, but that it is the only form which continues to be what ancient Judaism already was, yet imperfectly: the religion not only of a Word once spoken, preserved in its meaning but no longer in its living actuality, but on the contrary, the religion of the Word and of the definitive and total Word, which is still always living, always present, always spoken here and now ... but Protestantism, insofar as it is opposed to Catholicism, only admits this present actuality as being wholly interiorized, and to that extent individualized.[238]

The "always present" nature of Catholic spirituality to which Bouyer refers is Christ's *actual presence in the present*. The concept

---

[238] Bouyer, *Introduction to Spirituality*, pp. 24–25.

of "real presence" is built into the Church, itself based upon the still-present Jesus Christ. Without the sacraments, after all, how could Christ remain with us? Protestantism by and large lacks this real-world connection and thereby lacks an authentic sense of "Church."

Any true humanism—centering on Christ—must mark this Church-based, sacramental theology as its reason for being. Or else it defines "human being" on a mistaken basis. Humanitarian problems with "personhood" show up very shortly thereafter (slavery, abortion, eugenics, etc.).

Judaism was the religion built upon *sacrifice*, before such a concept as *sacrament* was conceived of. Sacrifice means "to make holy" and entails *man* offering something to *God*, in order to seek grace (through a human act, e.g., killing a bull); sacrament, conversely, is an offering of grace *by* God to man as, in Saint Augustine's coinage, "an outward and visible sign of inward and invisible grace."[239] Sacrifice and sacrament turn out to be opposites when we consider which party—man or God—is active and which is passive.

While God's covenant with the Jews has "never been revoked" (CCC 121), it changed from being evidenced in the Old Testament as *sacrifice* to being evidenced in the New Testament as *sacrament*. From Abraham to Moses, sacrifice stands as the most important way, in the Old Testament, for man to curry favor with God. Let's look at the two most famous examples of Old Testament sacrifice. Abraham was ordered by God's angel to

---

[239] To obtain a supernatural end we must use supernatural means. At the Council of Trent (sess. VII, can. 4), Saint Augustine's definition and reasoning were clarified by the declaration that sacraments are necessary.

sacrifice Isaac, just as later Jews—led by Moses—were ordered to sacrifice Paschal lambs and to smear the lambs' blood on their doorposts on the night of the Passover.

Sacrifice requires action on the part of man. Had Abraham failed to begin preparation for sacrificing his son, or had Moses' people forgotten to offer the lamb's blood at Passover, the Lord would not have delivered them. They would have been out of luck. All would have been lost. Everything depended upon the work done by *man* through sacrifice.

Because Abraham "passed" the test God set out before him, God rendered Abraham's "descendants as countless as the stars of the sky and the sands of the seashore" (Gen. 22:17). Because Abraham's descendants, led by Moses, "passed" the test of the Passover, they survived the Angel of Death and were eventually delivered from their Egyptian captivity.

It should be remembered that the Jews during and after Jesus' day who refused to accept Christ's fulfillment of the Old Testament continue to employ sacrifice as their primary way of relating to God.

But through Christ's fulfillment of the Scriptures, through His own Paschal (*Passover* in Greek) act of self-sacrifice, he inverted the concept of sacrifice into a new concept: sacrament.

Christ became the new Passover,[240] the blood offering of the New Covenant. For the first time in salvation history, God, and not man, performed the labor of the sacrifice: divine *self*-sacrifice.[241] In fact, this is precisely the meaning of the Incarnation: God's own Son, the Incarnate Word, came to earth to relieve

---

[240] O'Connell and Stoutzenberger, *The Church through History*, pp. 5, 6.
[241] Ibid.

man of his duty as the sacrificer. (This certainly does not mean that the central liturgical action in the Catholic Mass is not the Sacrifice at the Altar; indeed it is. But the liturgical rite is based upon Christ's act of *self-sacrifice*, not upon some Judaic sense of the priest's sacrifice.)[242]

Through Christ's self-sacrifice, God inverted the concept forever.

The Christian's existence has *already* been made holy, as of the first Easter, with no further blood to be spilled (the "blood-less sacrifice").[243] All that the sacramental Christian (i.e., the Catholic) must do is to *accept* the benefit of Christ's sacrifice, open not only to a "chosen people," but to all the world, Gentile and Jew alike.

Therefore, we recognize one, and only one, means of accepting His Son's sacrifice: sacrament.

[242] Klaus Gamber, "The Reform of the *Ordo Missae:* Could the Council's Decisions Have Been Implemented without Changing the Rite of the Mass?" In this article, Gamber gives the reader a cautionary example of the sense in which the faithful Catholic should *not* want to deny the real sacrifice of Christ at the altar (even if we want to remember constantly that such a sacrifice is the sacramental work of God and not the sacrificial work of man). He writes: "Without doubt, Martin Luther was the first person who reformed the liturgy; he did so systematically and for theological reasons. He categorically denied that the Mass was a sacrifice, and in doing so, he also rejected various parts of the Mass, most notably the offertory prayers."

[243] Saint John Chrysostom. *In Epistolam ad Hebraeos Homiliae,* Hom. 17, 3: "We always offer the same Lamb, not one today and another tomorrow, but always the same one. For this reason the sacrifice is always only one.... Even now we offer that victim who was once offered and who will never be consumed."

This warrants the role of Church—necessitated by Christ's otherwise absence.

Whereas the Jews never accepted as Messiah Jesus, who was born to transform *sacrifice* into *sacrament*, the post-sacramental Christians, or Protestants, do so along with Catholics. But curiously, they doubt that He meant to institute a new world order based upon sacrament. One can then understand Bouyer when he says that "in Protestantism, everything goes on, or seems to go on, as if the Incarnation had ended with the Ascension of the Savior."[244]

Protestantism does not take the sacrificial claims of Judaism seriously (even as it gladly accepts Christ's erasure of sacrifice). For the Protestant, sacrifice did not become sacrament. It simply vanished, became nothing.

Sacramentally speaking, the dominant form of Protestantism in the world today (the "reformed" theology of Ulrich Zwingli) rejects the idea of sacrament as a literal one. Protestants doubt and even reject the literality of Christ's Eucharistic admonition and the sacramental theology that it enculturated. Thus, Protestants are post-sacramental Christians. (This is very strange, because Protestantism is generally marked by a heavily literal scriptural emphasis.)

Although Protestants celebrate in Scripture the Triduum, the Sermon on the Mount, and the Beatitudes, they lack most or all of the sacraments, which place such salvific events into their proper context. During the Reformation, which rejected most of these sacraments, the mysteries of faith were all reduced by *sola scriptura* to the historical page, a "dead letter."[245] None of these

---

[244] Bouyer, *Introduction to Spirituality*, p. 25.
[245] Ibid., 45.

sacraments continued, in non-Lutheran Protestant countries such as America, to be recognized as otherworldly.

For the Protestants, the *body of Christ* was reduced to that of a single, historical individual. There is *no such thing,* for them, as a Eucharistic people, headed by Christ and united as the Mystical Body of believers who consume His Body and Blood through daily and weekly sacraments. Conversely, Catholicism, as Brant Pitre made famous, takes far more seriously the "Jewish roots of the Eucharist."[246] That is, by the Incarnation, the promise made to the Jews was opened to all the Gentiles of the world by reversing the activity of sacrifice: with one final self-sacrifice by God Himself. Christ allowed Himself to be killed by His enemies and thereafter consumed by His followers, telling them at the Last Supper to "gnaw the flesh of the Son of man and drink my blood [in order to have] eternal life" (see John 6:53).

This self-sacrifice ushered in a new era marked by sacraments—but only for those who choose to accept it!

How to live a fully human life—one in the fashion of Christ's true humanism—evades any Protestant Christian who abandons the sacraments: *How to break bread in fellowship each day; how to say "I'm sorry" outside Confession; how to face down death each day ("in the midst of life there is death"); how to be and how to stay a part of the Body of Christ; how to foster vocational holiness—either "in the cloth" or through marital procreation.*

Protestantism blithely ignores the truth that when these seven central items of human life are not considered in their otherworldly sense, they will be overlooked in their worldly sense. Even

---

[246] Brant Pitre, *Jesus and the Jewish Roots of the Eucharist: Unlocking the Secrets of the Last Supper* (New York: Image Publishing, 2011).

the mitigated, "symbolic" sense in which Protestants claim to uphold the sacraments will eventually devolve. It will be notable in its respective republic and culture.

Today's secular Left, grandchildren of the Enlightenment, operate on the *same basic assumptions as the Protestant Reformation*: post-sacramental theology. In other words, the secular world borrows the assumptions from the mainstream Protestant world that the Catholic sacraments are "merely" symbolic (which eventually expresses their utter meaninglessness). But, of course, the secular Left intends more consistently than Protestantism to destroy all semblance of the Church left over after the destruction of the sacraments.

Prot-Enlight "Demystification"

Famously, the violent progressivism of the Enlightenment "demystified" the life of man. Its loyal proponents claimed that it *shed light* upon the "darkness" of the Middle Ages (the "Dark Ages") ruled by the Church. The Enlightenment achieved this demystification, as the story goes, by "freeing" man from his membership in Church, family, and neighborhood—three *natural communities* to whom he would presumptively no longer owe any duty. At that point, man could enjoy his new "freedom" without hindrance.

Now freed from the yoke of natural duty, Enlightenment thinkers reasoned that men could go on to assert their radical individualism. They could thereby create a secular, humanist utopia. Think of this as the first rearing of the ugly head of progressivism, early in the modern era.

In the context of the natural community of the Church, Enlightenment de-mystification was surprisingly literal: the *musterion* (sacraments) were actually attacked and excised as outmoded superstitions of a bygone era. De-mustification *equals* desacralizing.

Perhaps even more literally, the Protestant Reformation demystified (literally *desacralized*, stripped away) most of the Catholic sacraments as well. Among Protestantism's thirty-eight thousand sects, the vast majority agree that half or more of the sacraments are mere symbols. And to call a sacrament a "mere symbol" is to divest it of all of its potency, as noted above.

The same notion is worth putting in a slightly starker way: following the Reformation, most Protestants came to believe about their own biblical sacraments basically the same thing as did the Enlightenment thinkers (who rejected Christianity outright!). And this is to say that Protestants came to view the sacraments as symbols.

For an introduction and three chapters now, the reader has interpreted the compound term "Prot-Enlight" as a kind of *analogy*, a drawing together of two or more distinct things.

But now, for the first time, I submit the notion to the reader that Protestantism is actually just a Christian form of the Enlightenment—that "Prot" and "Enlight" are simply two species of the same genus, *demystification* of the sacraments. Demystification divorced the Protestant congregations from any ability to connect, sacramentally, to one another via the Church. This created a new Protestant humanism.

By the end of this chapter, the reader will see the historical basis for such a claim. So far, I've shown *that it happened* (philosophically). Later on, we will see *how it happened* (historically). American history—American legal history, no less—shows it in an undeniable manner. The Prots and the Enlights (enemies as they eventually came to be) were indeed bedfellows for most of American history.

But first, let's take a brief look at the Reformation itself, to understand why it engendered such a splintered group of congregations.[247]

The Protestant Reformation as a Series of Unintended Consequences

We must spend another moment describing precisely what *was* this Reformation, upon which America was largely constructed, two centuries later. The twenty-first-century American must remember that, from its beginnings, *the Reformation was a series of unintended consequences*, not a coherent, directed movement. Martin Luther, the first Reformer, did not set out to accomplish what the Reformation eventually accomplished: wholesale removal, within Protestantism, of two of the Catholic Church's three teaching mechanisms (Sacred Tradition and the Holy Magisterium, the latter of which included the removal of the sacraments).

No, this eventual occurrence was a historical happenstance. The three teaching pillars of the Church are Holy Scripture, Sacred Tradition, and the Holy Magisterium. Although by our own day, one acknowledges that Protestantism clearly grew into a type of Christianity deferent to *Scripture alone*, Luther had not originally intended to eradicate Tradition and the Magisterium — and thereby the sacraments and the true sense of Church. But Luther did set such events into motion, just as he failed to back down after he recognized the untoward direction of such events.

In the very early stages of the Reformation in the late Renaissance, the Augustinian monk Luther had opposed the Dominican

---

[247] As opposed to, say, the Great Schism, whose schismatic action was comparatively intended and unitary.

monk John Tetzel's method of fund-raising on behalf of the commission of St. Peter's Basilica: the selling of indulgences. Luther's dissent against the Church was not initially unprecedented: intra-Catholic dissenters had arisen often throughout Church history. Until the Diet of Worms, the Church *itself* trivialized this conflict as a mere squabble between Catholic religious orders, which was altogether common in those days: Luther, an Augustinian, versus Tetzel, a Dominican.[248]

Luther opposed the Church's robust power structure, which enabled the selling of indulgences. His narrowly tailored Ninety-Five Theses revolved around that complaint and a few others. The Theses were by no means a broadside against the Catholic creed (including Tradition) or the Holy Magisterium. To mount a rather specific attack on the sale of indulgences, he complained somewhat generally of too much power within the Catholic Magisterium. But Luther certainly did not intend from the outset to rid the Church of its Magisterial hierarchy — and definitely not its sacramental theology, which even after his excommunication in 1521, Luther would mostly uphold.

Similarly, as time went along, Luther's extemporaneously developing theology — immediately following the Diet of Worms[249] — had to cover the "gaps" that his Ninety-Five Theses created. If the Magisterial structure of the Church was to be attacked a bit more broadly than he had originally designed, who would fill the role of the priestly class? The response suggested as much by Luther's deafening silence as by the increasingly extremist Protestantism around Northern Europe: everyone in the pews.

---

[248] O'Connell and Stoutzenberger, *The Church through History*, pp. 189–190.
[249] Ibid., p. 190.

The Reformation in that way bore an undeniable "Power to the people!" flavor.

Thus, without really wanting to do so at all, Luther thereby "democratized" Christianity. From Wartburg Castle, he translated the Bible into German, which enabled common people to read it without filial dependence upon the clergy and the liturgy. And without the liturgy and the priestly class, sacraments in fast-Protestantizing Northern Europe could not be effectively administered. But once again, Luther explicitly defended the notion of the sacraments.[250]

Northern European copycat Reformers such as John Calvin and Ulrich Zwingli jumped in and carried Luther's work to radical new theological extremes in France and Switzerland. New reformers, especially Zwingli, violently attacked the sacraments. At the Colloquy of Marburg, Luther met with Zwingli and pled a desperate defense of the sacraments. Most importantly, Luther made the case for the real presence of Christ in the Eucharist, which Zwingli demystified as radically as any Enlightenment contemporary would. And did.

Unsurprisingly, Luther and Zwingli came to no agreement.[251] Luther had begun a theological revolution based upon extemporaneous dissents—whose ramifications he had not initially wanted or anticipated at all! The Protestant Reformation quickly spun out of control: *attack the power of the Church in a slightly*

---

[250] John B. Payne, "Zwingli and Luther: The Giant vs. Hercules," *Christianity Today*, www.ctlibrary.com/ch/1984/issue4/408.html.

[251] Luther considered Zwingli a "fanatic" since Zwingli disavowed the real presence of Christ in the Eucharist. Zwingli responded, "You would have cleansed the Augean stable, if you had had the images removed, if you had not taught that the body of Christ was supposed to be eaten in the bread." Ibid.

broader manner than the specific target first imagined by Luther, and
wind up getting rid of both the sacraments and the clerical order of
priests; attack the tradition of the Church's thinkers in order to ready
the way for the printing of vernacular Bibles, and wind up getting rid
of Natural Law within Protestant Christianity.

At the level of sacramental theology, it is now clear that Prots
and Enlights during the sixteenth century took more or less the
same dismissive approach to Catholicism. But does this mean
that they *actually* teamed up during the ensuing seventeenth and
eighteenth centuries? Doesn't this go too far?

Not at all. The story of American Protestants and secularists,
from the founding and framing eras onward, is a shocking one:
they joined forces against Catholicism in such a specific manner
as to suggest they were more historically in line with each other
than we would recognize today.

American Prots and Enlights Team Up:
The Separation of Church and State

In chapter 1, we examined the history of English Whig anti-
Catholicism. Here follows the account of the goal, for which Prots
and Enlights teamed up *in America* after the founding of the country (remember, they had joined forces in general against the Catholic Natural Law and the sacramental theology of Catholicism).

As you read the following section, keep in mind that our
American attitude on the "separation of church and state"[252]

---

[252] Pope Leo XIII called the separation of church and state, in its
pure form, "the Americanist heresy." He lamented that church
and state were strongly "dissevered and divorced" and wanted a
closer relationship between the two (*Testem Benevolentiae Nos-*
trae, 1899). He did not specify with much nuance how closely
church and state should run in order to avoid the heresy. But

was considered until very recently an extremely violent, anti-religious position. We're about to see that even many religious Americans still wrongly think that full separation of church and state is a neutral, or even a good, thing. Consider Pope Leo XIII's words and assumptions in his *Humanum Genus* (1884), widely condemning the more extreme forms of secularism:

> They work ... obstinately to the end that neither the teaching nor the authority of the Church may have any influence; and therefore they preach and maintain the full separation of the Church from the state.[253]

But even the Constitution itself, as originally ratified, did not require separation of church and state! Nor did the "religion clauses" of the First Amendment.

---

this book suggests the broad rule that American First Amendment jurisprudence was not guilty of "Americanism" in 1791 or in the decades immediately following but was indeed guilty of "Americanism" well before the outright codification by the Supreme Court in 1947 of Jefferson's century-old "wall of separation" language. As such, one can think of a "hard form" of separation as heretical, and a "soft form" (nebulously addressed at the Second Vatican Council) as nonheretical.

[253] *The Letter "Humanum Genus" of the Pope, Leo XIII, Against Freemasonry and the Spirit of the Age* (April 20, 1884). This encyclical antedated Leo's other encyclical on the matter, *Testem Benevolentiae Nostrae*, by fifteen years. The response came from Albert Pike, Sovereign Grand Commander of the Scottish Rite, Southern Jurisdiction: "[The encyclical was] a declaration of war, and the signal for a crusade, against the rights of man individually and of communities of men as organisms; against the separation of church and state, and the confinement of the Church within the limits of its legitimate functions; against education free from sectarian religious influences." Hamburger, *Separation of Church and State*, p. 397.

Examining the unconstitutional doctrine of American separation of church and state ends up showing more about the historically strange relationship between the religious Right and the secular Left than it does about the Constitution's First Amendment.

As of 1791 when the First Amendment to the U.S. Constitution was ratified, there was no intended separation between church and state. None whatsoever: the "separation" verbiage appears nowhere in the Constitution or in any of the Amendments.[254] And there is virtually no argument on the matter, among Bill of Rights scholars. In fact, more than half of the thirteen states, in 1791, had an established, official religion, a state-sanctioned sect of Protestantism![255]

The doctrine of separation of church and state eventually became "read into" American law through the unlikeliest alliance against American Catholicism: secularists and Protestants. (Perhaps one should say that such an alliance appears "unlikely" to all *except* those who have read the first half of this book!)

One man's studies of this misalliance have been particularly helpful. In his authoritative book *Separation of Church and State*, legal scholar Philip Hamburger sets out to (and does effectively) show that the First Amendment of the U.S. Constitution was

---

[254] Hamburger, *Separation of Church and State*, p. 1. Jefferson's infamous letter to the Danville Baptists, as noted by Hamburger, created a metaphor that would be widely misused until eventually, an entire faulty legal principle was made out of it.

[255] "These established Churches (Episcopal in southern states and Congregationalist in most New England states) were established through state laws that, most notably, gave government salaries to ministers on account of their religion." Hamburger, *Separation of Church and State*, pp. 9–10.

intended by its creators to do just the opposite of what it does today: bulwark, rather than hinder, religion in America.

More importantly, Hamburger's book shows *why* the opposite result was produced: because of the influence of the American Prot-Enlight (though he does not use my term).

Based on his close attention to the gradual historical reversal of the legal meaning of the First Amendment by American Protestants and secularists over two hundred years, Hamburger ends up coming very, very close to announcing something identical to what the first half of this book has consistently called "Prot-Enlight." It is a historical and legal account of the very same misalliance discussed philosophically and theologically in this book!

The reason Hamburger stops short of specifically announcing this is probably that such an idea lies outside his legal and historical "wheelhouse." On the other hand, this book's — and more specifically this *chapter's* — goal lies in drawing out the implication that Prot-Enlight is actually a single, two-sided coin rather than two separate coins. And this point is best made by highlighting and drawing upon Hamburger's ambitious point that "in America anti-Catholicism adopted some of the assumptions of liberal theology."[256]

As far as this chapter is concerned, Hamburger's well-premised statement is pretty much the whole ball of wax. *Protestantism is secularized, desacralized, Enlightened Christianity.*

That's precisely what liberal theology is, Hamburger all but notes![257]

---

[256] Hamburger, *Separation of Church and State*, p. 194.
[257] Hamburger seems impressively keen on demonstrating a historical curiosity noted also in this book: American Protestantism

One is amazed to come across Hamburger's staggering insight and intuition, which articulates the following proposition, not from philosophical-theological assumptions but from legal ones:

> Rather than follow the path of European liberals in going to the extremes of anti-Christian skepticism, American liberals explored the further reaches of individualistic Protestantism and questioned the authority of churches, clergymen, and creeds.... American Protestants had departed from established churches, including those of Rome and Canterbury, but now increasing numbers of American Protestants [even] questioned the authority of entirely disestablished Protestant churches.[258]

The Protestant clings to Christ without clinging to the Church (or, as Hamburger points out, to clergy or to creed). And, as this chapter has attempted to show, such a thing cannot be done in the long run: Christ cannot be retained without *Church*, *clergy*, and *creed*.

Only this is the true Christian humanism, as Hamburger all but insinuates in his legal look into American religious history.

---

took virtually every play from the Enlightenment "playbook" except the very last one, as many European Protestants did (i.e., getting rid of Christ Himself). Hamburger uses legal reasoning to show that while nineteenth-century European Protestants became fully secularized kids of the Enlightenment, American Protestants became ... simply more individualistic, "Enlightened" Protestants—but not political liberals, like their European counterparts! They became instead "the religious Right." From any angle—legal or philosophical—it is an unexpected outcome.

[258] Hamburger, *Separation of Church and State*, pp. 194–195.

He discusses what he considers to be the *Americanist*[259] rejection of "Church" in terms of Prot-Enlight anti-clericalism. This fast became a nineteenth-century game in America of: "Are you Protestant enough?" American anti-Catholicism turns out to be a Puritanical fear of the "Romish"[260] sense of Church (even Episcopalian clergies "looked too much like"[261] Catholic ones, as American Puritans became more radicalized).

More specifically, the Prot-Enlight fear of clergy, creed, and Church *caused* the increasing radicalization and continuing atomization of American Protestantism. The loss of the culture of sacraments, following upon the loss of these "three Cs," was the *effect*. And it proved to be an ever-accelerating process. American denominations became more and more Protestant, more anticlerical, as time went on.

Hamburger comes as close as any legal historian to announcing the existence of something called "Prot-Enlight" ... without actually doing so. He begins what has been called "the best and most important book ever written on the subject of separation of church and state in the United States [by announcing that] the notion of separation gained wide acceptance in the 19th century primarily due to the pervasiveness of American anti-Catholicism."[262]

---

[259] The term "Americanism" is here referenced in the same context in which Pope Leo XIII would use it — or as in Hamburger's closing statement, "Americanism versus Roman Catholicism." *Separation of Church and State*, p. 445.

[260] Hamburger, *Separation of Church and State*, p. 445.

[261] Ibid., p. 387.

[262] Stanley N. Katz, review of *Separation of Church and State* by Philip Hamburger, Harvard University Press, reviews, http://www.hup.harvard.edu/catalog.php?isbn=9780674013742&content=reviews.

But Hamburger thoroughly shows that the First Amendment was not originally ratified in 1791 to achieve any anti-Catholic end, or even any separation of church and state.[263] He recounts that, notwithstanding even framing-era anti-Catholicism, "Separation first appeared in popular American debates about religious liberty not as a demand but as an *accusation*."[264]

Neither party, even the most fervently anti-Catholic Protestants or secularists, wanted separation that early on. In the founding- and framing-era politics, in other words, a platform of separation of church and state would have been campaign suicide.

Protestants and secularists would eventually, by the mid-1800s (well before Pope Leo XIII would get wind of the "heresy"), begin perverting the First Amendment to befit their increasing anti-Catholicism. Hamburger writes:

[263] Early on, Hamburger explains that, from even before the time of the Constitution's ratification, an "Americanist" notion of individualism (based upon a hard separation between church and state) seemed to unite Protestants and secularists against hierarchical Catholicism. Both parties feared the entrance by Catholicism into America. Clearly, differing species of individualism — religious (Prot) and political (Enlight) — seem to have united the two types of purists (or Puritans, if you will). Both parties wanted none of the Catholic Church in America. The American Protestants, as we all know, were religious Puritans and *sola scriptura* individualists; similarly, Hamburger depicts the post-Enlightenment secularists as political "puritans" who wanted to rid American culture of all forms of non-individualism. This implicated Catholicism, in both the Protestant and the secularist minds. Both the Protestant and the secularist of the day cited as being central to America the "intellectual independence" (*Separation of Church and State*, p. 202) that they presumed to be so utterly opposite to Roman Catholicism. So, for a time, they became bedfellows.

[264] Hamburger, *Separation of Church and State*, p. 65.

In the middle of the 19th century, some Americans employed the idea of separation of church and state against Catholicism and thereby made it a popular "American" principle. During the beginning of the century, as has been seen, some secular political writers had occasionally advocated separation as a constitutional principle in a spirit … that was anticlerical but not specifically anti-Catholic. By the middle of the century, however, Protestants began to employ separation in a manner more likely to have widespread appeal.... Increasing numbers of Protestant leaders therefore opposed the Catholic "union" of church and state by urging a separation of these institutions.[265]

The story that Hamburger tells is that separation of church and state began as an American byword, employed by Prots and Enlights, to preclude Catholic but not Protestant "exercises of civic clericalism, which immunize[d] and le[ft] standing only the purest and most individualistic forms of Protestantism."[266]

As an example, Hamburger puts forward the baffling view of the Junior Order of United American Mechanics, who believed that "free education opposed any union of church and state, [and that this itself required] maintaining the Public School system and preventing sectarian interference therewith, [by] the reading of the Holy Bible therein."[267]

Separation *required* the reading of the Bible in public schools? Only in Prot-Enlight America!

Further, in order to prove that "separation" was a highly nuanced byword, Hamburger offers the view of "the notorious

[265] Ibid., p. 193.
[266] Ibid., p. 65.
[267] Ibid., p. 455.

American Protective Association, [which] cooperated with the Ku Klux Klan against Catholicism ... and preached the glorious trinity of the Bible, the Flag, and the School"[268] as *requisites* rather than *exclusions* of the First Amendment.

Too strange.

In today's all-encompassing sense of the term, "separation" means separation. But not back then, at which point it seemed to mean, "Protestant, but not Catholic, exercises of civic clericalism were A-okay." As counterintuitive as it is, Hamburger proves that from the mid-nineteenth through the mid-twentieth century, both American Prots and American Enlights agreed that the First Amendment required distinctly Protestant exercises in civics—for example, reading the Protestant but not the Catholic Bible in school.

But, as all strange bedfellows are fated to turn against one another, Prots and Enlights began butting heads in the late 1940s. Their unification against any Catholic influence in America dissolved into a bitter rivalry, culminating with the landmark Supreme Court case concerning the publicly funded busing of Catholic schoolchildren, *Everson v. Board of Education*[269] and its "aftermath."[270] The case marked a decisive sea change after which point the secularists turned against the Protestants. Evidently done with their alliance, the secularists began to insist that the "separation" should be interpreted literally, not as a Protestant-sparing byword. All religion, all Christianity, then came under the secular attack. In other words, the changing legal culture brought by the secularists began, after *Everson*, to

[268] Ibid., p. 456.
[269] Everson v. Board of Education 330 U.S. 1 (1947).
[270] Hamburger, *Separation of Church and State*, p. 199.

insist that neither the Catholic *nor* the Protestant Bible should be taught in schools.

And with that, a more recognizable interpretation of "separation" emerged. No longer threatened by the prospect of immigrating Catholics, Protestants and secularists turned violently against one another—as we easily recognize today. More accurately, the secularists turned against the Protestants. But not before creating an intensely anti-religious (formerly, it was only anti-*Catholic*) First Amendment jurisprudence.

And to be fully honest, a plain textual reading of the phrase "separation of church and state" favors the newer, post-1940s secularist view over the idiosyncratic, pro-Protestant "loaded" one that had prevailed for one hundred years. Today's religious Right should not complain about what happened: they helped to *create* the loophole, after all. Only the Catholic can complain.[271]

---

[271] Also highly relevant to *Everson*, Hamburger spends some time describing the role of Hugo L. Black's anti-Catholic cooperation with Protestant, nativist "protective leagues" and Southern Masonic groups (*Separation of Church and State*, p. 422). Indeed, it was cooperation by one very peculiar member among the Supreme Court's jurists to hear the case. Hamburger skewers the infamous Ku Klux Klan member-turned-Supreme Court Justice, as he describes Hugo Black's nakedly anti-Catholic agenda in cases such as *Everson*. Black, a notorious hater of Catholicism, "could make the best anti-Catholic speech you ever heard" (*Separation of Church and State*, p. 427), according to his lifelong friend, Klan Grand Dragon James Esdale, who told Black to "give me a letter of resignation and I'll keep it in my safe against the day when you'll need to say you're not a Klan member" (*Separation of Church and State*, pp. 426–427). Esdale's full quotation, as cited by Hamburger, about the Ku Klux Klan's central role in Black's successful senatorial bid, reads: "I arranged for Hugo to go to [all 148] Klaverns all over the state

Clearly, Hamburger shows, separation cases such as *Everson* were not being decided on the basis of blind justice, but instead on the heavily biased basis of Prot-Enlight anti-Catholicism.

Hamburger closes his case by noting that after *Everson* "even traditional Presbyterians felt they had to fight off manifestations of liberal theology."[272] In other words, even the *least* progressive American Protestant denominations realized (shortly after the atomizing Puritan project had backfired) that Protestantism seemed to borrow far too much from the Enlightenment.

Irrespective of Hamburger's differing approach from this book's, he seems to understand what almost no one else in

---

[of Alabama], making talks on Catholicism. What kinds of talks? Well, just the history of the Church and what we know about it. Not to talk on politics. Hugo could make the best anti-Catholic speech you ever heard." While the aftermath of *Everson* would come as a surprise to Black and his KKK "dragon" and "wizard" friends—along with virtually every American Protestant—the holding of the case was not, considering Black's highly leveraged, outcome-determinative position on the bench (*Separation of Church and State*, p. 434): "Black's association with the Klan has been much discussed in connection with his liberal views on race, but in fact, his membership suggests more about the ideals of Americanism and, especially, American religious liberty that he shared with so many of his countrymen. The combination of progressive, Protestant, and Klan sentiment that brought Black to the Senate illustrates how anti-Catholicism and, more broadly, fears of ecclesiastical authority transcended the differences among vast numbers of Americans, creating loose alliances that Black, the Klan, and many others cultivated on behalf of themselves and their ideals. In this context the separation of church and state flourished as a Constitutional ideal, bringing together disparate groups by appealing to their aspirations for America and their loathing for Rome."

[272] Hamburger *Separation of Church and State*, p. 197.

America does.[273] Prots and Enlights are rivals indeed. *But at some very real level, they are rivals on the same team. Perhaps they are even rivaling moods within the same psychology, different sides of the same Prot-Enlight coin.* They both reject Catholicism's natural community of Church. Both parties are *protesters;* both parties are *enlightened.*

Conclusion

So it's quite simple, really: the Church is the natural community that administers sacraments. In so administering, the Church binds one Christian human to another, in a way indispensable to true republicanism. It shows human beings *how* to be human beings, individually and in groups. The Protestants reject elements of the Catholic Church, such as creed and clergy, which enable the sacraments. And by rejecting a formal creedal or clerical structure within their congregations, the Protestants sever their ties to the sacramental Church (even if they point out within

---

[273] The only angle that Hamburger seems to miss in his excellent book is whether Prot-Enlights were anti-Catholic because they were anticlerical, or vice versa. At times, he seems to assume both positions. But given the difficulty and the scope of this question, he should be more than forgiven. As a legal historian, he merits high praise for getting even as far as pointing out the theological strangeness of Protestantism's desire to abandon the three Cs of Catholicism — clergy, creed, and Church — while keeping the fourth, Christ. After all, it is rather impressive for a nontheologian subtly to insinuate so much theological truth: namely, that in getting rid of clergy, creed, and Church, Prots were only slightly less secularized than the Enlights (for having attempted even haphazardly to retain Christ). In a restrained legal-historical sense, Hamburger seems to squint toward this chapter's thesis: that, bereft of those three Cs, a Prot will always slide toward being an Enlight.

their services some worthless and symbolic sacramental surrogates, bearing the same names as the Magisterial sacraments).

In conclusion, we can now see the connection between the worldly and otherworldly aspects of each of the sacraments. The connection is perfected by man's natural community of the Church. Without the Church, man is helpless to identify what is truly noble in himself and to render a proper definition of "human being." Such a humanism—one operating without the Church—cannot then be Christian. It ultimately proves to be a secular, Enlightenment humanism *going by the name* "Protestant" or "Biblicist."

If the sacraments do not make holy our lives in a communal Body of Christ, they are worthless symbols indeed. If the sacrifice of the Eucharist, mimicked within this or that Protestant congregation, is not sacramental, then that Last Supper tells us nothing special about day-to-day meal-taking, the most regular and best-kept daily routine in man's life. The worldly is revealed through the otherworldly, just as the otherworldly is concealed in the worldly.

Further to this, if the sacrament of Holy Orders is removed from a Prot-Enlight society, as it has been from ours, then there exists no role within congregations for administering the sacraments.

If the sacrament of Confession is needless, then the daily act of honest apology to one's family and friends, and even to our enemies, is needless as well. If we do not need to properly apologize to *God*, why in the world should we apologize to *man*? Society depends on humans who can reconcile one with another, without going to blows or to court.

If Baptism and Confirmation are merely symbolic rituals— and not an actual type of ingress into a fixed community, the

Mystical Body of Christ—then the Church is plainly not any sort of nature-provided community at all. Why, then, from a Protestant perspective, engage in the "symbol" of Baptism (why all the fuss over *infant* versus *adult* Baptism) and why bother to go to "church" on Sundays at all? Without the otherworldly view of Baptism and Confirmation, there can be no worldly view to guide us. There would be no natural community of the Church into which one would enter.

If there is nothing sacred or worthy in our acknowledgement of death through Last Rites, then all the more dubious is the prospect that our death is a portal and not a terminus.

Last but not least, if Holy Matrimony is received as a contract only, then it is breakable by the same methods found in all contract law. A marriage would be tormented at all times by "scorekeeping," an indispensable element of contracts. The outlook on procreation would change. There would be no natural community of the family at all (further discussed in the next chapter).

Prot-Enlight demystified the sacraments of the Catholic Church and thereby destroyed the fullness of Christian humanism. While the religious Right and the secular Left initially teamed up against American Catholicism, these two halves of Prot-Enlight were motivated by different ends in attacking the sacraments. The latter desacralized the entire world and meant it. The former (although it had not formulated all the consequences entailed by its goal) sought only to desacralize Christianity, while retaining Christ.

But in still another sense, these two aims were similar in that they imposed upon the Church the modern sense of the individual over the collective unity of the sacraments.

Chapter 5 explains how the unintentional Protestant degradation of the family followed closely upon the collapse of the American sense of the Church.

CATHOLIC REPUBLIC

Why, in conclusion, is such a specifically Catholic humanism a necessary element in American (or any) republicanism? Because, of course, it is the *only* true humanism, insofar as it connects the *supernatural* with all the "dots" required by republicanism! Culture, composed of human beings, cannot be based on natural concepts alone: it is not in our nature. All of the higher natural concepts discussed in the chapters of this book require a supernatural nexus—the sacraments.

The practice of the supernatural sacraments requires natural rights (chapter 1); presupposes a social structure of subsidiarity (chapter 2); dictates and refines morality (chapter 3); and constitutes natural communities, the Church in the first place (chapter 4) and family in the second (chapter 5) as necessary conditions for their own maintained existence.

The only remaining question is whether these elements of republicanism can be authentically created *without* recourse to the sacraments. The reader should already know the answer!

A society that attempts to uphold natural rights must always invoke Catholic Natural Law, which points us to the sacraments. Without the guidance of Catholic Natural Law and the daily grace of the sacraments, the resultant secular "rights regime" will be nothing more than preferential treatment of certain favored parties. A society that attempts to uphold the family as the central unit—or "local rule" without recourse to the vocational-sacramental concept of familial subsidiarity—will wind up with a centralized government (like ours!). A society that attempts to codify morality in the Prot-Enlight sense will lack the sacramental grace that perfects the will to do right. Only the specifically Catholic sense of moral theology habituates true virtue. A society that attempts to center on "church" without sacraments will not honor—or even correctly define—what the Church is.

The Church is the natural sacralizing community. And finally, leading us straight to chapter 5, a society that attempts to center on family without the sacraments will conceive of Matrimony as a "worldly thing," as Martin Luther said, a contract utterly devoid of holiness and sanctification. As such, it will descend into sterility and materialism.

Chapter 5

Staking the New Regime in the American Culture

The Crypto-Catholicism of American Family and Economy

The essence of a fallen world is that [in marriage] the best cannot be attained by free enjoyment, or by what is called "self-realization" (usually a nice name for self-indulgence . . .), but by denial, by suffering. Faithfulness in Christian marriages entails that: great mortification. For a Christian man, there is no escape.

—J. R. R. Tolkien, letter to his son Michael Tolkien

While it has been rightly emphasized that increasing per capita income cannot be the ultimate goal of political and economic activity, it is still an important means of attaining the objective of the fight against hunger and absolute poverty. Hence, the illusion that a policy of mere redistribution of existing wealth can definitely resolve the problem must be set aside. In a modern economy, the value of assets is utterly dependent on the capacity to generate revenue in the present and the future. Wealth creation therefore becomes an inescapable duty, which must be kept in mind if the fight against material poverty is to be effective in the long term.

—Pope Benedict XVI, Message for World
Day of Peace, January 1, 2009

The fifth element of crypto-Catholicism in Prot-Enlight America is *family*, called by the Church Fathers the "Church of the home," the "Church in miniature," or more recently, "the domestic Church."[274] During the Vatican II debates, several council fathers stated that the "final division of the Church was not the parish, but the family."[275] Sadly, the modern conception of the family no longer sees it as a *calling* or *vocation*.

Accordingly, the twenty-first-century American rarely thinks of family as a natural blessing. Without the Catholic, sacramental, vocational context of Holy Matrimony, the sanctifying mortifications called for by marital life have most often been viewed as useless sufferings to be avoided or excised wherever possible.

And by today, the family's fall from grace has become so obvious that even many non-Catholic Americans have taken notice. Symptoms may be plainly observed, yet (as the reader now knows) diagnosis and remediation requires consultation of the Catholic Natural Law.

After all, what could possibly explain the counter-instinctual trend among American twenty-, twenty-five-, and even thirty-year-olds *not* to marry? Unwillingness to suffer, even slightly, for a greater goal is tantamount to abandoning the goal. If and when these young people eventually marry, it seems too often to be without a willingness to undergo even the slightest suffering. Hence the eventual collapse of so many American families.

---

[274] John Paul II, Apostolic Exhortation on the Role of the Christian Family in the Modern World *Familiaris Consortio* (November 22, 1981), no. 65.

[275] Joseph Atkinson, *Biblical and Theological Foundations of the Family: The Domestic Church* (Washington D.C.: Catholic University of America Press, 2014), pp. 301–315.

In this chapter, we will see how the emerging Prot-Enlight view of marriage and family as a "worldly thing … like any other secular business,"[276] rather than as a heavenly thing, has destroyed not only the family, but also our Western understanding of the economy.

Remember how closely related to family the concept of the economy is. In Prot-Enlight America, the economy has not properly been seen, as it should be, as a function of the family. It is precisely this. When the family is viewed as a vocation and a sacrament, it is recognized as a complete, productive unit. (For example, Aristotle's *Economics* was even subtitled "On the Good of the Family.") We will see how "the natural economy"—Catholic Natural Law's capitalistic, free economy—is the *only* kind that properly arises from a view of the family as the central unit of society.

Just as chapter 4 showed that *Church* is no longer received as a natural community in the Prot-Enlight American mainstream, this chapter will show that the concept of the American *family* suffers from the same degradation. Like the Church, the family has been desacralized and denaturalized. Mainstream American culture views the family not as a central fixture of human nature but rather as *something synthetic*—something to be "planned," very often mocked, set into unnatural contexts, opportunistically put off until "more convenient," manipulated as a means to an end, and sometimes even eliminated entirely.

Prot-Enlight American culture views the family as everything from an occasionally enjoyable if inconvenient tool, to a harmless but silly relic of a bygone era, and all the way to an outright nuisance to be extirpated. But almost *never* in America

[276] Luther, *Weimar*, vol. 12, p. 131.

is family recognized for what it truly is: man's first, sacramental, most natural, and most intimate community.

And just as chapter 4 showed why the Church is misunderstood in American popular culture, and how to replenish a natural view of it, this chapter will ask the questions *why* is it a problem and *how* to fix the problem. Of course, the reader already has a clue that both answers in this arena involve replacing Prot-Enlight crypto-Catholicism with outright, Natural Law Catholicism. All restorative efforts outside of Catholicism are doomed to futility.

Just as all the previous chapters of this book anticipated responses by its skeptics with a simple enumeration of the *symptoms* of the problem today, so shall this chapter. From even before the cradle to the grave, the "burden" of the family is rejected by the American culture.

Beginning with near-ubiquitous contraception and widespread abortion, young and even middle-aged men avoiding marriage and family, nearly "fifty-fifty" odds of divorce throughout the American populace, right up to the cottage industry of nursing homes (and sometimes euthanasia) at the end, one simply cannot deny that America rejects a sacramental view of Matrimony and family.

Following upon American society's desacralization of family — its treatment of marriage as Martin Luther's "worldly thing" — the culture has become detached from any cohesive sense of family duty.[277]

---

[277] This chapter will trace the widespread eradication of family duty to the eradication of membership in the Church described in chapter 4. Reformation congregations more or less borrowed the Enlightenment principle that membership in the one true Church is superfluous. But the Protestant eradication of family

Here follows the simple account as to why erasing the sacraments of the Church is tantamount to erasing natural duty to one's family. Whether the Protestants accomplished this willingly or not, the unexpected consequences to society and its economy were both severe and undeniable. Just as the breakdown of the popular sense of the Church leads indirectly to the breakdown of the family, so also does the breakdown of the family lead indirectly to a misunderstanding of the *natural economy* (or capitalism). Of course, the problem in America is soluble only via the Catholic sacramental view of the family.

America's Prot-Enlight Elimination of Family as Natural Community

The sacrament of Matrimony is like family "glue." As Pope Francis publicly noted, young families often approach him, saying: "But today, Father, [marriage] is difficult," to which he responds, "Of course it is difficult! That is why we need the grace, the grace that comes from the sacrament!"

The easy pitfall here is to imagine that the concept of sacrament—specifically Holy Matrimony—means glue only *between spouses*. But Holy Matrimony is far more than that. We need "glue" to keep us together with our family of origin, as well. Although we belong as humans to the class *mammalia*, one recalls that mammals are wired merely to raise their young to survive

---

membership sprang up as an unintended consequence of the rejection of the Church in the cultural mainstream. The one thing led to the other.

Unlike the secular Left, who craved radical autonomy (even to the point of conceptual orphanage, i.e., rejection of all familial duty), the religious Right never intended this. Nevertheless, it came to pass.

to maturity. To stick together in a uniquely *human* way, a family of grown-up siblings (with their growing children and their aged parents) requires the help that comes from the sacrament.

Think of how sharply in America this contrasts with the popular "W.A.S.P.," or Prot-Enlight, sensibility about grown-up family. Think *Everybody Loves Raymond*: grown-up family is received as a nuisance and nothing more.

But from the perspective of the Catholic Natural Law, family constitutes a natural type of community; it equals the community won by Christ's *triumph over nature*. Marriage does not cease to be a natural community just because it is also *extra*-natural. To the contrary, the naturalness of marriage depends upon the supernaturalness of the sacrament, as chapter 4 laid out:

> Those who celebrate the sacrament [of marriage] say, "I promise to be true to you, in joy and in sadness, in sickness and in health; I will love you and honour you all the days of my life." At that moment, the couple does not know what will happen, nor what joys and pains await them. They are setting out, like Abraham, on a journey. And that is what marriage is! Setting out and walking together, hand in hand, putting yourselves in the Lord's powerful hands. Hand in hand, always and for the rest of your lives. And do not pay attention to this makeshift culture, which can shatter our lives.[278]

Matrimony is a mystical bond, a becoming "one flesh" (Eph. 5:31), in which spouses partake of the divine love shared among the Trinity. Holy Matrimony is based on the Holy Family's model:

[278] Francis, address to the participants in the pilgrimage of families during the Year of Faith, Saint Peter's Square (October 26, 2013).

Mary and Joseph said *amen* to the unanticipated and, from their own perspective, startling "family planning" of God. They did not substitute their judgment for that of God: a child was to be born unexpectedly to them.

Faithfully they welcomed the child. Christians of all kind are called to the same procreative obedience.

Remember, like all the other sacraments discussed in chapter 4, marriage bears both otherworldly (theological) and worldly (daily, human) implications. Recall also from the last chapter the Greek and Roman sacramental concepts of *musterion* and *sacramentum*.

We must avoid Prot-Enlight America's misunderstanding of Holy Matrimony as a mere *contract*, which strips it of its magic, its sacramental gloss. The blithe reduction of mystical relations to the contract principle of "mutual consent" in marriage is one of the great sicknesses of the twenty-first century; it crowns *choice* as the high principle of our age.[279]

In other words, the Enlightenment created the dangerous, false notion that two human beings could get together and call up "down," by some perverse agreement. Think of the emperor's new clothes, which were in reality *no clothes* at all: no mutually secured consent could alter the king's nakedness. Today's secular Left — with begrudging agreement by today's religious Right — has come to believe that extramarital, premarital, or homosexual sex, if mutually consensual, is not wrong. In other words, the mere consent of two adults determines what is sexually "right."

---

[279] It is even older than this, being one of the recently reinvigorated maladies of the sixteenth century. Mutual consent, in this context, was a specifically designed product of the Enlightenment, the now familiar movement that first popularized the notion of metaphysical relativism discussed in chapter 3.

CATHOLIC REPUBLIC

Today, American popular culture acknowledges these vices as wrong only when *nonconsensual* (i.e., sex appears to be "immoral" only when it is rape). According to such reasoning, man, not God, is the measure.

And while the familial issues of divorce and contraception do not ideologically separate the Prots and the Enlights by much anymore, the concepts of homosexuality and fornication still often do. Increasingly, however, many Protestant congregations have, to varying extents, accepted these as well. For the sacramental reasons described in chapter 4, one looks to the future expecting to see such remaining moral distinctions between Prot and Enlight eroded.

At any rate, *all* of these faulty views stem from the Prot-Enlight, nonsacramental, nonprocreative view of Matrimony.

The Enlightenment standard of *mutual consent* equates to nothing other than the moral relativism discussed in chapter 3: anything that is consented to passes muster. According to the relativistic new premises being embraced by America and the West, if two adults of consenting age have come together and decided to call an immoral sexual relationship "moral," then society *must* accept it as moral. Mustn't it?

Of course not.

If Protestants once seemed to join Catholics in criticizing the Enlightenment reconceptualization of consent, divorce, and procreation, then how has the attack on the family recently ensnared them too?

The answer comes straight from our last chapter's discussion about desacralization! The false notion of Matrimony as a *contract* is equivalent to desacralizing the Eucharist. The difference between sacralized marriage (Catholic) and desacralized marriage (Prot-Enlight) is humongous! It often means the difference between "staying the course" and getting a divorce. And seeing as the Prot-Enlight conception of marriage maintains that a spouse should, more or less, "always" excite or please you, it is quite amazing that the divorce rate hovers *only* around 50 percent!

No marriage, no family, has successfully been constructed upon never-ending thrills. But the Prot-Enlight culture expects, even demands, constant marital titillation.

After the politically conservative Protestant congregations joined the secular, liberal Enlightenment thinkers in discounting Matrimony as a sacrament—abandoning the *supernatural* connection—the popular view of the American family was thereafter lost as a *natural* community. That is, in America the deck is now stacked against marriage.

This illuminates one of the lasting Protestant weaknesses on the issue of family in the debates that eventually arose between Prots and Enlights.

How and why should we defend marriage against *certain* (i.e., homosexual) pretenses, as Protestants most often do, if not against the *other* pretenses (divorce and remarriage)? Marriage, as ultimately impermeable by such perversions, is either sanctified by Christ[280] or it is not. It cannot be something in between.

From the sacramental Catholic perspective, divorce is not only immoral; it is technically *impossible*. It suggests the falsity that two married people did not come together before God as one flesh,

---

[280] The wedding feast at Cana (John 2:1–11) reveals the sacramentality of Matrimony. Sacramental marriage relates somewhat to natural marriage, but as a distinction of kind, not a distinction of mere degree (as it may at times seem). In other words, Christ's institution of marriage as a sacrament reveals marriage's altogether new status of being in the world after Christ, even though marriage was *always*—even before Christ—a natural, intelligible nongovernmental thing.

with the purpose (whether or not it was their intent) of creating an unalienable community of more than just two, of family. *This is the case whether or not a given marriage has produced children.*

The family, when taken out of the context of the natural—and supernatural—community, will produce unnatural fruits. And one readily recognizes these despoiled fruits in today's America: heterosexual marriages between partners who refuse to spend time together, or with their children (especially fathers escaping to work to avoid "time at home"); homosexual "marriages" being conducted, with and without adoptive children, as an experiment.

These bespoiled fruits abound everywhere in America: in both the cities and the suburbs.

The False Dichotomy of Burbs versus Urbs

On the basis just described, there is a resultant problem with manliness and fatherhood common to both halves of Prot-Enlight (the Protestant religious Right and the Enlightenment secular Left). The current problem is that men in both camps either *reject* or *resent* the vocation for which their manhood was appointed: fatherhood.

Generally, each party inhabits its own domain of the American landscape: the religious Right sticks to the suburbs, and the secular Left sticks to the city. The popular culture imagines the suburbs and the city as opposites. Like each half of Prot-Enlight, however, they turn out to be made of the same stuff. One should think of this false dichotomy as the "burbs versus the urbs."[281]

[281] Timothy Gordon, "Questioning American Exceptionalism," *Imaginative Conservative*, November 7, 2013, https://theimaginativeconservative.org/2013/11/taking-exception-american-exceptionalism.html.

And, just as the reader sees in multiple other corners throughout this book, Prots and Enlights have bitterly turned against one another in America, although they were once close allies against Natural Law Catholicism. In our last chapter, we examined how Prot-Enlights turned against one another within America's legal culture. In our next chapter, we will examine how they have turned against one another in the realm of science and technology.

But when one turns here to the ongoing American debate about the family, the battleground is the popular culture in the "burbs" versus the popular culture in the "urbs."

Contrary to claims by generally liberal urbanites and mostly conservative suburbanites—and some very confused crossbreeds —"real America" still lives in the big and beautiful spaces. The crypto-Catholic American spirit of tough religiosity still lives in these rural places (which enjoy geographical majority with demographic minority).

Liberty interplays inextricably with old-fashioned self- and family-reliance in rural America. This is subsidiarity. It is virtually the only place nowadays where the concept of "holding property" is not laughable. The moral self-reliance of the *true* "Americanism"[282] is ever present there. One assumes that it will continue to be so, as a minority position, as long or as short as our republic in name only continues to exist. Rural America should be the haven of crypto-Catholicism.

Like the other twenty-first-century dichotomies in America mentioned in this book, "the urbs versus the burbs" turns out to be a false one. Urbanites and suburbanites, being non-rurals, have far more in common than either side likes to admit. The

---

[282] This is in contrast to the heresy of Americanism.

urban-suburban false dichotomy perfectly reflects that of the two "variant" sixteenth-century ideologies that composed the early Union and became its ideological grandparents. The reader knows these ideologies, of course, as Prot-Enlight: the religious Right and the secular Left.

Just like each camp of Prot-Enlight, urbanites and suburbanites only *think* they are cultural opponents.

Urbanites hold up as beautiful their cramped vertical lodgings and "freedom" from the strictures of childrearing, in a sterile display of American hubris: cubist ugliness, metropolitan familiarity, downtown "squalid chic," and heinous avant-garde art. (Compare this architecture with classical European buildings!)

Suburbanites take pride in comparable ugliness, but in its suburban form: a neuter and adventureless repudiation of the pilgrim nature of the Christian life (via unbending routine), an inorganic and calculating sort of "family planning," comfier (compared against urban architecture) but equally unseemly assemblages of concrete and glass, and abundant soccer fields.

It's pretty much all bad. But none of this analysis is as simple as, say, mocking the iconography of dorky "dad jeans" or "mom minivans" ... or, for that matter, the metrosexual's "selfie." It bears far more profound and more interior meaning for America.

Each characterizing the other side's malignancy, both the religious Right and the secular Left miss the point: American cities and suburbs are *both* wimpy. Our cities and suburbs are *both* ugly.[283] Each is profane, irreligious, and desacralized.

---

[283] Oh, you're not wimpy just for living in a "burb" or an "urb," as almost all of us unfortunately do: you're wimpy if you celebrate the nasty ethos of either the American suburb or the American city. Each one stands against the manly, independent spirit and the procreative culture of life of our republic, such as it originally

Between the city and the suburb, one is unsure what is worse for republican civics: the half-gentrified squalor, the sterilized sense of the sexual organs, the vapid conversationalism, the ubiquitous arrested development, and the cartoonish androgyny of the *city* ... or the effete risk-aversion, humdrum of routine, mother-knows-best socialism in sports, "play dates," and petty acquisitiveness of the *burbs*.

Not an ounce of it bears the mark of true religious faith. Nor is there a strand of Jeffersonian DNA in any of it. Not the vaguest specter of Washington or Mason hovers over it; not a drop of blood or a single summoning of the vigorous spirit.

The real problem seems to be the lack of religiosity in both the city and the suburb. The urban or suburban man who figures there is nothing worse than death (i.e., the irreligious man) will cling to survival and to lifestyle accoutrements with the coward's iron grip. Thus, the solution to our problem seems to be *loosening* the grip on life, which not coincidentally has been the ostensible reason for the flight to the countryside.

Think of the words of Curly in the movie *City Slickers*: "You city folks spend about fifty weeks a year getting knots in your rope—and you think two weeks up here [out of the city] will untie them for you. None of you get it. Do you know what the secret of life is?... One thing. Just one thing. You stick with that,

---

was. Compared with our (far less than perfect) founders, we are the "lesser sons of greater sires" (as King Theoden of Rohan says). The cities and suburbs of America are merely the garishly overproduced sets where the actionless melodrama of our fast-declining Prot-Enlight America winds itself out. We are not ingenious. Our countryside estate-dwelling founders were—or, at least, they were "ingenious" enough to plagiarize from the best sources available.

and the rest don't mean s---."[284] (Sadly, Curly fails to identify the redemptive love of Christ on the cross as the "one thing," but it's Hollywood … one takes truth where he can get it.)

Aside from the reluctantly childbearing household, there is another familial trend in the suburbs, one notch over on the spectrum: a childless, urban-admiring, yet married household. This increasingly typical household includes *only* two monogamous people, contraceptively childless and wanting to treat marriage as "one long date." This trait—once thought of as an exclusive characteristic of the urbs (minus the monogamy)—makes plain the larger false dichotomy.[285]

And as is implied above, even in the suburban households that *do* contain children, the worldly drive to emulate the more stylish, urban mind-set remains visible, if subtle.

But whether children bless a suburban household or not, something deeper in the roots of Prot-Enlight impels folks in the American suburbs (and the cities as well) to turn their eyes away from their families and toward their jobs and possessions. The next sections will explore that phenomenon in detail.

Protestant Work Ethic: The False Equation of Vocation and Profession

The average Catholic will receive six out of the seven sacraments. This is because there exists a fork, as it were, in the sacramental road. One chooses *either* the vocation of Holy Orders *or* the vocation of matrimonial family. As we saw above, too many

[284] *City Slickers*, directed by Ron Underwood (Columbia Pictures, 1991).
[285] Like all other aspects of Prot-Enlight, the ostensible acrimony between its two halves (in the metropolitan landscape) will in time be replaced by their comity.

Catholics today borrow Prot-Enlight assumptions constituting a nonprocreative, nonvocational married life. In milder cases, this might even be so in households that *have* children (which has worked profoundly negative effects even in the semi-traditional suburban household).

Barring serious medical problems, a marriage is called to holiness through offspring. As a married Catholic, your vocation lies in your spouse and family. *Childbearing* is the true alternative to the ordained, priestly life. Remember Mother Teresa's famous words: "Not everyone is called to be successful; everyone is called to be faithful." One way or another. Neither priest nor lay should attempt to escape it.

Today, the false vocation — wildly popular in America — is "your job."

If it is taken to be a vocation, then *labor* (and not *family*) comes to be seen as sacred. Such a view degrades the average suburban family in today's America.

In reality, family is the end, and labor (wealth) is merely the means. It is not the other way around. In other words, family is the vocation; labor and wealth merely support it. How did the average American — many Catholics included — come to view his job as his vocation and his family as basically ancillary to it?

As the reader can probably guess, the answer to this question has everything to do with American foundations in Prot-Enlight. As the reader might *not* guess, it has more to do with Prot and less to do with Enlight (which is the opposite of what we've seen thus far, wherein the latter usually tricked or goaded the former into following its camouflaged progressive doctrines).

Recall from the beginning of this chapter how Martin Luther called marriage a "worldly thing." After the Reformation in the sixteenth century by and large rejected the sacraments, the average Protestant still craved the daily grace that the sacraments conferred. A need for a "substitute" for the sacraments — as if this were possible — was felt by most Protestants.

Recall Thomas Aquinas's teaching that all of man's cravings are natural, within the proper context. The flip side of that coin is that even natural cravings can be placed into unnatural contexts: in those cases, the appetites are satisfied with disordered substitutes. This is precisely what happened to the Protestant — particularly the American Calvinist — yearning for daily grace, following upon the Reformation's rejection of the sacraments.

Paraphrasing Max Weber, who wrote *The Protestant Ethic and the Spirit of Capitalism*, *World Heritage Encyclopedia* suggests that the Reformation profoundly affected the view of work, dignifying even the most mundane professions as adding to the common good and thus blessed by God, as much as any "sacred" calling. A common illustration is that of a cobbler, hunched over his work, who devotes his entire effort to the praise of God.[286]

But what has labor necessarily got to do with sacraments, after all? It was an attempted Protestant substitute for them. The same insightful synopsis of Weber's argument explains:

> Weber traced the origins of the Protestant [work] ethic to the Reformation.... The Roman Catholic Church assured salvation to individuals who accepted the Church's sacraments and submitted to clerical authority. However, the Reformation had effectively removed such assurances. From a psychological viewpoint, the average person had

---

[286] "The Protestant Ethic and the Spirit of Capitalism," *World Heritage Encyclopedia*, http://community.worldheritage.org/articles/ The_Protestant_Ethic_and_the_Spirit_of_Capitalism.

difficulty adjusting to this new [desacralized] worldview, and only the most devout believers or "religious geniuses" within Protestantism, such as Martin Luther, were able to make this adjustment, according to Weber. In the absence of such assurances from religious authority, Weber argued that Protestants began to look for other "signs" that they were saved.[287]

In other words, in the Calvinist Protestant world of America, diligent labor replaced—at some psychological level—the role formerly played by the sacraments. This was the world of the early Puritans, who influenced the American economy at the beginning of the American experiment.

Labor ostensibly became "an outward, visible sign of inward, invisible grace." Strangely enough, the misdefinition and false sacralization of labor crowns "Americanism." What is stranger still is that many American Catholics have accepted the latent but strong Puritanism involved in such a substitution.

Weber himself draws out the final implications, predicting the ultimate outcome of the Puritans' materialistic substitution for the sacraments:

The Puritan wanted to work in *calling*; we are forced to do so. For when asceticism was carried out of monastic cells into everyday life, and began to dominate worldly morality, it did its part in building the tremendous cosmos of the modern economic order. This order is now bound to the technical and economic conditions of machine production, which today determine the lives of all the individuals who are born into this mechanism, not only

[287] Ibid.

those directly concerned with economic acquisition, with irresistible force. Perhaps it will so determine them until the last ton of fossilized coal is burnt. In Baxter's view, the care for external goods should only lie on the shoulders of the "saint like a light cloak, which can be thrown aside at any moment." But fate decreed that the cloak should become an iron cage.[288]

Translation: material ownership is not evil, but it is not for everyone, in spates. That is because, for the rich man *or* the poor man, bountiful ownership is not necessary to do what he was made to do: achieve holiness through fatherhood (if not priesthood).

Mother Teresa, one more time: "Not everyone is called to be successful; everyone is called to be faithful."

But *most* rich folks forgot the part about universal faithfulness while *all* socialistic, envious folks forgot that some good people will achieve material success.[289] And this is the story of American and Western materialism in the city and the suburbs. It is embraced by secularists, and even by many Catholics, almost as universally as by the Protestants who engendered it. The "light cloak" of the American provider, the father, became an "iron cage," which would ultimately rend the American family asunder *rather than draw it together*.

[288] Max Weber, *The Protestant Ethic and the Spirit of Capitalism* (New York: Scribner, 1953), p. 181.

[289] "The great mistake ... is to take up with the notion that class is naturally hostile to class, and that the wealthy and the working men are intended by nature to live in mutual conflict. So irrational and so false is this view that the direct contrary is the truth.... Each needs the other: capital cannot do without labor, nor labor without capital." Leo XIII, *Rerum Novarum* 19.

But it will be seen below how only the Catholic view can realize the vision of material goods in their proper context, a "light cloak" valued, but not overvalued, by its owner.

At this point, one must put the facts into their proper context. Materialism is the "first nature" of secularists, who in America followed the lead of Protestants, instead of vice versa. Secularists will always be attracted to materialism as a sort of perverse first principle: after all, material goods and material comforts are the only solace consistent with their ideology. This same materialism is somewhat second nature for Protestants, who wanted all along to keep Christ but to jettison His Church-based sacraments. Weber hit the nail on the head in identifying labor as central to the Protestant attitude about daily grace. But most surprisingly, under Puritan influence, wealth acquisition became "third nature" for American Catholics, who assumed two aspects of materialism—careerism and consumerism—not as a purposeful substitution for Christ (as with the secular Left) *or* for the vocation of family (as with the religious Right), but in the *name* of their disordered commitment to each.

This seems to be why so many American Catholics embrace Prot-Enlight materialism.

To put this in the terminology of the previous section, one might confidently say that careerism and consumerism characterize both the burbs and the urbs in America. And virtually all Americans—the secularist, the Protestant, and the Catholic—bought into the consumerism-careerism "combo" for mostly different reasons. Catholics and, in a nonsacramental way, Protestants bought into such materialism *in the name of* family. Secularists did so generally *instead of family* (simply because materialism is the only effective atheist pleasure sufficient to distract one from his inevitable grave).

But not a whit of this careerism or consumerism should be seen to condemn capitalism, which absolutely *can* be ordered around the family.

We will examine exactly how to do this. The blame belongs with the *manner* in which Calvinist Protestantism (and secular Enlightenment thought) approached capitalism. They did so with careerism and consumerism, which stem from the Prot-Enlight American failure to locate the true source of daily grace — the sacraments. Hold that thought, regarding careerism and consumerism. Before discussing these two dimensions of materialism further, we must briefly discuss what capitalism *is*. On that matter, there seems to be a great deal of confusion.

Subsidiarity and True Capitalism

Because we've already seen that true republicanism and true Catholicism require natural rights (chapter 1), subsidiarity (chapter 2), an independently moral citizenry (chapter 3), and a commitment to natural community (the *Church* in chapter 4 and *family* here in chapter 5), the sort of political economy required by all this is already fixed: a "free" and "natural" one. This means capitalism.

A free, natural economy requires moral oversight by family, not by government.

Government rule of the economy, or the "centrally planned economy," is fundamentally incompatible with each of the elements of true republicanism named above.

Here the reader should not make the easy mistake of misinterpreting what Max Weber said above. All capitalism is not inherently Calvinist. Similarly, all capitalism is not inherently materialist. But everywhere, even in the Catholic world, just such a mistake seems to permeate the assumptions about political economy.

Au contraire: proper capitalism is very Catholic.

Whereas any one of the above-listed chapters' content could be used to disprove the moral validity of the centrally planned economy, the simplest way to view political economy is through recourse to the three natural rights (life, liberty, and property), which we've already examined so thoroughly.

Leaving aside life, for the moment, the natural rights of private liberty and private property, being *rights*,[290] should not without strong cause be removed by government. Rejecting the centrally planned economy—"capitalism," or whatever else one names that rejection—involves one thing only: the principle of governmental noninterference with those two rights.

[290] Although Thomas never used the word *ius* (right) in the context of private property, as pointed out by Brian Tierney in *The Idea of Natural Rights*, he nevertheless called it a "necessary" power and a "natural dominion" of mankind. In other words, something both *necessary* and *natural* for humans may be simplified as a "right." These are the two key elements of the concept of right. Some scholars seeking to diminish Thomas's natural sense of property, like Thomas Gilby, attempt to temper Thomas's insistence not only upon the human right in proprietary *acquisition*, but also upon the human right in proprietary *transaction* (i.e., liberty of contract), with the presumptively chastening Thomistic proposition that "the enjoyment of the fruits of the earth should be for all.... A man in dire necessity did not steal who helped himself from another's goods," Thomas Gilby, *St. Thomas Aquinas Philosophical Texts* (London: Oxford University Press. 1951), p. 156. Sadly, this has been popularly mischaracterized. But this caveat has always existed in the unabashedly property-affirming tradition of English common law, via the tort law "doctrine of necessity": for instance, in a storm, a ship's captain has the emergency-based right to dock even in a private dock. The point is that Thomas Aquinas's caveat is *not at all* averse to the "capitalist" sense of private property.

Liberty in the economic sense most often means *liberty of contract*,[291] the people's freedom to bargain over the terms of their own contracts without unnecessary governmental interference.

Once we have affirmed, alongside Thomas Aquinas, that it is altogether natural and even necessary for man to hold private property (personal, real, financial, intellectual, labor, etc.), we acknowledge that it is equally natural for man to dispose of his property however he deems most profitable. Thomas Aquinas called this dual capacity *potestas procurandi et dispensandi*: the "power of acquiring and administering things."[292] For thousands of years, such disposal of property has been accomplished through the liberty of contract.

Crucially, Thomas names *two* powers: acquiring *and* administering property!

[291] In the Constitutional sense, liberty of contract is arguably the realm in which the right (i.e., liberty) appears at its most morally defensible: government should not interfere with the terms of contracts arranged between two individuals.

[292] *Summa Theologiae* II-II, 66, 2. Brian Tierney writes of this passage: "Aquinas wrote of 'natural dominion' that belonged to humans because of their faculty of reason 'in which the image of God consists.' He also wrote that it was by virtue of human free will, through which a man was master of his own acts, that he could be master of external things also. Aquinas explained that private property was an acceptable and necessary way of exercising man's natural dominion because common property was easily neglected and could give rise to confusion and discord. It was fitting, therefore, that external goods should be held by individuals as regards 'the power of acquiring and administering things,' but as regards use, they ought to be treated as common in the sense that they were to be shared with those in need." Brian Tierney, *The Idea of Natural Rights: Studies on Natural Rights, Natural Law, and Church Law, 1150–1625* (William B. Eerdmans, 1997).

Whether we are talking about a purchase-and-sale contract, a rental contract, an employment contract, an easement contract, or a business agreement, we are really talking only about the means by which two parties transact their *property*. And as we've already seen, subsidiarity requires that, ordinarily, the government should not interfere with such private parties or their decisions.

Contracting is fair because of free will: adults of sound mind should be able to *take their own risks*.[293]

Think of the famous 1984 NBA draft class: Michael Jordan was selected by the Chicago Bulls after—*after!*—the Portland Trailblazers passed up the opportunity to draft Jordan by selecting Sam Bowie instead. Bowie never became a star; Jordan, conversely, appeared on the cover of *Sports Illustrated* ("A Star is Born!") just one month into his career. He eventually won the Rookie of the Year award and, of course, would go on to win five Most Valuable Player awards. The Trailblazers could not, one month into the season, renege on their contract with Bowie and demand to take Jordan away from the Bulls. The fact that

---

[293] Opponents of capitalism, i.e., central-planning advocates of all stripes, fail to see the importance of the fundamental conditions of contracts: *temporality* and *contingency*. All bargains are struck in real time (temporality) and with no guarantees (contingency). Uncertainty marks human existence, and it equally affects both parties to every bargain. Almost always, one side winds up with the better end of the bargain, of course. But even so, contracts are still fair. Determining who came out "on top" is possible only afterward. Thus, it is only fair to honor the temporality, contingency, and yes—even the pure dumb luck—that go into the making of every bargain.

Capitalism does just that. On the other hand, central-planning systems seek to do away with it by unfairly reallocating the contract's benefits retrospectively.

the choice to select Jordan was originally the Blazers' to make is, of course, utterly immaterial. On account of the elements of temporality and contingency in the NBA draft, the Blazers made (historically speaking) the *wrong* selection and the Bulls made the *right* selection.

Temporality and contingency: capitalism is morally superior to central planning (i.e., all other political economies) since it alone honors these dimensions of real life, just as it alone honors the rights of liberty and property. Opponents of free markets, inside and outside Catholicism, refuse to countenance that plain fact.

In *Rerum Novarum*, Pope Leo XIII admitted the implications of human liberty: *bargains must be honored*! In one of the most famous lines from the encyclical, he says: "Let the working man and the employer make free agreements, and in particular let them freely agree as to the wages." While Pope Leo admitted that "if through necessity or fear of a worse evil the workman accepts harder conditions because an employer or contractor will afford him no better, he is made the victim of force and injustice" (45), Pope Leo was *not* saying that bargains between men should not be honored. He was merely saying that employers should act justly.

Article 1, section 10 of the U.S. Constitution discusses private contracts in the same terminology: the government there *admits* that it cannot "impair the obligation of contract." In other words, state governments cannot dissolve, abridge, interfere with, or interrupt existing contracts between private parties. (Today, of course, big-government American courts have reinterpreted that phrase to mean that, somehow, it *can* do these things: the landmark Supreme Court case *Blaisdell* said so!)[294]

[294] Home Building and Loan Association v. Blaisdell 290 U.S. 398 (1934).

The requirements of subsidiarity could not be any clearer. As noted in chapter 2 of this book, Pope Pius XI said in *Quadragesimo Anno* that

> just as it is gravely wrong to take from individuals what they can accomplish by their own initiative and industry and give it to the community, so also it is an injustice and at the same time a grave evil and disturbance of right order to assign to a greater and higher association what lesser and subordinate organizations can do. (79)

Take a moment and absorb that strong statement in the context of private contracts. *Any* assignment to government of a task capable of being done by a smaller association, like the family, is a grave evil!

In other words, it is "gravely wrong" for government needlessly to transfer *decision-making* from individuals to the community. And the rationale of subsidiarity is the same in the realms of *property* and *liberty of contract* (which is a subset of property): individuals and families were appointed by God for just this type of moral agency, the responsible acquisition and the transaction of property. Government was not! Government was constructed in order to *defend* this type of familial independence — and not much else.

So, governmental nonintervention in contracts is premised upon self-determination[295] and upon subsidiarity's interplay with the three natural rights.

[295] In contract law, self-determination is referred to as the "bargain theory" of contract: it stands for the idea that contracts function best under the "adversarial" system, whereby the greatest approximation of justice will be done by a system in which each party represents itself against others.

CATHOLIC REPUBLIC

Governmental nonintervention, it turns out, was not at all based upon Enlightenment theories of self-ownership,[296] as is

[296] This is the only major issue I can imagine upon which I would venture to disagree with Dr. Edward Feser: What has generally been called "libertarianism," mislabeled much more often than not, in its true form should not be premised upon Enlightenment theories of self-ownership, but rather upon the enumerated self-limitation of government power. All theories of governmental minimalism should be based upon government's inferior role within conflicting spheres of influence, governmental and popular. Even in a citizen's mildly vicious activities that do *not* exercise some natural right — let alone the citizen's righteous exercise of natural rights such as the liberty of contract — the enumerated nature of the federal government's power restrains its own purview to interfere (unless a specific or exceptional power to interfere had been enumerated, of course, like the most unfortunate Sixteenth Amendment to the U.S. Constitution). Theologically, the restriction on government power is a reflection of the very nature of authority. The restriction is premised on the government's inability, relative to the contrasting ability of the family and the father, to teach moral lessons. This means that so-called self-ownership is irrelevant.

In fact, the central government's inability to teach morals is so complete that its few legitimate enumerated exercises of power must be based on exigencies such as war or crime, according to Thomas Aquinas, not upon moral pedagogy. These are indeed the only two mentions that Thomas Aquinas makes of the legitimate operation of central government (alongside the reasonable reimbursement of civil servants via taxation). While it is incontrovertible that "one has no right to do wrong," as many Divine Command theorists are quick to point out, many wrongs must remain *legal* simply because the government lacks the moral and logistical power to regulate them. The wrongdoing actor or contractor in such situations will, presumptively, be held accountable *on the other side of the eschaton*, but not on this side. Augustine, Aquinas, and Pope Leo XIII all agree that not all venial sins ought to be regulated or admonished

sometimes asserted by Catholics. One does not have to "own oneself" in order to assert that governmental authority should be restrained. Why not? Because Catholic Natural Law's rule of subsidiarity (and emphasis on family authority) does not avail the government sufficient power to interfere with any of the three fundamental rights, except as a last resort—even if human beings do not "own themselves."

In other words, capitalism alone (among all political economies) fails to violate the Natural Law in these fundamental ways.

Subsidiarity Forgotten: Capitalism Blamed for Consumerism and Careerism

So, capitalism proper is not the problem. In America today, Prot-Enlight abuses and perversions of it constitute the problem. Only the Catholic view can put material goods and services into their proper priority, maintaining Weber's (and Baxter's) view of them as a "light cloak" that can at any moment be tossed aside by its unattached wearer.

Such a view requires the proper economic outlook, which itself requires a proper role of government. As chapter 2 showed,

---

by government: this semi-positivist delimiting of legislative power is uniquely consistent with the concept of subsidiarity (unlike Enlightenment self-ownership theories). As seen in chapter 1, Locke's plagiarism of hated Catholicism and his self-contradicting Protestant Whiggism (which by its discomfiture between goal and means *requires* said plagiarism) should be grounds for a general dismissal of his scholarship.

If that is not enough, then the obvious wrongness of his corpuscularianism, empiricist epistemology, crypto-materialism, and now, his unessential theory of self-ownership as the basis for "classical liberalism" ... should be sufficient to "cover the spread."

divine fatherhood is the nature of true authority—and the best image of earthly authority.

So, when one turns to the question of political economy—a subset of the family—it seems strange to find so many Catholics joining the secular Left in identifying our American economic problems as the fault of capitalism and not the family. Unlike the secular Left, these Catholics have at hand the social teaching of subsidiarity, under which all problems that can be solved at home (including economic ones) must be solved there.

How strange that those who caused the problem, the Prot-Enlights, blame the economic system for their own errors!

The blame should be cast upon the pseudo-capitalism being administered in Prot-Enlight America: evidently, families today are not teaching their children how to be moral producers and consumers. As long as a system protects economic freedom, one can be certain that its moral problems must be based on bad *individual* choices (which misspend that freedom).

Economic problems within a free economy are certainly fixable, at home through fatherly teaching. Just as certainly, they are *incapable* of being solved by the lawmaking powers of the government. Because these are problems of materialism, they are moral problems.

Goods and services in the American marketplace should not be seen as existing for their own sake. Material goods are merely a means to a nobler end: human flourishing, which depends upon morality. When a republic's people begin to believe that material goods are more important than they are, those people will become enslaved to the acquisition of such goods. That is *materialism*. Material goods should not be seen as items of such great value that one goes headlong into debt over them—that is *profligacy*. And such goods should not be fetishized so as to fill gaps in the moral and spiritual life—that is *smuttiness*.

From the moral perspective, within capitalism there are only two possible kinds of economic problems: supply-side abuse and demand-side abuse. They are an economy's only possible problems. America suffers from both kinds.

A basketball coach sarcastically quipped after a bad loss by his team, "Well, we had only two problems during the game tonight: *bad offense* and *bad defense*."

That's us. That's the American misunderstanding of economy.

The supply-side problem of American Prot-Enlight has already been discussed in the sections above: *careerism* is the new term described (but not used) by Max Weber. Out of a lack of deference to the sacraments, the head of a household comes to sacralize his career. Even as he probably began that career with his family's good in mind, his Prot-Enlight view of Matrimony, wealth, and labor transformed his career into his dearest focal point. He mistakenly came, as Weber indicated, to think of his *career* rather than his *family* as his vocation.

Thereby, career became the thing most treasured by the Prot-Enlight man, like the wedding ring more cherished by the unfaithful bride than her marriage itself.

Careerism is identifiable as the supply-side American problem because the career of the head of the household *supplies* the family's wealth, which enables the purchase of demand-side goods and services. While such a career is just as necessary for the sustenance of the family as the products it furnishes, the materialism of Prot-Enlight enlarges the importance of the material and diminishes the importance of the spiritual.

This brings us to the demand-side abuses in our Prot-Enlight American economy: *consumerism*. Consumerism fails to place material goods and services into their proper context, a critical task that only the Catholic view can accomplish. The Catholic view, uniquely, equates material goods to Weber's (and Baxter's) "light cloak"—useful but utterly expendable.

Our flawed (i.e., Prot-Enlight) American market demands are reducible to the three above-mentioned sub-traits of consumerism, which drastically overestimate the value of material goods: *materialism, profligacy,* and *smuttiness.*

In earlier chapters, we saw that Thomas Aquinas prefigured the robust defense of liberty and property rights (which today make up a free economy based upon subsidiarity).

As we saw in chapter 2, Thomas Aquinas affirms that kids belong to parents, not the state; not all virtue is capable of being legislated; financial and real property is personal rather than public (even if Catholic Natural Law bids us to share extra material goods); the main point of central government is martial law and the punishment of the criminal, and nothing more.

Thus, we have examined in various chapters how all these Thomistic factors together imply an unplanned economy and a minimalist government. The solutions of Thomas Aquinas are not big-government legislation and rule from afar, but rather, personal moderation and self-restraint.

So let's look at Thomas's solution for consumerism in societies (like ours) engorged by consumption. Thomas's "Five Ways of Gluttony,"[297] which deal with *literal* overconsumption, is the best medieval analogy for *figurative* overconsumption (in the marketplace). By examining these five ways of gluttony, we can see all the angles of Prot-Enlight consumerism.[298]

---

[297] Thomas Aquinas. *Summa Theologiae* II-II, 148.

[298] Since nuanced market economies were only a shadow of thought during Thomas's time, Thomas's treatment of gluttony can be used as an analogy to show how Thomas would characterize our economic overconsumption. Thomas locates not one, but

Materialism, in its narrower sense, is encapsulated in the first of Thomas's five ways of gluttony: *ardenter*—that is, consuming *too eagerly*. When one consumes, literally or figuratively, too eagerly, he attempts to make the object of his consumption into a source of profound and lasting joy. Material goods alone cannot confer an ounce of real joy. But material goods and services, when properly contextualized, certainly augment the real joys of human life. One sees how the way of *ardenter* characterizes American life today: the consumer is simply too eager to take his pocketbook to the marketplace.

Material wealth does not, as the Calvinists believed, accurately reflect, according to Catholic Natural Law, those who are saved and those who are not. In fact, Christ's parable of the rich fool (Luke 12:16–21) tells quite the opposite story from Calvin's notion of wealth-evidenced piety: "You fool!"

God said to the rich man. "You fool, this night your life will be demanded of you; and the things you have prepared, to whom will they belong?" At the end of the parable, Christ concludes, "Thus will it be for the one who stores up treasure for himself but is not rich in what matters to God." (Luke 12:20–21).[299]

---

five ways of committing the sin of gluttony—and these same five ways of overconsumption in the marketplace apply.

[299] The lines preceding these read:

Someone in the crowd said to him, "Teacher, tell my brother to share the inheritance with me." He replied to him, "Friend, who appointed me as your judge and arbitrator?" Then he said to the crowd, "Take care to guard against all greed, for though one may be rich, one's life does not consist of possessions."

Then he told them a parable. "There was a rich man whose land produced a bountiful harvest. He asked himself, 'What shall I do, for I do not have space to store my

The parable warns us against the particularly subtle, if under-standable, human tendency to stockpile, to try to take shelter from life's pains through material goods. Our single shelter should instead be the solace of Christ Himself. One must be very cautious about stockpiling, because — especially for family men — it runs very near to an advisable form of provision gathering. But one must always recall: "Wherever your heart lies, there is your treasure" (see Matt. 6:21).

Profligacy is encapsulated (somewhat redundantly) in the second, third, and fourth of Thomas's five ways of gluttony: *prae-propere*, *laute*, and *nimis*. That is: consuming *too soon*, *too expensively*, and *too much*. The profligate spender makes purchases too soon, before he has saved up the money for his purchase. He also makes purchases too expensively; even if he has saved up enough money to avoid debt, his purchases will usually cost too much. Finally, the profligate spender makes purchases too much of the time; he spends money too often, as a sort of pastime. Recognizing each of these three aspects of profligacy — *prae-propere*, *laute*, *nimis* — helps us to recognize what is essential to today's American consumerism, a substitution of material for spiritual wealth.

Smuttiness is encapsulated in the fifth and final of Thomas's five ways of gluttony: *studiose*. That is: *consuming too daintily*. In an abundant Prot-Enlight economy, products cease to be seen as useful commodities and come instead to be *picked among* as status symbols and "regarded with awe as being the embodiment of a potent spirit or as having magical potency."

---

harvest?' And he said, 'This is what I shall do: I shall tear down my barns and build larger ones. There I shall store all my grain and other goods and I shall say to myself, "Now as for you, you have so many good things stored up for many years, rest, eat, drink, be merry!"'" (Luke 12:13–19)

In other words, such products become *fetishes* (the definition of which appears in the previous sentence). Paradoxically, overly dainty consumption by the average consumer within the American economy leads to a fetishized version of goods and services. Not long after a society becomes a commodity-fetishizing one will it become a pornography-embracing one: after you begin by deifying objects, you end by objectifying people. The market for the basest human instinct, the sexual drive, will get accessed most grotesquely of all. In both cases — literal and figurative smuttiness — material goods are surrogated for spiritual and moral ones.

But if we cut away from American capitalist economy its Prot-Enlight careerism (i.e., sacralized labor) and consumerism (i.e., materialism, profligacy, and smuttiness), what, if any, portion remains? Will there remain a truer capitalist system, manifesting *proper moral and economic behavior, consistent with subsidiarity?*

Absolutely.

And this residual space will be identifiable as *Catholic capitalism,* regardless of what you call it.

The Confusing Proposition of Distributivism

In the name of a greater goal, I told a "white lie" above: "the simplest way to view political economy is through recourse to the three natural rights."

That was one simple and clear approach to political economy. But the *very simplest* approach to proving that all centrally planned economies are unacceptable morally is that they are variant forms of *moral consequentialism,* holding that the "end justifies the means," that, *if the goal is good enough, immoral acts are justifiable.*

Pursuing innately immoral means to achieve good ends is simply not allowed by Catholic moral theology. Irrespective of good intent, intrinsically wrong acts are always and categorically wrong.[300]

Now, all the many forms of central-planning economies claim to justify governmental stripping of liberty and property. The kind of central planning at question matters not. There are lots of different ostensible strains of it. But as Father Merrin in the 1973 film *The Exorcist* says (about the many names of Satan): "There is only one." Any political economy that strips the individual of his rights of private property and contract liberty is an economic form of *consequentialism*, attempting to make right out of wrong.[301]

One form of mid-twentieth-century economic consequentialism has re-arisen in the Catholic world with a dangerous enthusiasm: *distributivism* (or *distributism*). This form was endorsed by Catholic luminaries such as G. K. Chesterton and Hilaire Belloc and has falsely entranced many Catholics in the name of "subsidiarity" and "family." For this reason, distributivism merits our special attention at the moment.

---

[300] "But the negative moral precepts, those prohibiting certain concrete actions or kinds of behavior as intrinsically evil, do not allow for any legitimate exception. They do not leave room, in any morally acceptable way, for the 'creativity' of any contrary determination whatsoever. Once the moral species of an action prohibited by a universal rule is concretely recognized, the only morally good act is that of obeying the moral law and of refraining from the action which it forbids." John Paul II, *Veritatis Splendor* (August 6, 1993), no. 67.

[301] We saw earlier how even governmental abrogation of a private contract involves, at one level or another, the public appropriation of private property. This is nothing more, as Saints Augustine and Aquinas acknowledged, than legalizing "massive robbery" by the state.

Although difficult to pin down in a straightforward definition by its advocates, here is one of the most recent versions of
distributivism:

> Put succinctly, distributivism was the name that Belloc and
> Chesterton gave to the version of subsidiarity that they
> were advocating in their writings.... Unlike the socialists,
> the distributivists were not advocating the redistribution
> of "wealth" per se.... Instead, and the difference is crucial,
> they were advocating the redistribution of the means of
> production to as many people as possible.[302]

As above, distributivists regularly contrast their views with
those of other collectivists by pointing out, as above, that they
favor *universal* private-property ownership. Socialists, they correctly highlight, would not do this: socialists generally oppose
private ownership.

But the distributivists are never willing to say exactly *how*
universal property ownership should come to exist. Universal
ownership is not the present case. So the method of its achieve-
ment remains a mystery.

But not really.

In the passage quoted above, our distributivist author admits
all we need to hear, saying, "They were advocating the redistribution of the means of production." We infer that this indicates
government action: *government distributes private property to all* (by
taking from certain private-property holders and giving to others).

Here is the problem for the distributivists: Pope Leo XIII dealt
specifically and conclusively with such government action: "It is
surely undeniable that, when a man engages in remunerative labor,

---

[302] Pearce, "What Is Distributism?"

the impelling reason and motive of his work is *to obtain property* [emphasis added] and thereafter to hold it as his very own."[303]

Pope Leo XIII thus anticipates and rejects the distributivist argument: you work not only to *keep* property but first to *earn* it. Since man labors not only upon property already possessed, but in order "to obtain [said] property" in the *first place*, the distributivist premise is destroyed.

And at this point, even the most orthodox Catholic thinkers who advocate distributivism cannot avoid utopianism: *an ideal world of perfect equality and collectivism*. For example, the very same prominent distributivist quoted above, remarks:

> In an ideal world every man would own the land on which, and the tools with which, he worked. In an ideal world he would control his own destiny by having control over the means to his livelihood. For Belloc, this was the most important economic freedom, the freedom beside which all other economic freedoms are relatively trivial.[304]

Family, small business, small government, and subsidiarity are the watchwords on which the distributivists *claim* to hinge their project. But the unlimited amount of authority required by the government to force distribution stands as the perfect opposite of

---

[303] Leo XIII, *Rerum Novarum* 5. Nearby, Pope Leo XIII continues to narrow what he takes to be a distinction between the intelligent and the unintelligent members of creation: "What is of far greater moment, however, is the fact that the remedy they [socialists and collectivists] propose is manifestly against justice. For, every man has by nature the right to [labor, to endeavor to] possess property as his own. This is one of the chief points of distinction between man and the animal creation" (6).

[304] Pearce, "What Is Distributism?"

these four things (i.e., family, small business, small government, and subsidiarity). The *perfect* opposite.

In practical terms, the following would all be distributivist solutions to current problems: policies that establish a favorable climate for the establishment and subsequent thriving of small businesses, policies that bring real political power closer to the family by decentralizing power from central government to local government, from big government to small government.[305]

Yes, it would be fantastic if all of us possessed bullions of stock-piled gold and a swimmer's build. But we do not. If we *do* have those things — under a moral system, anyway — it is exclusively because we have earned them.

Moreover, the *policies* entailed by distributivism are never enumerated. Ask a distributivist, and he'll never answer how it all works (without a huge government). Only distributivism's allegedly miraculous *consequences* are ever listed. Instead of explaining what those distributivist policies are, or how they would bring about universal property ownership, distributivists are willing only to describe how rosy life with this "new" sort of "nonsocialist" collectivism would be.

In reality, this reticence about specifics is the very oldest trait of collectivism itself. Each time a new brand pops up, it focuses merely upon its desirable effects, and never upon the rights-stripping required to achieve such effects (or upon the certain aggrandization of the government to follow).

And all forms of collectivism slander capitalism in precisely the ways described at the beginning of this chapter.[306]

---

[305] Ibid.

[306] The term "capitalism" was actually a slur, in the first place, for our political economy by its critics. In reality, far better

CATHOLIC REPUBLIC

Because within the state of nature, all men are not born owning their own means of production (except hereditarily), a natural economy cannot *guarantee* ownership thereof. As in the passage above, the distributivists imply that the state should distribute the means of production universally. Of course, such distribution would involve both the state's interference with private property and private contracts: *voiding existent contracts and stealing private property.*

---

names for Karl Marx's slur "capitalism" are "natural economy" and "free enterprise." After all, what makes a free-enterprise economy natural is the fact that, within it, the government does not enjoy the power to interfere substantially in the economy of nature's assets. Within nature, the principles of scarcity and need motivate labor (just as the supernatural principle of charity motivates freely elected redistribution, i.e., charity). American capitalism has taken on precisely the monstrous image that Marx designed the slur to prefigure: a popular confusion of cultural problems such as careerism and consumerism for the role of political economy. And as our first four chapters show, the declining crypto-Catholic, Prot-Enlight republic of America has unduly helped to accelerate this confusion. Even if we all privately *root* for small businesses over big ones, the laws should be the same for the former and the latter. Natural justice demands that laws and principles apply universally. As such, the meaningful distinction between the public sector (i.e., the government) and the private sector (i.e., individual people and businesses) should be emphasized, not the distinction between "big business" and "small business." Natural economy favors not small business or big business over the other, but any private, legally operated enterprise over the rights-stripping power of the government. Justice, natural rights, and free will demand this. Any "new" political economy must concern itself with reconciling its premises with nature, which is left wanting with distributivism.

Power would thereby be centralized, not decentralized. The movement would enlarge, not minimize, government. It is more than a little bizarre that such minds as Belloc's and Chesterton's (and distributivism's modern proponent, Joseph Pearce) fail to see the patent cross-purposes at work between subsidiarity—"the principle at the heart of the forces of decentralization"—and distributivism, which further centralizes power in the government.[307]

Now, since distributivists never say exactly what their policies are, perhaps we could extend to them the benefit of the doubt: a certain kind of "distributivism," wherein property would be "redistributed" by freely elected private charity—instead of by the government—is just *properly functioning capitalism*[308] and

[307] Neither is the distinction between state distribution of wealth and state distribution of means of production meaningful. Finances, real estate, and personal property are all forms of "wealth," after all. So Pearce's distinction is really a distinction without a difference. Why and how does it matter whether the government, in order to give to Paul, steals Peter's money, his land, or his plow? All three constitute "robbing Peter to pay Paul."

[308] On the other hand, distributivism remains susceptible of another distinct meaning that, unlike its mainstream definition, would remain perfectly kosher, by the Catholic standards mentioned above. As long as the distributivists agree that government should not be given the power to interfere with private contracts or property, then indeed distributivism would describe a healthy functioning natural economy that Catholics and other anti-collectivists could endorse without hesitation or fear of collectivism. That is, it would be the system that we already enjoy, except perhaps reinvigorated by the cultural renewal (entailing even more charity) pushed for in all the other chapters of this book. In that case, the distributivist is not engaging in any new sort of economics, or even economics at all.

The distributivist, on that healthy (if unlikely) model, would simply be hoping for what is here hoped for: the eradication of

nothing more. To a limited extent, it already happens in capitalism every day, although a healthier republic would certainly bear
witness to even more charity than ours does. (To be fair, even
in the heyday of today's American secularism, America proves
year in and year out to be the most charitable country on earth.)

At its very best, distributivism *equals* natural economy—capitalism—under the renewed, moral, republican form of culture
described above. (We take no issue with that!) At its worst (and
most probable), it is the old beast: collectivism.

Conclusion: The Home Economy, Unexpected Feminism, and Free Enterprise

Before concluding chapter 5, there remains one final aspect of the
Prot-Enlight elimination of the natural community of family in
America that merits our attention. Just as today's America bears
witness to an overarching Prot-Enlight problem with manliness,
there stems from the same source a very severe problem with
American womanliness: *the combination of home economy and unexpected feminism*. It seems to extend from the materialism of Calvinism and secularism, described above, in the domestic context.

Feminism is all-pervasive in American culture. Although the
phenomenon is less *spoken of* now than in the culture of the late
1960s and early 1970s, it seems to be more securely *situated* within
the cultural mainstream. As such, feminism operates far more

---

careerism and consumerism within our already extant form of
capitalism! Such theorists would simply affirm what "capitalism"
set out to do within a healthy, nonmaterialist republic. But to
be sure, the perennial failure by the distributivists to articulate
which powers the government "deserves" makes one suspect
that there is no hope for such a healthy interpretation of the
movement's goals.

effectively, far more quietly. From TV commercials, to movies, to sitcoms, to sports, to the workplace, the American woman is expected to be outside the home. Women who remain at home to raise a family are hassled, discouraged, ridiculed, and even persecuted at every turn.

Most of this harassment is rather obvious to any moderately observant American today. But what merits the reader's attention is the wholly unexpected element of semi-Calvinist feminism found *even among the stay-at-home mothering culture*. In the toxic wake of the feminist movement, one notes a psychological defense mechanism by many of the non-feminists who opt for the mantle of traditionalism: they respond that their chosen homemaking *really is* a profession.

No, it is not!

As we saw in this chapter, it is infinitely *higher* than a profession: it is a vocation.

Therefore, on the basis of the homemaker's defensiveness against these constant onslaughts by the secular culture, the Calvinist premise of labor replaces the Catholic vocation — in the home as well as in the workplace (which we saw above). Consequently, the home is too often run "like a business." As such, the sacred vocation of mothering ends up mimicking the rote labor of the workplace. Of course, as a sanctified calling, *mothering* should be regarded as infinitely higher than, and completely different from, the workplace.

In other words, traditionalist mothers seem to have "protested too much" against their feminist detractors — viz., that "mothering is *indeed* a worthwhile, even a productive, profession" — and thereby desacralized it.

Why in the world would anyone lionize the boring shift they are forced, by the economic exigencies of life, to grind? Why would that same person criticize as "dull" the dynamic calling of motherhood? The situation should be the exact reverse, if anything: dull, rote labor should seek to emulate the ennobling and vibrant vocation of the home.

It is a strangely reversed appraisal of *what merits outright praise* (vocation) and *what merits mere toleration* (daily labor).

This modified form of domestic feminism seems to have produced the same toxic bromide as feminism proper: a war on men. Unhappy that not all women could be turned from the home to the workplace, the feminist movement evidently begrudgingly accepted its failure and winsomely adapted its critique to the household context. In the home, at least, they reason, a feminist critique of men can still be effective through the depiction of the *idiotic father figure* (in virtually every movie, show, or home-products commercial oriented toward the audience of the household mother). The *mother figure*, on the other hand, is depicted as the savvy, slim, and versatile "head" of the household.

Remember, this is just the bizarre byproduct of Calvinism and feminism, just as careerism is the bizarre byproduct of Calvinism and traditional masculinity.

All in all, the home and the family should be seen as both natural and supernatural, operating in a self-sustaining manner and residing at the very center of society. A society that puts family at its core will be marked by its natural economy (i.e., the *only* setup appropriate to republicanism and subsidiarity). This setup must be Catholic in its structure because it bears supernatural elements of the sacramental and natural elements of intelligible Catholic Natural Law principles such as rights, subsidiarity, morality, etc.

Outside of its Calvinist context, a capitalist political economy will not equate, as the secular Left alleges, to Upton Sinclair's

The Jungle—filthy, polluting smokestacks and all. Outside of its Enlightenment context, capitalism will not assume the look or feel of a filthy pornography hut. Outside of its Prot-Enlight double context of immoral consumerism and careerism, capitalism will take on a healthier relationship with the moral demands of both *buying* and *selling*.

The family teaches how to be a moral buyer and seller. In this sense, capitalism would be better represented by its seldom-used moniker, more consistent with Natural Law: "free enterprise."

Think of such free enterprise as a lemonade stand, run by little kids who use their parents' capital: lemons, water, and sugar. Their labor would deliver a nonguaranteed amount of profit, subject to all the contingencies of the curbside marketplace. This image includes all the important elements of subsidiarity: family property, private agreement between buyer and seller, and *total* governmental noninterference.

One would not expect the government to dictate to our child lemonade vendors how much (or how little) to sell their wares for or how many hours to work. Our young capitalists would attempt to earn as much money for their sold lemonade in as little time worked as possible. The inviolability of private agreements between vendor and vendee, along with the natural reasonable worth of lemonade to humans, is what ensures the eventually fetched price of their lemonade. (Along similar lines of thought, one would not expect our young capitalists to be "guaranteed" some minimal daily or hourly amount of profit: no possible guarantor—especially not the government—could capably make such a promise. Free enterprise dictates that attempting to do this would be as immoral as it would be impracticable.)

For example, when that initial twenty-dollar asking price for a glass of over-sugared brew inevitably fails, our fast-learning young vendors would certainly take the hint and gradually reduce the price to that which *nature has appointed* for lemonade (which is, of course, a flexible range rather than a precise amount).[309] This independence from external, governmental manipulation is what designates a free economy, one consistent with Catholic Natural Law.[310]

If one asserts in response to our example of the lemonade stand that it is not a capitalism-representative model because it's too childish, then let's bring it into a more common *adult* setting (common here in Central California, anyway): say, a family fruit stand. Here, the operative subsidiarity exercised by the vendors grows *stronger*, not weaker, than in our lemonade example.

Usually, small vendors operate on "the family economy," meaning that members of the family exclusively maintain their enterprise: reaping and sowing the fruit, transporting it to the stand, "manning" the stand throughout the day, electing a price structure, arranging the "wages" of the family's children, etc.

The schedule of the family stand will be reasonably influenced by both *business* and *nonbusiness* factors. In rendering managerial decisions, the "bosses" of the fruit stand, presumably the parents of the family, will automatically take into consideration the family exigencies of such things as holidays, time off, the extenuating

---

[309] "When," one asks, "will that natural price become apparent, signaling to its vendors to stop dropping the figure for a cup of lemonade?" Well, of course, when cars begin to stop and make purchases! That's when.

[310] Remember, Robin Hood did not "steal from the rich and give to the poor." He recovered from the king's tax collector and restored to the overtaxed middle classes. How deftly the secular Left modifies one or two words, and thereby turns a conservative fantasy into a liberal one!

circumstances of "employees" (i.e., children), and the allocation of the various duties.

As such, the family will be both productive and self-sustaining with virtually no input from legislative bodies, which would only serve to hinder the thriving fruit stand. *Importantly, the rules of fairness demand that the same standards of governmental non-interference should govern the ideal—small, family businesses—and the less-than-ideal—non-family businesses!*

These examples bear all the marks that ought to be demanded by any Catholic set of economic standards. This means consistency with the sacredness of private liberty and private property, the temporality and contingency of all bargains, subsidiarity, free will, and natural community.

In the context of Catholic Natural Law, we already know that the single natural community with supernatural implications (i.e., family) is a uniquely sacramental-vocational concept. But this also means, in the realm of the economy, that the self-regulated blend of productivity and spirituality can be achieved by the family's economic teamwork. Industry and family are *not* truly opposed as they are seen to be in the Prot-Enlight context—especially when the "bosses" have a parental relation to their workers. The bosses of the family enterprise are in the perfect position to "make the call" as to what needs to be done on any given day.[311] But once again, the same balance can be achieved in any

---

[311] But just because the family economy represents the most harmonious instance of subsidiarity within a system of free enterprise, it does not necessarily follow that today's more common subset of specialized labor, implying a single breadwinner, cuts against subsidiarity. It does not mean this at all. It just means that the breadwinning father will be away from the family (and usually, the neighborhood, the third natural community) as he works

CATHOLIC REPUBLIC

workplace—not only small or family businesses—under the guidance of Catholic Natural Law.

Now that the reader has come to understand the distinguishing marks of the "non-consumerist" (i.e., moral) consumer—and the consumerist marks of the immoral one—he is ready to take on the crypto-Catholic republican element of proper science and technology. This realm involves the most cutting edge and the most dangerous aspect of American consumerism. Today, this represents perhaps the "hottest" market issue, the *most* susceptible of Prot-Enlight perversion, misunderstanding, and corruption.

---

during the day, which is less than ideal. Ideally, one should work at or immediately near his home. But under even the "commuter" model, the principle of governmental noninterference obtains, just as the sovereignty of family subsidiarity remains. Subsidiarity is harmed only when the government, on the basis of legislative interference, begins assigning to individuals and families, jobs, product prices, wages, and real or personal or financial property.

254

Chapter 6

Staking the New Regime in the American Culture

The Crypto-Catholicism of Science and Technology

It is the steady, ongoing, never-slackening fight against skepticism and dogmatism, against unbelief and superstition, which religion and science wage together. The directing watchword in this struggle runs from the remotest past to the distant future: "On to God!"

—Max Planck

All hope cannot be pinned on science, technology, economic growth. The victory of technological civilization has instilled in us a spiritual insecurity. Its gifts enrich but enslave us as well.

—Alexandr Solzhenitsyn

By this final chapter, it has been well established that America is in steep decline. In concert with the previous five symptoms of decline in our crypto-Catholic culture, our twenty-first-century republic in name only has traded its formerly Protestant religious faith for something called Enlightenment scientism — the pseudo-scientific outlook of the secular Left.

In essence, American scientism is a fundamentalist doctrine that places quasi-religious faith in science alone, just as once-Protestant America believed in the Bible alone.

American *sola scriptura*, one might say, became *sola scientia*. While the reader probably already recognizes *that* this happened, at this point, this chapter will explain how, why, and *to what effect*.

Scientism is the post-Enlightenment belief that physical science will eventually solve all the problems of mankind. It runs closely alongside the moral relativism we discussed in chapter 3 and the secular humanism described in chapter 4. Along with every other dimension of the Prot-Enlight American apostasy—the withdrawal from Catholic Natural Law—discussed in this book, no true republic can survive by assuming that only the dictates of the five senses are true.

Scientism warrants a full response from the Catholic Natural Law (which is *not* encompassed within this short chapter!). This chapter highlights the crypto-Catholic element of *science and technology* in American culture. Until very recently, the only "loud and proud" response to Enlightenment science has come from its hated twin rival: American Protestantism. And that response has been vastly insufficient and even counterproductive at winning over the undecided American hearts and minds.

Only the *true science* of Catholic Natural Law can respond properly to the popular set of ideas embodied by scientism. However they may try, American Protestants can make practically no rejoinder whatsoever against Enlightenment science, since, as we saw in the Introduction, the two worldviews reject all three prongs of Catholic Natural Law: *human nature as free, and nature as intelligible and goal oriented*. Together, both halves of Prot-Enlight assume Catholic Natural Law to be false, except, of course, that Protestants aim to retain belief in Christ.

You can't do that.

As we saw in the last chapter, the Catholic answer to scientism lies in correcting the so-called scientific novelty of the early Enlightenment. This chapter will promptly tend to that, showing that anything "new" to the scientific outlook of the sixteenth and seventeenth centuries was not *improvement* but *error*.

One more word of caution: while scientism is a worldview held by *some* scientists, we must remember that many practicing scientists reject the viewpoint's implicit materialism. Many embrace the same meaningful view of nature put forward in this book. (That is to say, a significant portion of scientists affirm Catholic Natural Law.) For example, one Catholic philosopher of science, William A. Wallace, wrote: "A mathematical physics—to use the modern term—was for [Saint Thomas] a very real possibility, even if he had but the most rudimentary knowledge of how it could one day achieve the results we now associate with it."[312]

A few of the following theistic scientists were Christian, and a couple were even Catholic: Gottfried Leibniz, father of calculus; Max Planck, father of modern physics; André-Marie Ampère, discoverer of electrical current; Alessandro Volta, discoverer of the first battery; Albert Einstein, father of the theories of relativity; and Monsignor Georges Henri Joseph Lemaître, formulator of the Big Bang theory.

It should also be remembered that scientism is a *popular viewpoint* subscribed to mostly by nonscientists, among today's entertainment-obsessed consumers. It has become the default position of the *hoi polloi*—the uncritical, *received* viewpoint promoted in

---

[312] W. Wallace, "A Thomistic Philosophy of Nature," in *From a Realist Point of View: Essays in the Philosophy of Science*, 2nd ed. (Lanham, MD: University Press of America, 1983), p. 39.

anti-religious entertainment, television, and news. Such popular presentations of the natural world uncritically assume science and technology to be superior to the classical, Natural Law view of the universe (rejecting the three prongs of Catholic Natural Law by viewing nature as unfree, unintelligible, and nonteleological). In short, most people do not know why this is their point of view and could not defend it if they tried.

Most do not. Those who do so, do so badly.

Even scientists who affirm scientism are wrong, of course. This chapter will demonstrate as much. The topic of *causation — the relationship between cause and effect — must be the centerpiece* of any discussion of science or theology (or any other self-respecting academic discipline, for that matter). And typically, scientists who affirm scientism have a profoundly impoverished understanding of causation. As the secular Left regularly says in criticism of the religious Right, one can pose a proposition or theory only by reasonably showing how it has been *caused*. This is our criticism of the secular Left's scientism: they don't follow their own advice!

In America, the army of proponents of scientism have pushed their militant, fundamentalist worldview *without the ability to explain science's primary engine*: the principle of causation. As such, they have created a hollow devotion to something they call "science" and an even hollower obsession with its primary fruit, technology. Therefore, we close our critique of American Prot-Enlight with its creation of a technology cult.

The Ridiculousness of Denying Causation

Here in our final chapter — finally, officially — we defend the religious Right from the secular Left. In a delicious twist of irony, the principle of causation *condemns* the latter and *vindicates* the former.

To embrace causation—as secular Left scientism *claims* it does—is to embrace all the causes in a sequence, including the first cause of the universe: a.k.a. a creation by a Creator. (This does not vindicate the premise of the Protestant brand of Creationism—just its end.) While we will not delve too specifically into either the science or the philosophy of science, it suffices here to show that denying the existence of a first cause, as scientism does, is to pose a logical impossibility, an "infinite regression" (which denies that all causal series *must have* a first cause).

Given the elementary truth that all series of causes must be traceable back to a first cause, pre-Christian Aristotle held that such a first cause must be a "prime mover"[313] or an "unmoved mover," God. In other words, if one embraces the principle of causation at all, then it cannot *break down* (even at the beginning of time): some *beginning force* must have caused the first material thing in the world to come into existence. By definition, that first cause must have been outside space and time.

This much is beyond dispute, although the proponents of scientism stubbornly and superstitiously dispute it. Once one admits that much, embracing Divine Creation is tantamount to embracing our Catholic version of causation—creation *ex nihilo*, "out of nothing." In view of this, scientism reduces to the comical absurdity: *In the beginning there was nothing ... which exploded.* Only one element separates this superstitious scientism from the correct position: they're missing the middle step, God.

This Patristic (A.D. 300–500) concept, creation *ex nihilo*, received scientific confirmation over fourteen hundred years later, by Monsignor Lemaître's twentieth-century findings about the

[313] Aristotle, *Metaphysics* 1073a14–15.

"Big Bang." Literally, the universe came from nothing. Inconvenient as this may be for a worldview such as scientism, with foregone commitments to an uncreated universe, the "basics" of the Catholic Natural Law viewpoint are (at this point) virtually beyond doubt. It is a "done deal."

It turns out to be more than a little vindicating for such Patristic thinkers like Saint Augustine, who espoused creation *ex nihilo* long before science proved him right.

Similarly, so-called quantum mechanics is today confirming the Catholic point of view regarding the Creator's observation of and interaction with His creation. As Catholics, we refer to God as "Creator *and* Sustainer." Above, we pointed at science's proof of God as Creator out of Nothing; here, we point at its proof of God as Observing Sustainer.

Thomas Aquinas suggested that the universe requires an intelligent, creative Observer: God. This Thomistic concept is still receiving newer and newer scientific confirmation, 750 years later.

Thomas Aquinas's holistic view is best characterized by the very title of his most important work: *Summa*. It means "everything." The main idea of the *Summa* is that, compared with theological truth, scientific truth is totally, equally true, in differing ways: *science always arrives later to the party than philosophy and theology, is all.* Better late than never.

Catholic Natural Law holds that the truths uniting theology and science are inseparable. Properly done, each centers on causation. Improperly done, which is to say, done from the Protestant or the Enlightenment perspective, bad theology and science strip themselves of their commitment to causation (and thereby, to one another).

Consequently, mysticism and superstition come to characterize both Prot-Enlight halves.

Once more: *to embrace causation is simply to embrace the inevitable fact of Creation itself.* A material universe exists; something *not material* must have caused it. But modern, atheist scientism reduced itself to Enlightenment witchcraft by positing that causal sequences somehow "miraculously" broke down in respect to the universe's *great, godless beginning.* As noted above, infinite regressions are logically impossible,[314] although proponents of scientism seem to have forgotten that fact.

Each of these denials renders Prot-Enlight science ridiculous. But at this point in American culture, only the Protestant scientific position has been called such. It turns out to be far less ridiculous than the position of scientism.

Formal Cause and Final Cause

Let's now take a big step back and recall that America was once an overwhelmingly Protestant nation. From the Protestant point of view, which constantly quibbles with scientism in our era, science *seems* to make God look less and less plausible.

For a century and a half, the Protestant viewpoint dominated popular culture; now the Enlightenment outlook has overtaken it. While the "lead" has changed, American "intellectual" culture is still ruled by surges of the *Enlightenment-science versus Reformation-faith* debate. Most folks still define their positions as either one of the two extremes.

"Pick your poison," America concludes: reason or faith, science or the Bible. Obviously, this is a false dichotomy. As with

---

[314] Secular science quibbles with the first half of that proposition—concerning causation's demand for a beginning and a Creator; the Protestants quibble with the second half—concerning Divine Creation's implication of Catholic Natural Law.

all the other symptoms of decay in Prot-Enlight America, things cannot continue this way for much longer.

On account of the Protestant commitment to *sola scriptura*, the religious Right fearfully seeks to deny many advances of modern science;[315] after all, modern scientific innovation cannot be found in the Bible. Such a denial has worked the unintended consequence of a popular perception that Christianity *in general* fears scientific truth. But popular culture in America fails to recognize that not *all* forms of Christianity fear science.

Remember, the Catholic Church advances a view of nature that supposes its purposeful design and its intelligibility. These are the very conditions that good science requires, allowing (1) *a purposeful set of measurements* (2) *observed and theorized about intelligently*. Failing either element, science (or theology, for that matter) simply cannot be done. Without purpose and intelligibility, it cannot seek meaningful truth.

And this is where both Protestant Creationism and Enlightenment scientism come up short.[316]

---

[315] Although the Protestants agree with the Church as to the origin of the world—i.e., God indeed created the universe by and through Christ—they disagree with the Church as to the knowability of Creation—and the knowability of Creation's purpose.

[316] Catholic Natural Law assumes a goal-oriented view of nature: it is purposeful and points to some ultimate truths of the universe, as clues left by a Creator. Catholicism also assumes an intelligible view of nature, meaning that if we are clever enough "scientific gumshoes," we can make some natural theological meaning of the universe. This is, again, a simple review of the three prongs explained in the introduction. Thus, a Catholic Natural Law view carries with it both the reasonableness and the goal orientedness of nature, a proposition that describes the second and the third dimensions of Catholic Natural Law described in the introduction: nature as intelligible and nature

Scientism was inaugurated in the sixteenth to seventeenth centuries by the "Baconian turn" of science, named after Enlightenment scientist Francis Bacon. By eliminating the two important types of causality, Bacon altered the basic assumptions of science forever: "Man, the servant and interpreter of nature, does and understands only as much as he has observed, by fact or mental activity, concerning the order of nature; beyond that he has neither knowledge nor power."[317] Science became the realm of observing and recording only.

By its own admission, the new study of nature, physical science, *meant nothing.* Stripped of the Aristotelian view of nature's purpose and meaning (i.e., final and formal causes), Bacon asked: Why should the study of nature do anything more than measure physical properties of things, as useful to man? He thought that science should be altogether stripped of any reference to final and formal cause. So whether it was justified or not, he "purified" science of all connection to theology, philosophy, metaphysics, or meaning:

> For as we divided natural philosophy in general into the inquiry of causes and productions of effects, so that part which concerneth the inquiry of causes we do subdivide according to the received and sound division of causes. The one part, which is physic, inquireth and handleth the material and efficient causes; and the other, which is metaphysic, handleth the formal and final causes.[318]

---

as teleological. In other words, the Catholic faith holds that properly done science is true, but constantly urges us to a study of theology and of the final end of the universe.

[317] Francis Bacon, *Novum Organum Scientiarum* (1620), Aphorism 1.
[318] Francis Bacon, *The Works of Lord Bacon: The Second Book of the Proficience and Advancements of Learning, Divine and Moral* (London: Henry G. Bohn, 1854).

The Catholic Natural Law approach honors all four of Aristotle's causes: *material, efficient, formal,* and *final.* Four causes can be detected in every academic discipline, from theology and science to philosophy and sociology. As a matter of fact, the four causes can be discerned in any effect one sets out to study. Presently, we will examine how this failure on the part of Enlightenment scientism—in both reasonableness and goal orientedness—relates to two of the four types of causes described by Aristotle.

Think of these four causes in two groups: *two more important* (formal and final cause) and *two less important* (material and efficient cause). Indispensable to our exposé of Enlightenment scientism is the deliberate deletion—by its first practitioners—of the two more important causes,[319] formal and final, which lend an academic discipline its reasonableness and goal orientedness.

A material cause is quite literally the *matter* out of which something is made. Matter changes constantly and inevitably. Aristotle showed that the matter out of which something is made—the *marble* in a marble statue, for instance—*causes* it to be, materially.

In the second place, the efficient cause comes nearest to the common usage of the word "cause": the physical producer of a certain observable motion or effect. (Efficient causation is most commonly associated with motion: for a poolroom example, the cue ball acts as an efficient cause when it hits another billiard ball, causing it to move as well.) To return to our marble statue, the efficient cause is the *act of chiseling the statue.*

As we'll see, the Enlightenment retained these two less important causes, turning them into the focal points on which scientism would be practiced, going forward.

---

[319] This deliberate deletion can be called either "scientific positivism" or the "Baconian turn." This book uses the latter.

Now, we will describe the two more important causes: formal and final.

A formal cause is something's knowable "structure" or "arrangement," as it were, which an intelligent observer can understand. Plato called this knowable structure its *form*, which (unlike a material cause) is unchanging and eternal. To return to our marble statue, the formal cause is the *idea in the artist's head*, before he begins chiseling the formless block of marble. From the Catholic Natural Law point of view, nature is intelligible solely on account of its formal cause in the mind of God. Without recourse to a thing's — e.g., nature's — formal cause, that thing *by definition* cannot be meaningful to observers.

Last but not least, final cause is a thing's purpose or goal — the motivation, for example, of the artist's creation of the marble statue (say, the honoring of God). Only the analysis of a thing's final cause enables an observer to determine its purpose. Scientists and philosophers can reason about the function of nature only when they have a reasonable guess about its final cause, its *reason for being*. This is key.

As we shall recall later in this chapter, the Enlightenment (along with the Reformation) rejected formal and final causation in the practice of modern science. Only Catholic philosophy retained the crucial concepts of formal and final causation. Therefore, in our day, only the Catholic Church retains a truly "open-minded" view with respect to the fast-changing, technology-driven natural sciences in America.

The Protestant View of Nature and Popular Scientism

The knee-jerk rejection of well-established scientific theories — e.g., evolution, plate tectonics, the Big Bang theory, etc. — by the mainline religious Right has done great harm not only to the reputation of our Reformation brethren themselves, but to the overall purchase of Christianity (and even theism) in America. In short, it has made easier the job of those secularist TV shows and pundits: *to mock and discredit Christianity at every chance.*

Flat out, Protestantism has failed to answer secular science's atheistic claims (falsely based upon "recent scientific findings") to have rendered God mythic. Such a refusal has produced devastating results in the American popular culture. Secular science has falsely been made to appear infinitely "wiser" than Protestantism.

Once more, Catholic Natural Law alone can reverse this misunderstanding. Let's consider an analogy briefly.

Imagine that you are falsely accused of a heinous murder. You are to be brought before a jury of peers for your "day in court." Imagine that, at first glance, the facts of the crime *wrongly but strongly* make you look guilty. Let us even suppose it is the "perfect storm": a one-in-a-million mistake in which you, the innocent party, find yourself in serious danger of being falsely convicted. (Let's say the true murderer looks just like you and happens to drive the same type of car; you were near to the crime scene when it happened; for unrelated reasons, you appeared nervous and culpable when the police arrested you, etc.)

You curse your luck.

But you remember after being taken into custody that you are blessed with a saving alibi: at the time of the murder, you were at a pizza joint just beneath the crime scene, watching a basketball game with five strangers who remember you, all of whom are willing to testify on your behalf. Your lawyer consults with them and has secured all of them to testify on your big day in court.

By simply presenting their evidence, you will surely be saved from a wrongful conviction.

Now, imagine that just before your trial, you are suddenly and inexplicably taken with the crazy idea that you ought to testify on your own behalf, instead of using all the convincing and available witnesses to prove your innocence. You tell your lawyer to call off all your witnesses. You tell him that you can clear your own name.

Your lawyer cannot believe it and urges you against this madness. All the same, you go through with your ill-conceived plan: taking the stand, you freeze up, and on cross-examination, you plead the Fifth. As you do so, you look completely guilty—as guilty as everyone thought you were before the trial. On that basis, the jury wrongly convicts you.

This nightmarish scenario closely resembles what American mainstream Protestants have done to Christianity's reputation in the realm of scientific advancement (after the so-called scientific revolution of the Enlightenment). Instead of using scientific truth to accomplish a deeper theological and philosophical understanding of the world—for instance, the Big Bang theory and quantum theory, which have *vastly* anti-atheistic implications —Protestants have unintentionally assumed the look of "pleading the Fifth" in the face of a ruthlessly devastating cross-examination by scientism's "lawyers." And pleading the Fifth is not the mark of a winning party.

That cross-examination, by the way, wrongly presumes that science and theology are on opposite "sides." But saying so has not been part of Protestantism's defense. *Both* sides of Prot-Enlight have made it look to the rest of the world as if science wins and Christian theology loses. The average secular mind, "cultivated" by the five biases (noted in the first five chapters of this book) of the failing public school system, examines the parties to the debate and assumes that there is no rejoinder to the aggressive assertions of scientism: "if Protestant Christianity had any responses to modern science, surely it would use them."

That is a reasonable enough assumption.[320]

Protestantism hobbled itself by going along with the Enlightenment assumptions about the removal of formal and final causation. And that's precisely how the Protestant voice in America has proceeded during the last several decades: "against" science via an alternating campaign of silence and protest. Instead of accessing the scientific and philosophical truths *most* convincing of a goal-oriented, intelligible view of the universe—which leads quite directly to a *Catholic* view of it—they have "pled the Fifth" and made atheist scientism seem far more convincing than it really is.

Why in the world, one wonders, have the Protestants rejected even good science as if it could *possibly* contradict the core beliefs of Christianity? It cannot do so, in reality. As Catholic Natural Law famously holds, "truth cannot contradict truth."[321] Put more specifically: *scientific* truth cannot contradict *theological* truth. They are one and the same.[322]

---

[320] Everyone assumes that each party to an argument will put forward his best case in his own interest: that's why an "adversarial" legal system such as ours generally works so well. Parties tend to represent their own interest best. Conversely, no one assumes that a party to an argument has a devastating argument that he chooses to forgo. It's insane.

[321] Pope John Paul II picks up on this Scholastic aphorism: "Truth Cannot Contradict Truth," address of John Paul II to the Pontifical Academy of Sciences (October 22, 1996).

[322] In fact, truth reinforces other aspects of truth. But before one can gain access to this scientific route to religion, one must accept the Catholic Natural Law view of nature. Protestantism, on account of its rejection of Catholic Natural Law, has

While scientism views its task as the menial recordation of the senseless details of the world, Protestantism opts to ignore all such details (based on the assumption that *only* the final conclusion—Christ the *omega*—matters). While Enlightenment scientism defines its task to be to *toil in futile, material obscurity*, Protestant Creationism identifies its own task as *the discounting of all theological relevancy of the scientific world itself.*[323]

The astute reader notes the close connection between the Baconian turn of scientism (which studies nature only for its *utility*), described above, and the ego-centeredness of relativism and secular humanism, on the other.[324] We see it clearly when we turn to American technology.

---

not and will not. If it had, there probably would never have been a Reformation in the first place. In our final chapter, we review and refine the Catholic view of nature described in this book's introduction. Recall that the central assumption of both Enlightenment secularism and Protestantism involves an anti–Natural Law view of nature· this is the primary reason the Prot-Enlight, American version of nature cannot supply the necessary conditions for faith, republican citizenship, academic study, and day-to-day life. To both parties, for differing reasons, the universe is deterministic (no free will in nature), meaningless (no understandability in nature), and purposeless (no goal in nature).

[323] Details are important, as scientism insinuates, but the Church reminds science that details must be arranged and ordered according to their design. The end (*omega*) is important, as Protestantism recalls ceaselessly, but the Church urges Protestants to remember that the history into which Christ entered is a relevant composite of philosophical and scientific details

[324] A properly Catholic study of nature requires real science and real theology, without sacrificing one to the other. With the deletion of the two more important Aristotelian causes, Prot and Enlight even share the specific source for the idea that science

269

CATHOLIC REPUBLIC

Catholic Natural Law rejects the claims of both Enlightenment scientism and Protestant Creationism that the Word cannot be separated from the world.[325] As Anthony the Abbot first
articulated less than three centuries after Jesus died: "My book
is the created nature, one always at my disposal whenever I want
to read God's words."

So, the Church insists upon a study of nature that tends to
both details *and* the big picture simultaneously. As evidence of
this, today's "hot topic" in science is the search for a "grand unifying theory."[326] The human drive to truth presumes the unification
of theology, philosophy, and science in Catholic Natural Law.

Science cannot be practiced without it.

Science without Purpose or Meaning

In the early Enlightenment, physical science became its own dis-
creet discipline — no longer seen as useful for its "deeper" meaning

---

and religion are mutually exclusive. In asking why science and
religion are presumed to be poised against one another, one
gets to the heart of the matter. Both sides invoke ideas from the
late sixteenth and early seventeenth centuries, a.k.a. the early,
early Enlightenment. As chapter 4 stated, the Reformation was
simply intra-Christian Enlightenment, or Enlightenment retaining Christ. Although we correctly think of the Protestants and
the secularists as epic rivals, the reader now sees their shared
scientific pedigree: the eradication of the more important two
(formal and final) Aristotelian causes.

[325] Giuseppe Tanzella-Nitti, "The Two Books Prior to the Scientific Revolution." *Perspectives on Science and Christian Faith* 57
(September 2005).

[326] So-called grand unifying theories (GUTs) are sought to tie the
very small (quantum mechanics) to the very grand (Einsteinian
cosmology); infinitely more valuable is the GUT of the Catholic
Natural Law.

(formal or final causes), but only for the technology and utility it innovated. Some technological innovation, indeed, followed. But with technological gain came great pain: science was divorced from the deeper truths necessary even to its own propositions.

Prior to the Baconian turn, the classical Aristotelian worldview posited that all things, including the universe, aim at the purposes God designated for them. Physical scientists and theologians alike imputed meaning and purpose to the object of their studies. And the Catholic Natural Law, which incorporated this view of nature, enabled man to use his natural reason to conceive of abstract ideas about physical things. This included things he could not directly experience, such as the stars.

Scientific history up to the sixteenth century had assumed that nature's purpose was manifest within nature itself. And similarly, all of human history had assumed up to that point that the purpose of nature was knowledge of God.

For instance, scientism rejects any inquiry that asks the big question *why* (a function of jettisoned final causation). Simultaneously, popular science also views one of its foremost twenty-first-century challenges to be, say, the curing of cancer. Without access to the question that asks *why* cells divide in a runaway fashion, cancer is essentially incurable. If cellular division cannot be understood from an etiological point of view, then neither the efficient nor material cause of cancer can be discovered.

Other prominent areas of science ask: Why does light bear particle properties when observed and wave properties when not observed? Why is the universe so "finely tuned" for the cultivation of life? Why does life propagate itself at all? Why would the process of biological evolution begin from nothing?

All are utterly scientific questions — scientific questions of final causation — which post-Enlightenment science would deem a contradiction in terms. That is, even science must ask about nature's "goals." And yet, scientism stripped the "why" from the universe and unfortunately, we are left with just the hollow "that" things happen.

For its part, early Reformation thought seemed complicit in the new Baconian science's mechanistic view of the universe, but with an utterly ulterior motive: because *sola scriptura* required a denial of Catholicism's meaningful view of nature (a.k.a. "natural theology"). In other words, Bacon's criticism of Natural Law seemed helpful to early Reformation thought. Yet the pure convenience of the anti-Aristotelian, anti-Catholic arguments of Bacon had far-reaching, unintended effects upon Protestantism.

The Catholic tradition had long posited nature as a "book" that can be read through the practice of science and philosophy. But the philosophy of *sola scriptura* urged Protestants to embrace *only* those propositions articulated in the Bible, and to reject all else.

The Catholic view of a teleological universe—a universe with the fingerprints of the Creator all over it—implied that knowable truths about Creation and the Creator were vested in nature *outside* the Bible. And this was a great threat to the fundamental principles of the Reformation.[327]

---

[327] This much is true even at a very basic level. For instance, the fact of night and day conforms perfectly with humanity's need for both rest and productivity. While such a truth is spoken of at great length in Scripture, in Genesis, it is more immediately knowable to a person who has never read Genesis: from daily life, I know I must rest some and work some. The goal-oriented view of the universe derived from a knowledge of "night" and "day," however, is rejected by Protestants—when they're being truly faithful to *sola scriptura*—because they deem such truths to be extra-Biblical, pagan. If a Protestant of any stripe were

Sometime after the formation of the new Baconian science, Protestantism and scientism assumed starkly *different* historical paths, especially in America. The rest of the story is well enough told. One recognizes the bitter debate created by the increasing separation between Protestant creationism and secular science. But it is not remembered enough that bitter rivals are often made out of intellectual bedfellows.

As seen in literally every other chapter of this book, neither of these parties — Prots nor Enlights — realize how very close together their ideas run!

Perhaps now the predicament is more understandable: the mainline Protestant view, still the majority Christian view in America, urges its followers to deafen their ears to scientific developments, deemed irreconcilable with Christian belief. They won't use their lifeline (as in our example of the false murder accusation): extrabiblical Catholic tradition and doctrine *alone* can explain those scientific developments without forfeiting the truth of Christian theology!

Still more ignorant about Catholicism's inherently scientific worldview are the proponents of scientism. Most of these are meagerly educated, if at all, in the realm of logic, philosophy, rhetoric, or theology;[328] most know shamefully little, if any, of

---

to admit that nature is "readable" like a book, then something besides the words of the Bible would be affirmed in the discernment of truth. Catholic natural theology would then be vindicated, and a major portion of the Protestant qualm with Catholicism would be erased!

[328] For example, in his new book *Faith Versus Fact: Why Science and Religion are Incompatible*, militant atheist Jerry A. Coyne mistakes Thomas Aquinas as a Patristic and even seems ignorant of Thomas's fundamentally "pro-science" viewpoint.

the tendentious Baconian pedigree of their own Enlightenment scientism. All they know is the shopworn refrain that studying nature's purpose is "above their pay grade," even as they clearly deem it far *beneath* their profession.

They don't understand that "separation" and "rivalry" between religion and science is a ridiculous, laughable presumption (e.g., teleological science is what science is when done best).

Many well-respected scientists don't even seem to understand the gargantuan difference, in reference to nature, between a Protestant and a Catholic worldview. Nor do they seem to acknowledge, even faintly, the superstitious Enlightenment-era presuppositions about nature that inform their biases. All they really seem to know is mockery of Christianity based on an ignorant conflation of the Protestant view of nature and the Catholic one.

The Book of Scripture and the "Book of Nature"

In short, these two philosophies of science, "Prot" and "Enlight" —rival branches grown from the same anti-Catholic Natural Law timber—each seek to deny the other's greatest goal (Biblicism and scientism). The meaningless, mechanistic view of nature shared and bandied about by Reformation science and Enlightenment-scientism proponents forces either side to choose between their respective "prizes."

Protestantism values only the truth of Scripture on the one hand; secular science prizes the materialist methods of studying nature, on the other. Each of these is negated not only by the other, but by its own insistence on a meaningless conception of the universe.

But it is a false dilemma.

Trite as it may sound, the best of both sides can easily combine within the classical, Aristotelian-Thomist conception of the universe. The knowledgeable Catholic emerges amid all this bickering, thinking: "Both the Bible and science are *completely* valid — truth cannot contradict truth!"

But both camps require a principle that underlies the Bible and scientific data: the principle of *realism* (teleology and intelligibility together). Remember Aristotle: being is intelligible! Neither the letters, words, and sentences of the Bible nor the correlations of measured data mean anything if the universe is "random" or "unreadable."

On the one hand, if a Protestant posits nature as meaningless, such a view is necessarily attended by notions of a *futile creation*, instead of a beatific one pointing us toward the Creator. Suggesting that nature cannot or should not be "read" by man, nature's steward, suggests an almost *duplicitous* design by the Creator. Thus, the Protestants operate with a very tortured portrait of the functions of man's five senses and his ability to reason about the world. On this model, created nature becomes worthless at best — at worst, it's outright deceptive — not "good," as it is called in Genesis (1:31). Man's natural reason becomes impotent. He cannot discern anything meaningful in life besides the words of the Bible, whose values he cannot properly contextualize in the deceptive world surrounding him.[329]

---

[329] Moving upward to the higher functions such as the principles of pure reason, such as mathematics or logic, *sola scriptura* becomes even more absurd. As soon as man begins to "put things together" and develop systems of science, logic, and math, he must forthwith abandon them if they were not directly derived from the words of the Bible, which they are not (e.g., Noah certainly employed the principles of geometry, although he did not instruct us about them!).

Sola scriptura is quite the self-fashioned dilemma by the Protestants!

Even Scripture itself points at the solution of the Catholic Natural Law, in places mentioning nature's readability and textuality. As old as Christianity itself is an analogy about the pair of "books" making God's nature knowable to the mind of man. We behold two books: the "book of nature"—the created universe together with man's natural reason—and the "book of Scripture."

The world is a text. Consider just what texts, books, or scrolls are: "documents written by someone and addressed to someone else; a document that is intended to convey an intelligible content; a text that might require a certain effort to be properly interpreted and explained according to its author's original and genuine meaning."[330]

With just the slightest broadening of our definition of "text," nature can indeed be conceivable as *textual*. The above definition applies to nature as much as it does to the words of the Bible!

As noted above, even the Bible and the early Patristic heroes made reference to the book of nature. Among the following Patristics, all of whom antedated the canonization of the Bible (A.D. 393), "explicit references to the Book of Nature can be found: Saint Basil (A.D. 329), Saint Gregory of Nyssa (A.D. 335), Saint Augustine (A.D. 354), and Saint Ephrem the Syrian (A.D. 306)."[331] The prebiblical and biblical image of the book of nature proves to be infinitely more than a poetic metaphor or an artistic flourish. Both the book of Scripture—and those Fathers who organized

---

[330] Tanzella-Nitti, "The Two Books Prior to the Scientific Revolution."
[331] Ibid.

it—made explicit references to the book of nature. Protestants need to read it!³³²

Of course, the basic assumption of Catholic Natural Law reasoning enunciated in this chapter is that the book of nature is actually an older "text" than the book of Scripture. By its nature, the book of nature offers an independent mode of verifying many of the truths of the Christian faith. If the two modes of knowing God are *truly* independent, then they both stand on their own. (That's what genuine independence is, after all!)

Nevertheless, allusions to a natural "book" or "scroll" in the Bible (and even in the early Patristic period before the Bible was canonized) merit our attention, suggesting that *Scripture itself* tells us to "read" nature: "The heavens shall be rolled up like a scroll / and all their host shall wither away" (Isa. 34:4); "the sky was divided like a torn scroll curling up, and every mountain and island was moved from its place" (Rev. 6:14); and "another book was opened, the Book of Life, and the dead were judged according to their works, as recorded in the books." (Rev. 20:12).

Clearly, these Old and New Testament references to the Apocalypse suggest that the final destruction of nature at the end of time will be like ripping a giant page. If apocalyptic destruction is the act of *ripping* the book, we can clearly infer that creation is the ongoing divine act of *writing* the book.³³³

In short, not for nothing has God commonly been called the Divine Author by our Church. We see that the biblical image of a scroll applies with equal force to *any* perceivable works by the Divine Author, as they literally do to inscribed texts. This points us to the world, not only to the Word. Whether we call

³³² Ibid.
³³³ Ibid.

the universe the book of life, the book of nature, or in still other places, "the Book of History,"[334] we must remember that nature was "authored" in a way that *wants* to be "read." From such a reading, we know that our Father in Heaven created us in love. And in a loving creation, all manner of creatures have their proper function pre-appointed for them.

On the other side of the coin, a meaningless, non-purposive, Baconian view of the universe eventually stops the progress of realist science in its tracks (much as post-Enlightenment history suggests). The materialist conception of Enlightenment science assumes about reality that *only* matter—not "intangibles" such as ideas, rights, or souls—is real. Thus, as an academic discipline charged with making sense of certain ideas, scientism dooms itself. As we saw above, causation, allegedly scientism's *fixed and cherished idea*, is itself unobservable in nature.

Just as causation cannot be read about in the Bible, it cannot be known (except by inference) from scientific measurement. Secular science relies on the *pre-existence* of meaning, even as it derisively denies the concept. Without the immaterial, pre-scientific notion that X *caused* Y, then all post-Enlightenment science is destroyed. Naturally, this is very similar to the Protestant dilemma described above.

To posit either a meaningless universe or an uncreated universe is completely unscientific!

Albert Einstein set out to prove an eternal universe, one without a beginning, but admitted the atheist jig was up after it was demonstrated in 1927 that the universe was expanding and that energy was decaying. But on this matter, scientists with a nonteleological commitment grew stubborn, insisting (by taking

[334] Ibid.

a quasi-religious leap of faith!) that, as a matter of *sola scientia*, the investigation of space and time will eventually prove the universe to be an uncaused effect!

At this point, secular science *itself* "pleads the Fifth," just as it mocks Protestantism for doing: "although it *seems* clear that the universe was created," they will say, "eventually, science [instead of the Bible] will conceive of an explanation!" When Catholic Natural Law confronts scientism, scientism's advocates irrationally invoke their own version of a "god of the gaps" (their own epithet for Protestantism's point of view) by denying immaterial first principles[335] altogether. We must constantly remind the

---

[335] Think of the Aristotelian principle called "retortion," in the following context: scientism's claim that all immaterial things are unreal or imagined is itself demonstrably false. Retortion is considered an Aristotelian innovation with just a bit of modern enhancement: it is a logical proof of the existence of things that cannot be sensed, logical concepts called "first principles," which are ideas necessary to all other ideas. One leading proponent of retortion notes the doctrine's pedigree: "Aristotle invented this method, Augustine used it, Aquinas developed it, and Joseph Marechal emphasized it." Marc Leclerc, S.J., "Being and the Sciences: The Philosophy of Gaston Isaye," *International Philosophical Quarterly* 30, no. 3 (September 1990). Causation is one example of these first principles that can be demonstrated beyond a shadow of a doubt, by retortion; the principle of non-contradiction is another. The "catch" is that retortion shows first principles to be necessary only when someone attempts to disprove them. Let's imagine that the contrarian advocate of scientism (or any other materialist camp) asserts that "there are no real assertions." While I cannot syllogistically "prove" to him that assertions exist—since we are dealing with one of the first principles that underlies all thought—our contrarian was forced to employ an assertion to assert that there are no assertions! Thereby, he shows the falsity of his own view, even

if I cannot do so using standard logical arguments. This is called a performative contradiction, and it is the mechanism that makes Aristotelian retortion work. Retortion evidences the "principle of objectivity" (Leclerc) in immaterial understandings of the material universe, subsequent to the Baconian turn. The principle of objectivity lies at the very "foundation of knowledge" (Leclerc). For example, while I cannot strictly "prove" the principle of noncontradiction, it is operative in every sentence or thought I've expressed. Its truth is presupposed by even the false proposition: "The principle of noncontradiction is false"! Moreover, even though I cannot with my senses observe that a cue ball "causes" a billiard ball to move, upon striking it, I can rationally insist upon the necessity of that perfectly consistent correlation—the cue ball seeming to impart its motion to the billiard ball it strikes, every time. Science relies vitally on such inductions. Yet inductions are immaterial, and so, if science played by its own rules (just as we said above of *sola scriptura*), then it would have to deny even the idea that it claims commitment to: causation. All inductions, including the principle of causation, are ideal and strictly belong to the realm of ideas rather than to the realm of observable things. Causation cannot be "observed" by science any more than it can be "given" by Scripture. The principle of noncontradiction is not addressed within the Bible, of course. But a perusal of the Bible requires it, in order that, say, the first three sentences of Genesis may have a singular meaning! The first principles operate as part of our natural reason and as part of Catholic Natural Law (denied by Protestants and Enlightenment thinkers). De facto, *sola scriptura* is impossible because we need extrinsic, interpretive principles even before we can read! *Sola scientia* is impossible on precisely the same basis. The point is that Aristotelian retortion works equally well against scientism's skepticism as against *sola scriptura's* dogmatism. Each of the interpretive or logical canons used when a reader reads a text—even the Bible—exists outside of that text. The analogy of the "two texts," the book of nature and the book of Scripture, helps us to see that neither text, neither the Word nor the world, can interpret itself.

secular Left that, when backed into a metaphysical corner, they recur to the very tricks and obfuscations for which they criticize the religious Right.

Smart Devices, Dumb Folks

The main takeaway principle from this final chapter is that good science cannot be accomplished by scientism. Scientism is to true science what astrology is to our proper understanding of the cosmos. And, as the secular Left has effectively communicated, good science is certainly not accomplished by practitioners consistently associated with the religious Right either.

Proper science can be accomplished only by the party that, without contradiction, affirms the three prongs of Catholic Natural Law. The list of important scientists at this chapter's beginning should remind the reader what the strong implications of that last sentence are: *nature cannot be studied unless it is first understood as moral free, understandable, and goal oriented.*

Now, one of the most important "fruits" of good science is technological innovation. Unfortunately, technology is also one of the fruits of bad science and scientism. So, how then are we to tell the difference between good technology and bad technology? Often, the particular technological innovation in question may hail from either Natural Law science or Enlightenment science; the most important distinction lies in the *cultural* approach to

---

Scientism and Biblicism each require extrinsic meaning makers. This is the unique role of the single intelligent creature, man. Both Prot and Enlight, the religious Right and the secular Left, vitiate themselves by denying first principles. Only with a view to first principles can either biblical or scientific meaning survive.

and reception of the niceties made possible by a given technological advance.

Does the given culture incorporate technology in a balanced, spiritually healthy manner? Or does it consume technological innovation obsessively, replacing spirituality with the cheap functionalism that accompanies new apps on the iPhone? One way to answer these questions in today's America is by asking, "Has the 'smart device revolution' seen what we would *expect* to see with enhanced calling, texting, and e-mailing availability?"

Although my answer is anecdotal, it is basically undeniable: *No way!* Think about it: people call back, e-mail back, and text back far less than they ever did. *The easier technology makes life, the lazier and more self-centered its users become.* Prot-Enlight American culture can receive science in only this way.

After reading six chapters full of criticism of Prot-Enlight American culture, the reader will be tempted at this point to take pride, for a moment, in America's technological advances over the last decades. Such advances are beyond reproach, are they not? Who, after all, dares impugn the technological advancements of the digitized age?

To the contrary, our increasing dependence on post-Enlightenment technology seems only to have intensified most of the problems listed in these six chapters.

Science enhances technology, which in turn enhances science. Using science itself, machines are created to accomplish more scientific work. And the better our technology gets, the more efficient our methods of expression and telecommunication become (whereupon, ironically, human beings seem gradually to *stop* speaking to one another).

Always near at hand today are "smart devices." Such devices serve to unite—even to sharpen—the various criticisms of the secular Left offered in this book: in a secular-humanist republic failing both spiritually and morally, the most God-supplanting form of consumerism proves to be the science-based *cult of technology* we see in America today.

No sort of mass-consumption product could possibly offer Americans more deceptive *false hope* than technology's alluring devices, which do not cure the American failure of spiritual or bodily health. Oh sure, we may live slightly longer than we did before, but every human life promises the same natural ending.

"Technological man is an alienated being,"[336] Martin Heidegger wrote in 1927 in *Being and Time*. Technology alienates us from being *because it makes us forget our death*. Or, as Alexandr Solzhenitsyn put it, our "spiritual insecurity"[337] alienates us from what is most essential in our lives: the redemption and eternal life won by Jesus Christ on the Cross. What Heidegger and Solzhenitsyn—a non-Christian and a Christian—meant was that technology tempts man everywhere to seek spiritual solace *outside its proper source*.

Since already "being is that which hides"[338] from mankind, the stupor resultant from smart devices presumably serves only to make being's hiding spot safer. Nor does technology do anything salutary for civics and republican involvement by citizens.

Technology mediates culture and nature so unyieldingly as to threaten permanently to divorce them: as American culture shows, our popular culture has forgotten every one of the

---

[336] Martin Heidegger, *Being and Time* (New York: Harper Perennial Modern Thought, 2008).
[337] Quoted in Joseph Pearce, *Solzhenitsyn: A Soul in Exile* (San Francisco: Ignatius Press, 2001).
[338] Heidegger, *Being and Time*.

(otherwise simple to learn) truths of nature. Kids stay indoors playing video games instead of running around outside.

Technology has not brought people together; it has separated us from one another.

And even among those Americans unconcerned with our *ontological status* (as Heidegger or Solzhenitsyn were), most of us at least remain somewhat attuned to our *anthropological status*. In other words, most people care how the human race is getting along with itself.

So, the point is: even if we are willing to accept that our smartphones make us dumb, we probably should not be willing to accept that they render us *exiles living contemptuously among, yet apart from, humanity*.

We ought to care about the state of utter ruin in which we find the natural communities described in chapters 4 and 5.

Or perhaps, if we are willing to live apart from other human beings, we ought to have the courage of our convictions and seek *actual* exile, abandoning our desolation only on rare occasions to "play knuckle bones with passing children," as the Weeping Philosopher was rumored to do.[339]

Only a Catholic Natural Law approach to the fruit of science and technology properly contextualizes our advances without deifying them. Nature must interact in a temperate way with technology, just as technology must interact in a temperate way with what's left of our republican culture. Each of these is connected to the other.

[339] This section is heavily excerpted from Timothy Gordon, "Alienated Technology: Smart Phone, Dumb Folks," *The Imaginative Conservative*, April 1, 2014, https://theimaginativeconservative.org/2014/04/technological-alienation-smart-phone-dumb-folks.html.

Conclusion

Today, as seen in every other chapter of this book, American Prot-Enlight misleadingly seems to be a dispute between two rivals. Crucial to remember, however, is that every way in which Protestantism and Enlightenment thought seem ostensibly rivalrous turns out to be born of *similarity*, not of *difference*.

The paganism of the American scientific and technocratic view will only accelerate without some sort of popular intervention on behalf of the Catholic Natural Law.

Except for the occasional "one-off" where American "religion" and "science" come together in the popular culture to yell past one another (recall "creationism versus evolution"), the parties are no longer even on speaking terms. This is very similar to the almost *total* lack of communication, today, between "Church" and "state."

As per our murder trial analogy earlier in this chapter, the ordinary American is being duped more and more by the alluring promises of scientism. After all, scientism appears flashy and sounds glib to the uncultivated mind, which is not trained to ask probative questions. Unless we "put on our best defense" of the Catholic view of the world, Protestant Christianity (and even Christianity in general) will continue to appear unappetizing to the popular culture.

The conditions promise to worsen without the intellectual influence of the Catholic Natural Law tradition for which America is groaning.

All America can do is to hire a heavy-hitting "attorney" to make the case for a scientific theism of the Cross: the Catholic Natural Law position *alone* articulates a Christian viewpoint open to truth and agreeable to scientific advancement. The Catholic position *alone* can reverse the advance of scientism and its implicit atheism.

Nothing attests to this fact better than the *mere existence* of the Vatican's Pontifical Academy of the Sciences, refounded in 1936 by Pope Pius XI, dating all the way back to scientism's birth in the early seventeenth century. The academy includes the membership of such Nobel laureates as Ernest Rutherford, Max Planck, Otto Hahn, Niels Bohr, and Charles Hard Townes. Most Americans do not know the substantial resources the Church has invested in an open investigation of the universe.

Most Americans, if made aware of this, would receive such evidence as vindicating the Catholic Natural Law: *only* the Catholic Church can supply a golden mean between scientism and Biblicism, just as only the Church can properly contextualize the other necessary elements of life in a republic.

Acknowledgments

This book is dedicated to my best friend, my editor, and my wife, the lovely Stephanie Carissa Gordon, without whom it simply would not have come to exist. In the summer of 2016, together she and I rewrote the entire book in its present form. Her fealty and robust encouragement made her, among other things, the book's greatest natural advocate. (Moreover, she has been finishing my sentences for me since April 11, 2003, an "edit" that changed the course of both of our lives forever.)

I would also like to acknowledge the great dialectical contributions to this book by my brother David Gordon and my dear friends Chris Plance and Joseph Polizzotto. Other professional or dialectical friends to the penning or publishing of this book include: Dr. Taylor Marshall, Michael Voris, Jay Richards, John Zmirak, Steven Jonathan Rummelsburg, James Carrisalez, Sean Panick, Brian Cobb, Martin Raymond, Ashleigh Rossi, Anthony Bedoy, Bradley Birzer and *The Imaginative Conservative*, John Vella and *Crisis Magazine*, and Carmen, Christine, and all the good folks at Church Militant.

I would like to thank Milo Yiannopoulos and Dangerous Books for first publishing a truly dangerous book, which bounced from publisher to publisher.

I would also like to thank my philosophical mentor, Father Kevin Flannery at the Pontifical Gregorian University, and my legal mentor, Professor Thomas A. C. Smith at the University of San Diego School of Law. "Game-changing" additions to my analysis were provided by the publications of Dr. Edward Feser (chapter 1), Dr. Laurence Claus and Dr. Thomas Pangle (chapter 2), and Professor Philip Hamburger (chapter 4).

Finally, I would like to thank all the good people at Sophia Institute Press for running this second edition.

About the Author

Timothy J. Gordon, J.D., Ph.L., M.A., studied the philosophy of Aristotle and Thomas Aquinas in pontifical graduate universities in Rome, taught it at Southern Californian colleges, and then went on to law school. He holds degrees in literature, history, philosophy, and law. He resides in Central California with his large family, writing, teaching, and speaking on philosophy and theology.

For leisure, he wears the furs of endangered species, eats preservative-rich and plastic-wrapped foods, and adamantly refuses to recycle. In these dark times in the Church and the world, he lives by this maxim of G. K. Chesterton: "Solemnity flows out of men naturally, but laughter is a leap. It is easy to be heavy: hard to be light." *Risus est bellum*.

CRISIS Publications

Sophia Institute Press awards the privileged title "CRISIS Publications" to a select few of our books that address contemporary issues at the intersection of politics, culture, and the Church with clarity, cogency, and force and that are also destined to become all-time classics.

CRISIS Publications are *direct*, explaining their principles briefly, simply, and clearly to Catholics in the pews, on whom the future of the Church depends. The time for ambiguity or confusion is long past.

CRISIS Publications are *contemporary*, born of our own time and circumstances and intended to become significant statements in current debates, statements that serious Catholics cannot ignore, regardless of their prior views.

CRISIS Publications are *classical*, addressing themes and enunciating principles that are valid for all ages and cultures. Readers will turn to them time and again for guidance in other days and different circumstances.

CRISIS Publications are *spirited*, entering contemporary debates with gusto to clarify issues and demonstrate how those issues can be resolved in a way that enlivens souls and the Church.

We welcome engagement with our readers on current and future CRISIS Publications. Please pray that this imprint may help to resolve the crises embroiling our Church and society today.